Everyday Racism

———— ✻ ————

"In Philomena Essed's book *Everyday Racism* we finally have a publication that provides substantive and satisfying responses to the most frequently asked questions about racism and how it operates in our daily lives. No matter how provocative, tedious, simplistic, profound, or sublime the query, this book offers lucid answers, detailed explanations, and striking examples.

"The book is based on intensive interviews with Surinamese women in the Netherlands and African-American women in the United States. The author's well-documented presentation illuminates the ways in which racism is woven into black women's everyday contact with whites, and how culture impacts upon this interaction.

"In her brilliant analysis of how oppression and discrimination affect women of color in their workplace, on public transportation, in finding housing, and in their shopping, Essed describes the actions and reactions of the victims of racism, and discusses the psychological consequences. The theoretical aspects of the book and the interviews are skillfully written, in a manner that will appeal to both the everyday public and professionals.

"I recommend this book to everyone who has any questions about how racism operates on a daily basis. In particular, feminists and non-feminists, students in Women's Studies Departments, and women's organizations—grassroots and global—should use this book as a major resource. It is an important contribution to our awareness of the problems and conflicts stemming from racism, which still abounds in our academic institutions, social groups, and political organizations."

Dr. Gloria I. Joseph
Author of *Common Differences: Conflicts in
Black and White Feminist Perspectives*

About the Author and Translator

Philomena Essed was born in Utrecht, the Netherlands. In 1983 she received her Master of Arts in Social Anthropology from the University of Amsterdam, with a minor in Women's Studies. She later received her Ph.D. in Social Sciences from the same institution. She gives regular lectures and seminars at the Centre for Race and Ethnic Studies in Amsterdam, where she also holds a yearly workshop called "Women and Racism" in which she explores many issues discussed in this book.

Ms. Essed has contributed a number of articles to academic journals and to popular magazines, and her work has been published in the Netherlands, Britain, Canada, Germany, and Italy. She lives in Amsterdam and is currently working on another book, *Understanding Everyday Racism*.

Cynthia Jaffé received her Bachelor of Arts in English from Wesleyan University, Connecticut in 1980. She also holds a Master of Arts in Teaching from the School for International Training, Vermont, with a specialty in Teaching English to Speakers of Other Languages (TESOL). Ms. Jaffe lived in the Netherlands for nine years, working as a writer, translator, and English instructor. She now lives in Boulder, Colorado, where she works as a translator.

EVERYDAY RACISM

Reports from Women of Two Cultures

Philomena Essed, Ph.D.

*Translated from the Dutch
by Cynthia Jaffé*

Library of Congress Cataloging-in-Publication Data:

Essed, Philomena, 1955–
    [Alledaags racisme. English]
    Everyday racism : reports from women of two cultures /
by Philomena Essed. — 1st U.S. ed.
    p.   cm.
    Translation of Alledaags racisme.
    Includes bibliographical references.
    ISBN 0-89793-068-1 : $19.95 — ISBN 0-89793-069-X (pbk.) : $12.95
    1. Women, Surinamese—Netherlands. 2. Sex discrimination against women—Netherlands. 3. Racism—Netherlands. 4. Netherlands—Race relations. 5. Afro-American women. 6. Sex discrimination against women—United States. 7. Racism—United States. 8. United States—Race relations. I. Title.
    DJ92.S8E67 1990
    305.4'0973—dc20
                                          89–26770

Book and cover design by *Qalagraphia*.
Cover photographs: Mark Yamada.
Cover subjects: Gislene Mariette, Ardrena Thomas
Editors: Jackie Melvin & Kiran S. Rana
Editorial coordinator: Corrine M. Sahli
Production manager: Paul J. Frindt
Set in 10/13 Palatino by 847 Communications, Claremont, CA
Printed and bound by Patterson Printing, Benton Harbor, MI
Manufactured in the United States of America

9 8 7 6 5 4 3 2   1st edition

CONTENTS

———————— ✳ ————————

Acknowledgments

———————— ✳ ————————

I would have liked to personally thank each of the women I interviewed, for the trust they showed me and for all I was permitted to learn from them. In the interest of their privacy, however, they will have to remain anonymous.

I wish to thank Kitty Lie and the "Work Group of Black Women Against Racism" for the discussion about our struggle, our work, and our experiences. I am also grateful to Anja Meulenbelt, Tineke Jansen, and Irma Garconius for their comments on the manuscript. I owe Teun van Dijk a great deal of thanks for his stimulating interest in my work, our many theoretical discussions about it, and his comments on a portion of the manuscript.

I am very pleased that, finally, many of my English-speaking colleagues and friends can read this book. In particular I would like to mention my friend Cassandra Hayes, whose enthusiasm for my work has been very supportive. Special thanks are due to Cynthia Jaffe, who translated the book into English, for her commitment and loyalty under difficult circumstances. Last but not least, I am grateful to the editors at Hunter House: Jackie Melvin, whose scrutinizing pencil improved my text tremendously, and Corrine Sahli, for pulling it all together—and for her trans-Atlantic support!

FOREWORD

———————— ✳ ————————

This book is a popular reworking of academic research. Through intensive interviews with Surinamese women in the Netherlands and with African-American women in the United States,[1] I wanted to present the problem of racism from a new perspective: to show the many ways in which racism is woven into black women's everyday contacts with whites. Hence the title *Everyday Racism*.

Americans may be surprised to hear that there are people of color in the Netherlands and that the Dutch have a problem of racism. After World War II it became taboo to even mention the word *racisme*, which is Dutch for racism, in the Netherlands. This had largely to do with the Dutch revulsion against ideologies and practices reminiscent of the Holocaust. Also, the Dutch traditionally considered themselves tolerant of different cultures. These and other factors created the myth that racism—though it was a problem in other European countries, the United States, and South Africa—did not exist in the Netherlands.

When *Everyday Racism* first appeared in the Netherlands in 1984, its publication was reported widely in the mass media and it set off heated debate among whites: How dare someone accuse 'us' of racism! However, for many others—whites as well as people of color—it became an eye-opener.

The book exposed patterns of paternalism, hostility, and exclusion against people of color in the Netherlands. These manifestations of racism have historical roots. The Dutch were a colonial power, and their colonies were exploited economically and dominated culturally. The native peoples were forced to live with Dutch institutions, such as the law, politics, and school system, and they were made to adopt Dutch as their formal language. This situation did not change much after the colonies became independent.

Some Americans may have heard about Indonesians in the Netherlands, but probably not about the people of the former Dutch colony of Surinam. When, after 400 years of Dutch colonialism, over 200,000 Surinamese migrated to the Netherlands in the 1970s and 1980s, they were branded as "intruders," as people who did not belong. It took many of them years to realize that Dutch tolerance is a myth that hides the realities of racism.

Dutch images repeatedly portrayed the Surinamese as inferior, and these images were reproduced over generations. Though their crudest forms, such as the idea that people of color represent inferior races, have softened, the idea that the Dutch are superior has survived.

It was not easy to do research on Dutch prejudice and discrimination in the early 1980s. Neither the women I interviewed, nor I, managed to completely avoid the repressive impact of the Dutch denial of racism. My writing style remained cautious, reflecting the expectation that my views and findings could cause emotionally charged reactions from the readers. It was also difficult for the Surinamese women I interviewed to verbalize their experiences of discrimination. They had suppressed many of these experiences, thinking that to take offense or to point out the problem would amount to "complaining."

In order to broaden my own perceptions on racism, I also interviewed, in 1981–82, a group of African-American women. Unlike the Surinamese women, who are first generation immigrants, African-American women have lived for many generations in a white-dominated society. They can build on a strong tradition of resistance against racism, and therefore they are more used to talking about racism. This research was also presented in the Dutch edition of *Everyday Racism*.

For the U.S. edition, I have included additional, more recent American interviews, which I conducted in 1985–86. The American data served initially as a comparative and interpretative framework for understanding the Dutch data. However, it also has a much broader value. African-American women shared with me a knowledge of black and white relations developed and passed on from generation to generation. The additional data gathered four years later confirmed the relevance of the earlier research. One woman phrased this nicely when she commented about the past decade of U.S. race relations: "The script is constant"—in essence, nothing much has changed.

It may be challenging for the U.S. reader to be confronted with stories about American racism collected by a non-American. I have tried to turn the disadvantage of lacking "intuitive" knowledge about the system, because I was not born and raised in the U.S., into an advantage: As an outsider I could ask the women about common, sometimes even trivial experiences without giving them the feeling that they were relating stories I already knew. As a result, the U.S. material is rich, exposing many of the hidden inequities one usually only reads about in literature or in autobiographies.

I have written *Everyday Racism* for the general public as well as for professionals who are interested in real-life experiences of contemporary racism. I have tried to balance theory with practical discussion, to satisfy both categories of readers. The first chapter of the book is more theoretical, while in the other chapters we hear the stories of the women themselves, in the same everyday language as they were told to me.

Philomena Essed
Amsterdam, September 1990

Introduction

* * *

Black Women Speak Out

"They act as though they don't discriminate. But all the while they're discriminating like mad. It may be with a smile and real nice words, but if you listen well and see where it's leading, you see the discrimination. I'd rather a Dutchman say it straight out: 'You can't go here and you can't go there.' Then I know it and I'll fight back.

"But instead they say: 'Sure, come right in.' Then, once you're there, they treat you like shit!"

These are the words of a Surinamese woman. She speaks from personal experience. In plain, everyday language she offers us a striking profile of everyday racism.

Little has been written on the subject of racism in the Netherlands, certainly in comparison to the United States or Britain. Almost no attention has been paid to the black woman's view of racism—which is why this book was written.

Most whites today, consciously or unconsciously, have a tendency to cover up and deny their own racism. It is precisely for this reason that the perceptions of black women experiencing this racism are so important. If we consider the ways in which an individual experiences racism personally, we must address a question that has rarely been touched upon before, namely: How can blacks prove, both to themselves and to others, their sense that racism exists even when it is not being overtly expressed? The question is a crucial one all over the world. As we shall see, everyday reality teaches us that many instances of racial and ethnic discrimination are difficult to "prove." Yet the experience and consequences of racism are no less real or far-reaching because the racism occurs in hidden and seemingly impalpable form. On the contrary, the effects of everyday racism may be even more damaging in the long run than those of blatant discrimination.

On the basis of interviews with 25 women—14 Surinamese and 11 African-American—I will discuss the effects and meaning of racism as viewed from the perspective of these women's everyday experiences with whites. The stories told by these women illustrate how deeply racism is rooted in society today, and what kind of mark this leaves on the everyday lives of people of color. Almost all of the women interviewed here are young: between 20 and 30 years of age. As blacks in a predominantly white society, they are involved with white people on a daily basis simply as a matter of course. During their formal education, they have had whites as teachers and classmates. At work, there are colleagues, supervisors, or clients. At home there are neighbors; when shopping, there are salespeople and other customers; and then there are the white real estate agents, the landlords, the range of civil servants. The list goes on. All of these are average, "ordinary" white people. For black women, the encounters with them often involve contending with prejudice and discrimination.

These interviews took place in the Netherlands and California during 1981 and 1982. In 1985–86 I carried out follow-up research in California. Two interviews from that period have been included here.

I intended the study mainly as an exploration and did not attempt to be representative. I was introduced to some of the women by colleagues and acquaintances and was referred to others by women whom I had already interviewed.

The Surinamese women I interviewed were, for the most part, not highly educated. Almost all of the African-American women I interviewed were more highly educated than the Surinamese. This was a conscious choice. It is very common in explorative research to make use of the insights of people who have practical experience and awareness of the problem under study. I intended to use the American interviews to gather more general knowledge about racism, in order to promote greater recognition and comprehension of the phenomenon in the Dutch context.

There was another reason for my interest in speaking with better educated women. I wanted to break down the myth that more educated whites are less prone to racism. The interviews with these educated black women who have daily contact with educated whites shed much light on this aspect.

I wanted the women to describe and illustrate their experiences at length. With this in mind, I tried to direct the interviews as little as possible.

> In non-directive interviewing . . . the interviewer's function is simply to encourage the respondent to talk about a given topic with a minimum of direct questioning or guidance. The interviewer encourages the respondent to talk fully and freely by being alert to the feelings expressed in the statements of the respondent and by showing warm, but noncommittal, recognition of the subject's feelings.[2]

Obviously the above passage offers an "ideal" image of a non-directive interview. There is an important difference between this interpretation of non-directive interviewing and my own attitude, namely, that I could not and would not separate "showing warm recognition of the subject's feelings" from a genuine, heartfelt involvement.

I did not avoid all suggestive questions. In fact, because of the open nature of the interview, suggestive questions often led the women to contrast their own opinions to mine, or, through digressions and examples, to explain why they agreed or disagreed with particular propositions. It was of primary importance that the women be stimulated to choose *for themselves* how they would elaborate on their own opinions and testimonies.

Doing research among one's own group has the advantage of making it easier to discuss negative views about an "out group," in this case whites. Thus I was in an advantageous position as a black researcher of experiences of racism. As it turned out, the women also voiced open-hearted criticism of other blacks. Both in their positive and negative descriptions of experiences with other black women, the interviewees were able to transcend inhibitions toward me as a black woman. However, a disadvantage in interviewing a group of which you are also a member is that the interviewees tend to refer to things that are commonly taken for granted with the comment, "You know what I mean," leaving out its interpretation. In particular, discussing experiences that were painful or humiliating, the interviewees referred to them as "those kinds of things" and often said, "You know." At that point it required clear intuition on my part to know whether continuing the line of questioning would embarrass the woman or call up experiences that she could not or did not want to verbalize at that moment. This problem played a larger role in the interviews with Surinamese women than with African-American women. In the latter group, although I was black, I was still a relative outsider. It was therefore easier to ask "naïvely" for more detailed explanations.

Since the interviews formed my only empirical information, they were recorded on tape. This made it possible for me to retain the precise words the women used to convey their experiences. Furthermore, it allowed me to listen more calmly during the interview itself and to react to what I heard.

In the interests of readability, both the interview questions and the women's responses have been edited for this book. In doing this, however, I have adhered faithfully to the women's original intentions and interpretations. Explanations in brackets have been added by the translator.

In a book about experiences of racism, it is important to define concepts such as ethnic prejudice and discrimination clearly, so that we can agree on what is being discussed. Under what conditions can we speak of racism, and what is the connection between this term and the more general phenomenon of ethnocentrism? Does being prejudiced necessarily mean that you discriminate? I will address these and other questions in Chapter I. Important terminology and the designations of various forms of racism, such as individual and institutional racism, are illustrated throughout with examples. In view of the frequent confusion about the concept of racism, explicit definitions are likely to be of some help.

In Chapter II, 14 Surinamese women from Amsterdam tell of overt and covert discrimination and of the prejudice against them as black women. Since the group of women is small, it is possible to look in considerable detail at diverse aspects of their experiences. It becomes evident that the reality of racism is not limited to what each woman lives through personally. Discrimination against other Surinamese, especially children, or prejudices expressed against "foreigners" in general, also have an influence on them. It soon becomes clear that the whole climate of life is pervaded with racism.

In terms of their education and professions, the women interviewed are representative of young Surinamese women in Amsterdam. The majority are working-class women, about half of whom work as nurses, either for the elderly or in hospitals. A few work as typists, switchboard operators, or secretaries. Others are enrolled in college or have just graduated.

The racial/ethnic origin of the women varies. They describe themselves as "Creole," "mix" or "mixed," "Hindustani," "Negro," or "just Surinamese," in proportion to their kinship with one or more of Surinam's ethnic groups.[3]

The Surinamese have the same ancestors as the blacks in the U.S. and the same history of slavery. A fundamental difference, however, is that the slavery of the Surinamese took place not in the Netherlands but in the Dutch colony of Surinam. After the abolition of this slavery, large numbers of contract laborers were brought to Surinam from China, India, and Indonesia. In Surinam —then called Dutch Guiana—people of color comprised the majority of the population. The Netherlands, however, held the actual economic and political power, represented by the church, the army, and a small business elite. This white elite group lived in the wealthiest neighborhoods and had their own social clubs, to which people from the Surinamese elite also belonged. The average Surinamese, however, had little or no contact with these Dutch. Only after coming to the Netherlands did Surinamese begin to interact extensively on a day-to-day basis with whites. Hence it was quite a new experience for the Surinamese, for the first time members of a black minority, to be confronted daily with actual discrimination from whites.

In view of the delicate nature of the subject of racism in the Netherlands, I could not discuss it with the Surinamese women in direct terms. In order not to bias the women, I introduced my research to them as a study of experiences of Surinamese women with the Dutch. I preferred not to pose questions such as, "Did you think that was discrimination?" The women were discussing the issue of racism in a cultural context in which this hardly seemed admissible, and this imposed obvious limits on the information I could obtain.

I also wanted to conduct interviews, however, with a group of women who had been socialized since childhood to define themselves as members of an oppressed black "minority group" and who, as a result, were accustomed to speaking openly about white racism. Therefore I interviewed 11 African-American women in California. Black Americans from this state had been intensely involved in the struggle for equal rights and the rise of the Black Power movement in the 1960s. I could therefore expect that they would be willing to discuss the subject of racism openly. In these interviews, I felt free to pose more provocative questions such as, "Do black women envy white women?" The women advanced and illustrated their views on this matter extensively.

Everyday racism in the lives of African-American women is portrayed in Chapter III. The impression these women give of their socialization and of their heightened consciousness about racism clearly differentiates the American situation from the Dutch. Yet their actual experiences in everyday contact with whites show similarities to those related by the Surinamese women and confirm the Surinamese women's interpretations of these experiences. Frequently, these interpretations are not only confirmed but further illuminated by the perceptions of the black American women.

The feminist belief that women can recognize and learn a great deal from each other's experiences runs as a central theme throughout the book. This was the initial reason I, as a Surinamese woman, asked other Surinamese women about their experiences. I spoke with African-American women in order to obtain more information on the meaning of racism, and I have compared the experiences of the two groups of women in order to better understand and illustrate both situations.

Although this book describes the experiences of only two groups of women, other women of color will recognize themselves here as well. The same is probably true for men from ethnic groups. I hope that the insights and experiences of these black women will stimulate a discussion of similar experiences, and that this identification across national boundaries can strengthen the common struggle against racism.

CHAPTER I

_____ ✳ _____

Racism in Today's Societies

Racism: What Is It, Anyway?

It is human nature to experience an identification with and a feeling of belonging to our own particular group: the "we group."[4] This we group can be our family, our class at school, our home state (_we_ Californians), our generation (_we_ young people), our gender (_we_ women), and so on. Specific "others" (_other_ families, _another_ class, _those_ mid-Westerners, _all_ senior citizens, etc.) or, more generally, all people who, for whatever reason, are not included in the we group, may be perceived as the opposition. These others belong to the "they group."

The "we-they" way of thinking is the basis of the phenomenon of _ethnocentrism_. At the heart of this lies the attitude or opinion that one's own ethnic group is not only unique but "better" than other ethnic groups.[5] The norms and values of one's own group are taken to be the "good" norms, and the culture and customs of other peoples are then judged from this point of view. In a well-known example of Western ethnocentrism, cornrowing, a hairstyle traditional to black Africa, was picked up by a white movie star and presented as new and chic: the "Bo Derek" style. By acting as though it were a modern Western style, whites could adopt it without having to change their opinion that blacks are primitive, and certainly not worth imitating.

Ethnocentrism is often evidenced in the inability of anthropologists to take the point of view of the ethnic group they are researching. For instance, in a recent study, black women in the Netherlands were portrayed as cold and calculating when the researchers concluded that "they do not always blame their husband if he carries on another relationship, as long as he keeps fulfilling his financial duty to her."[6] Pain, anger, care, love, and the other human feelings of the black women vanish behind the quick generalizations of these white anthropologists.

Another characteristic of ethnocentrism is that the attitude toward one's own group is tolerant compared with the attitude toward other groups.[7] Unemployed whites are rightly seen as a victimized group, but when it is a question of unemployed Surinamese or African-Americans, suddenly "they don't want to work." Similarly, what is called "clever" when it refers to one's own group is called "cunning" if it applies to others.

In summary, ethnocentrism is concerned with the thoughts, feelings, and judgments that come from the ethnic "we group" being seen as "good" and normative. It is a positive bias toward one's own group. The not uncommon opinion that "blacks don't want to work" demonstrates that ethnocentrism is fertile soil for the germination of ethnic prejudice.

In contrast to ethnocentrism, which is directed against any "they group," *ethnic prejudice* concerns itself with specific ethnic groups. The emphasis is not on thinking from the point of view of the "we group," but on a negative attitude toward a particular "they group." Here we are not only concerned with ethnic prejudice, but also with *racial prejudice*. Since it is not always easy to distinguish between the two, from now on I will speak of racial/ethnic prejudice. However, we should be aware of the differences between the designations "racial" and "ethnic."

The question of how the concept of "race" came about and what we understand by it has stimulated much discussion among scholars.[8] One important conclusion they have drawn is that, from a biological perspective, we can only speak of one race of humans: the human race itself, Homo sapiens.[9] This does not alter the fact that in a popular sense people still make distinctions between "races." What they actually mean by this is racial types or racial groups, i.e., groups that are marked as different from other groups on the basis of physical traits such as skin color, hair, eye color, and physique. The choice of which traits are significant for the distinctions between racial types has developed historically and, to a certain extent, arbitrarily. In other words, there might as well have been a "redheaded" racial type, or a race of people more than six feet tall, if all redheads or tall persons from generation to generation had lived as a separate group and reproduced their specific traits in groups.

Since the term "racial" in a linguistic sense still suggests the existence of several races, I am not very happy with the designation "racial type." I am at a loss for a theoretically unambiguous wording, however. The academic literature uses the term "racial" quite often as well, with the explanation that it refers to a social and not a biological designation.

The concept of "race" is therefore referred to as a social construct. In essence, though it may seem to be about dividing people into groups with a characteristic appearance, it is really about associating specific racial groups with certain kinds of character traits and a certain kind of behavior. This deterministic attribution of specific behavior and specific human possibilities to different racial groups is at the core of racial thought.[10]

Opinions are divided as to the meaning of the term "ethnic." Concepts like "ethnicity" and "ethnic group" have become especially popular since the 1970s. This revival, which is apparent both in the jargon of social scientists and in everyday usage, has also been referred to as the "discovery of culture."[11] The tendency is to group people not only on the basis of physical characteristics but also on the basis of the history, language, religion, way of life, norms, and values shared within a group. Thus, the ethnic origin of individuals is not necessarily immediately recognizable from their external appearance.

The cultural history and ancestry shared by members of an ethnic group does, however, mean that an ethnic group can simultaneously be a racial group. In that respect it is often difficult to recognize ethnic origin as distinct from a particular racial type.[12]

Racial/ethnic prejudice, then, is a negative attitude toward a particular group or its individual members, on the basis of the racial/ethnic origin of that group. This negative attitude (negative ideas, concepts, opinions, feelings, dispositions, desires, and the like) is based upon unfounded generalizations and an incorrect image of the group. Prejudices are not just examples of "wrong information." A typical trait of prejudiced persons is that they tend not to be open to balanced information. They want to hold onto their negative attitudes and will often react emotionally when contradicted.[13] As an example, consider the following dialogue:

A: Those Surinamese are living off our taxes.

B: I'd be more inclined to think that most Surinamese work and *pay* taxes themselves.

A: Sure, and there should be more of them at it. First they don't want to work, and then you can bet they'll be thinking of tax evasion schemes.

B: How can you say they don't want to work when so many Surinamese are registered at the employment office, and when they don't stand a chance of getting a job because employers don't want Surinamese in the first place?

A: That's just what I mean. They're lazy; they'd rather just get welfare. No wonder people prefer to hire a Dutch person.

Clearly A is listening selectively to B, seizing B's arguments only to defend his own prejudice.

Prejudice is often wrongly described as a phenomenon based on irrationality. This implies that the mere fact that prejudice is emotionally laden makes it the opposite of rational. The fictitious example given here shows, however, that prejudice can be based on strategic arguments. Particularly in politics, founding prejudice on such rational (which does not by definition mean "correct") arguments has major consequences. The rational arguments appeal to the so-called common sense of the people. This semblance of common sense and so-called logical thinking, in turn, makes specific prejudices seem acceptable.[14]

The presence of prejudice toward a certain ethnic group does not by definition imply the presence of *racism*. The barely hidden antipathy of some Dutch toward Germans or Americans indicates prejudice, but not racism. In contrast, the prejudiced belief that Surinamese would not want to work *is* an example of racism, because the Dutch, as the dominant group, hold the *power* and hence the means to put into practice their own idea of superiority and their sense of being more deserving of certain rights and privileges. Thus, because of the prejudiced belief that

Surinamese do not want to work, the right to a job—a basic human right—becomes a privilege subtly reserved for Dutch people.

The concept of "power" (the oppression of other racial/ethnic groups based on one's own position of power) is fundamental to understanding the meaning and function of racism. Without access to the power to actually harm the "other" as a group, one may be guilty of pre-judgment — believing wrong or negative information about that group — and of individual discrimination, but not of racism. I will elaborate upon this later.[15]

Racism is a complex aggregate of prejudice and discrimination based on an ideology of racial domination and oppression. Racism denotes the definitive *attribution of inferiority* to a particular racial/ethnic group and the use of this principle to propagate and justify the unequal treatment of this group. The other group is seen as intrinsically strange and different. Racism is often coupled with the idea that the other group is out to "snatch away" and "walk over" the rights of the dominant group. Hence the close connection between racism and xenophobia—the fear of anything or anyone "foreign." The combination of contempt for people of color and the idea that "too many " black people in the country threatens the sense of community among whites (i.e., the "purity" of white culture) is sometimes referred to in Britain as the "new racism."[16] The function of racism is to justify the oppression of specific racial/ethnic groups. In this way, differences in power based upon racial/ethnic background are perpetuated.

Types of Racism

Those who believe that racism consists in explicitly saying or writing, "Black people are inferior," are likely to conclude that there is little racism in the world. Yet the message that blacks are less bright, less civilized, less sensitive, and less human, and that they may be treated in a less friendly and less humane manner than whites, is communicated in numerous, often invisible, ways.

For the sake of gaining a deeper insight into the premise that a society is racist, we will distinguish here between different types of racism: *cultural, institutional,* and *individual.*

Cultural Racism

Cultural racism—sometimes called ideological racism[17]—has to do with the image of blacks portrayed in media such as books, periodicals, and travel stories, through the language itself, as well as through religion, art, or cultural festivals. Cultural racism has a long history and precedes other forms of racism in society.[18] At its core is the contrast between "civilized" whites and "savage, undeveloped" people of color. Cultural racism involves the step from the "we" mentality (ethnocentrism) to the classification of black cultures, customs, and values or the "nature" of various peoples of color as inherently inferior. An early manifestation of cultural racism was the direct association of dark skin color with the word "black," and thus "ugly," in comparison with the pink and white of Northern Europeans. This association became established soon after the first encounters between white people and the so-called Negroes from Africa in the sixteenth century.[19] A plausible explanation for this is that the concept of "white" (in Dutch, *blank*) was traditionally associated with "good and pure" and "black" with "dirty and bad." [The Dutch word *blank*—like the English word "white"—can have any of the following literal denotations: bright, clear, pure.] Whites felt themselves to be more civilized than other peoples, whether they were native peoples, Asians, or Africans. In contrast to the "Indians," who were viewed as "savages" primarily for their religion and culture, in the case of "Negroes," the "lack of civilization" was inextricably bound up in the "black" skin color.[20]

For the people of Europe, tales of travels sent back by their voyaging countrymen formed an important source of information about the lives of peoples elsewhere in the world. The image of the "uncivilized native" was passed on to the mother country by Dutch people traveling in various parts of the globe.

Here are a few examples taken from *De aarde en haar volken* [The world and its peoples], a periodical with travelogues and the impressions of various authors. Citations from episodes appearing at the end of the nineteenth century[21] give the following information about the "nature" of various racial groups.

"A great disadvantage in the diamond fields is the thievish nature of the Negroes," writes a woman in her travel memoirs of South Africa. A Dutch man writes from "Far India" on the extreme "stupidity" of the elephant that takes orders from "a puny savage by comparison, who, . . . though certainly less intelligent than the animal, makes him go wherever he desires." In a story sent from Egypt, we read about "the naïve and good-natured Easterners," and in one from Palestine, about a population that is "by nature so unruly and rambunctious." It is indignantly reported from Haiti that the "poor chiefs of the colored and black people were bewildered, and lost their heads over the nonsensical babbling over human rights, by the worse-than-hollow ring of equality and freedom." (This referred to the "negative" influence of the French revolution on the affairs in Haiti in the late 1700s.) Finally, of "Mistress Senki" in China, it is said that she was "indeed a beauty . . . for a Chinawoman."

By the end of the nineteenth century, travel reports take on a semi-pornographic function as well. Young white men send postcards, made in the colonies, of naked African women to their friends and family in France, Belgium, and Germany.[22] Magazines, such as *The National Geographic*, produced in the U.S., start to publish pictures of African women with bare breasts, or scarcely dressed women from other non-Western countries.[23]

The idle hope that such racist (and sexist) descriptions of peoples of color are outdated and belong to history vanishes when we see the views fed to children through children's books. After analyzing more than 100 children's books—about 65 of which were written in the 1960s and 1970s and were thus lesson material for the present generation of youth—Roline Redmond[24] came to the conclusion that the depiction of black people is often negative, denigrating, and racist. The materials she analyzed included Dutch language books as well as a substantial number of Dutch translations of books that originally appeared in the U.S. or Britain. She offers persuasive examples. For instance, the dark skin color of Africans is emphasized by being compared to a snow-white tablecloth or the bright white of a shirt.[25] The implication is that the dark skin color is the opposite of "clean." Blacks are also called ugly, outright: "Ugly to see: with a flat nose and a broad face."[26] There are constantly recurring images of their subservience to whites. Blacks are also presented as lazy, aggressive, and unstable—Negroes cry and are subject to moodiness by nature.[27] When blacks are called names, they are not called "brat" or "bitch"; instead, racial slurs are used: "ugly darkie" (*lelijke zwartkop*), "sootface" (*roetmop*), or "ugly soot-black thing" (*lelijk roetzwart ding*).[28] The association of blacks with animal characteristics and with animals themselves occurs often, the monkey being a favorite comparison. In addition, blacks are regarded as barbarians, cannibals with whom it is difficult to communicate because of their deficient use of language. Whites, on the other hand, are the adventurers and bringers of civilization. The perpetuation of such racist images is sanctioned by the public at large. Thus, even a Newberry Award winner such as *The Slave Dancer* by Paula Fox contains racist language.[29] This book was highly acclaimed, yet the author insults blacks by referring to Africans as "niggers" and Africa as "nothing by a bottomless sack of blacks."[30] In view of the above, it should not be surprising that the song about Zwarte Piet (the black servant of Santa Claus in the Dutch Santa Claus legend) says: "I may be black as soot, but my intentions are good."

Cultural racism is presented to children in a variety of forms. The children themselves have no control over this and little control over what they will ultimately do with the acquired racism once it has become a part of their way of thinking. Thus, for example, even recently it was possible for a well-educated Dutch boy of about 16 to tell the following story spontaneously to a group of friends. "A kid from my class was in Arabia. His father was working as an engineer over there. Well, they had this ice-skating rink installed out there right in the middle of the desert. Ridiculous, all those *inboorlingen* [a derogatory Dutch word for "natives"] wanting to skate too!" Yet when white people allow themselves the luxury of heated swimming pools—even furnished with all the atmospheric trimmings of the tropics, as in some pools in Amsterdam—it is considered just plain fun.

When we see the image of the Third World as it is presented to children through school textbooks, the origins of such racist attitudes among the young become clearer. Harry van den Berg and Peter Reinsch[31] analyzed 25 textbooks chosen at random from those in use at various Dutch elementary schools. They found that racist views came up repeatedly in the books, particularly in the subject area of geography. In describing the tent dwellings of desert nomads, for example, one writer commented that white people ("a camper like you") would turn up their noses at such an existence. A bit further on, the tenor of the book suggested that these nomads might not even be real people; a female inhabitant is described as having toes that "grope and grab" and hands that were "as ape-like as her feet."[32]

This example is so obviously racist that one would assume everyone would immediately see it for what it is. But because such descriptions weave fluently through the text, the rest of which is not in itself negative, it takes extra attentiveness to identify the prejudicial parts. Schoolchildren are thus induced to take racist notions for granted unless the individual teacher or alert pupil actively points them out and questions them. Moreover, this kind of explicit racism is not nearly as prevalent in the textbooks as is the implicit racism, referred to by van den Berg and Reinsch as "racist associations."

Through her detailed analysis of British school textbooks, Gillian Klein has shown how Eurocentrism and racism operate through education.[33] The history of non-whites begins when whites "discover" them. Human civilization is portrayed as an evolutionary process in which Euro-American culture, that is, the Western legal system, democratic forms of government, and a capitalist economy, is considered the best the world has seen so far. Colonialism is justified by saying that the Europeans were bringers of civilization. Moreover, many of these textbooks obtain their illustrations free from the South African Embassy.[34]

Similar images are transmitted through U.S. school textbooks. But, in all fairness it must be mentioned that one of the most active and critical centers of school textbook analysis is located in the United States. The New York Council for Interracial Books for Children (CIBC) regularly publishes information on and guidelines to help prevent racism and sexism in school textbooks.

The impression we are left with (and which we apparently *should* be left with) after having studied children's textbooks on history, language, geography, and other subjects, is that colonialism was an inescapable outcome of historical circumstances, that Third World countries have only themselves to blame for their inferiority, and that the Western world is generous to offer aid and send people to provide guidance and leadership.

This ideology of white superiority, along with its "logical" implication, the inferiority of people of color, is expressed not only in elementary school texts, but also in textbooks for higher education.[35] So it should not surprise us when the white engineer's son speaks arrogantly about "natives" wanting to skate.

Cultural racism is also propagated through other channels, such as advertising. A few blatantly racial commercials have been shown on television or featured in magazines in different European countries. In one TV commercial for Chiquita bananas, a screaming black woman in a banana skirt is chased by a bunch of white sailors. One does not need too much imagination to understand the racism and sexism in the suggestion that the sailors are hungry. Recently, a more subtle example appeared on English television, offering a mixture of neo-colonialism and sexism: exotic "brown beauties" with long legs, dressed in see-through silks, smile and look at you with seducing almond eyes while they pick the Nescafé coffee beans that white Europeans are going to buy.

In the Netherlands, blacks have only very recently been "permitted" to participate in film or television commercials, and then only if they are lighter skinned. Since the discovery of ethnic minorities as a consumer group, white people have had to get used to the idea that X drink tastes delicious even when it is a Surinamese man trying to convince them of this. I wonder when we will see commercials that will tell us that by using Y suntan lotion one can become just as stunningly brown as an Antillian or Moluccan woman? Or about home perm Z, which can produce the same splendid head of curls for you as seen on the African-American woman appearing on the screen? At present, we have an ideology that preaches that what is aesthetically beautiful can only be an attribute of whites.

Similarly, in the Netherlands, serious news can only be announced by whites. The result? White newscasters, white program hosts, and white announcers. In the United States there is more representation of people of color on television, but positive images still remain exceptional, and there is a great deal of problematic stereotyping.

While little systematic research has been conducted on the image of people of color in advertising and television,[36] that is not the case with regard to reporting in the daily press. In his study of racism in the press, Teun van Dijk[37] points out that in news reporting in Britain and the U.S., events that are seen as threatening to the interests of the white majority are generally featured most prominently. Situations that are threatening to the interests of people of color, on the other hand, are not as fully reported. In much of the U.S., the media tend to convey the message that, since the civil rights movement, racial problems have been solved. Now that black resistance and struggle is no longer expressed as forcefully as it was in the 1960s, the newspapers seem to have lost interest in racial issues. Moreover, the presence of racism is often ignored or covered up with euphemisms such as "disadvantaged" or "underprivileged." Much of the coverage of blacks, Latinos, and other people of color still deals in stereotypes. Apart from sports and entertainment coverage, African-Americans are often portrayed as people who either *have* problems or *cause* problems. They are pictured as too lazy to work, failures in school, and prone to substance abuse. Success stories are rare. Similar trends prevail in Britain. Whereas a large part of the routine news about racial affairs in Britain is quite neutral, the headlines usually show blacks in a negative light. This is particularly true of the right-wing press, which does not hesitate to refer in their columns and editorials to blacks and any others they perceive as "the enemy" as murderers, tyrants, ayatollahs, and scum.

News reporting in the Netherlands is less overtly racist than in Britain. However, the Dutch media have their own ways of denigrating people of color. On the basis of consistent analyses of five national and two provincial dailies over a period of one month, van Dijk[38] concluded that these papers offer the Dutch readership very few positive images of ethnic minorities in the society. News articles are written from the dominant (white Dutch) perspective. With an occasional exception, mainly in the area of crime reporting, there is very little explicit racism. The implicit message, however, is quite clear. Much is written *about* citizens of color, but hardly anything *by* them or from their point of view on events that have bearing on their lives. Moreover, for the most part they are portrayed as a problem group: again, either they *have* problems or they are the *cause* of problems. Of course, in keeping with the "we group" (white) perspective, news articles rarely go into the problems created by Dutch people for citizens of color, specifically the issue of racism and its often drastic effects.

The findings of van Dijk's study can be summarized in the conclusion that Dutch newspapers, although not blatantly racist, are by no means anti-racist. Numerous articles bear witness to the extent to which anyone can air racist ideas under the cloak of "freedom of speech." The antidotal comment that was usually inserted by editors or reporters when the newspaper disagreed with a view expressed does not appear anymore.

The wave of attention the papers devoted to the Centrum Party [an extreme right Dutch political party, with a platform based on racism] in their reporting on the Parliamentary elections of 1982 was not used to further any consciousness-raising, sadly enough. Instead, a common front was presented. Coming from the "we" ("non-racist," "normal" white) perspective, the press pretended that only a small, identifiable group had allowed itself to be influenced by the ideology of white supremacy. But how can one know for sure that it was not a best friend or neighbor who "voted wrong"? There was also the embarrassing spectacle of news interviewers who let themselves be cornered by outspoken people who openly declared their racist opinions. Was this a sign of the interviewer's powerlessness, or worse, an indication that every so often he or she sensed that the speaker had struck a forbidden chord of recognition?

It would be absurd to place extreme racism on the same plane with more moderate forms, just as it would be wrong not to recognize that many people actually abhor racism. Yet precisely for that reason it is important to reveal the extent to which disrespect and indifference toward blacks are culturally propagated (consciously or unconsciously), taken in by the public, and transmitted anew. Society reproduces racism from one generation to the next. Though the sharp edges may have been filed down, the core of supposed superiority has been maintained by whites over the centuries.

Cultural racism seems to be based only on ideas: a deeply rooted prejudice against black people. Individuals, for example, can be prejudiced without necessarily being able to put their preference for whites into practice. In other words, theoretically, prejudice can exist without resulting in discrimination. In a racist society, however, the ideology of white superiority has a profound impact on the way institutions function. For this reason, cultural racism cannot be viewed separately from institutional racism.

Institutional Racism

Institutions are government agencies, businesses, and organizations that are responsible for legislation and for maintaining labor policy, political policy, health care, education, housing, social and commercial services, and other frameworks of society. When these institutions function in such a way as to limit certain racial/ethnic groups in their opportunities for growth, granting them fewer rights or limiting their opportunities to make use of these rights, then institutional racism exists.[39] In practice this means that, while there are many regulations ensuring that whites can work, receive training and education, obtain social and medical help, enjoy the protection of the law, and appeal to the police as citizens, these regulations are less accessible and are extended less as a matter of course to citizens of color.[40]

Two key concepts necessary for understanding the workings of institutional racism are *direct* and *indirect discrimination*. Racial/ethnic discrimination is the adverse treatment of members of a particular group on the basis of their racial or ethnic origins. The difference between direct and indirect discrimination will explain why I define discrimination as "adverse" treatment in comparison with the dominant white group, instead of using the more common term, "unequal" treatment.

Direct discrimination refers to the familiar concept of unequal treatment in equal circumstances: Stanley may not, because he is black; John automatically may, because he is white. The consequences are adverse for Stanley because of his origins.

Indirect discrimination also refers to adverse effects on people of specific racial/ethnic descent, except that in this case the discrimination is due to *equal* treatment. How does this work? The word "treatment" with reference to indirect discrimination is misleading. It is more often a matter of equal enforcement of unequal procedures or rules.[41] We find a clear example of this in a bill that some legislators in the Netherlands tried to get through the Dutch parliament in the early 1980s. Though the law was not passed, it provides an interesting example of our argument. The proposal stated that children of Dutch parents who live abroad are entitled to less child support than children who live in the Netherlands. This appears to be a "neutral" regulation. Yet applying it to all employees in Dutch service shows that it would affect a specific group: Moroccan and Turkish children. Such a law would not have been necessary for the Dutch alone; most Dutch parents have their children at home with them. The racist intention of such a proposal became that much more blatant when it was additionally suggested that children of Dutch diplomats be exempt from this regulation. This was also an attempt at direct discrimination (unequal treatment in equal circumstances): employees who work for the Dutch state, but whose children live outside the Netherlands.

Indirect discrimination doesn't proceed only from the establishment of "new" universal rules; the equal enforcement of existing procedures can have an "ethnically adverse effect" as well.[42] The many legal conditions that must be satisfied before one can register an independent business, or as self-employed, place foreign-born citizens at a disadvantage, if only as a result of the language barrier.[43] Indirect discrimination also need not be consciously intended as such. It often arises automatically, by force of habit, as it were, when an institution has only taken white people into account for many years. We can no longer regard it as innocent, however, when we see that for specific ethnic groups, the multi-ethnic character of Dutch society imposes numerous obligations but offers few social services or rights.

Western job and labor markets reveal many forms of direct discrimination against racial/ethnic groups. We can illustrate this better with the aid of another distinction: between *overt* and *covert discrimination*. An example of *overt discrimination* would be the situation in which an employer says directly to a Surinamese woman that he doesn't hire "coloreds." An instance of *covert discrimination* would be if the same employer did not openly express his prejudice against Surinamese women, but instead confessed "with regret" that someone else had just been hired.

Covert discrimination is clearly hard to "prove." However, in experimental research—i.e., situations designed for the purpose of testing certain assumptions—covert racism among Dutch employers has been shown to exist. In one such situation in the Netherlands, the personnel in temporary employment agencies said they had no work available for a Surinamese or a Spaniard who applied, while a moment later there *was* work for a white Dutch person with equal qualifications. Employers were found to react negatively to letters of application signed with an obviously ethnic name, yet they reacted positively to a letter that was identical except for being signed with a typical Dutch name like "De Vries."[44]

These are not isolated cases; they are regularly occurring forms of discrimination. Unemployment rates among racial/ethnic groups are considerably higher than among whites. Furthermore, the labor market shows ethnic "segmentation": a proportional overrepresentation of ethnic groups in low-paying, heavy, irregular, and unskilled kinds of work.

In addition, ethnic groups have little vertical mobility.[45] In some cases, people from ethnic groups are permanently denied certain opportunities. For example, the state employment office in the city of Utrecht will no longer help "older" foreign women with their job search.[46] This is not a question of women who are close to retirement age: "older" in this case means first generation immigrants. As a result, for Turkish and Moroccan women the chance to work is nearly gone before they reach forty. Other sinister practices have also come to light, such as remarks like "stupid Surinamese" scribbled on the registration cards of Surinamese who register at the employment office in Amsterdam.[47]

Discrimination in housing often occurs in covert ways. Rents or prices may be set so high that the majority of people of color cannot afford them anyway. Individual homeowners may lie about vacancies, or housing agencies apply some form of screening. We will come across many examples of these forms of discrimination in the stories of both the Dutch and U.S. women I interviewed. A notorious example of covert racism in the Netherlands is the "distribution policy." Although not formally set down on paper, the distribution of municipal housing in various large cities has proved to be discriminatory. As though it were a matter of pests or radiation hazards, a percentage was determined in advance of how much ethnicity white Dutch people could be exposed to, for instance, a maximum of six black families in one building. (It has not been considered that ethnic groups live with an enormous percentage of "strangers"—whites—around them.) A direct outcome of this policy is a longer average waiting period for citizens of color seeking housing. In effect, an extra criterion must be satisfied before the housing is allocated. Covert discrimination, formalized through the "right" of individual landlords to protest, is yet another barrier.

Discrimination by housing associations and other private enterprises also makes it more difficult for ethnic groups to find housing. The result is again visible: They get the worst housing, or they pay a lot of money to live in boarding houses that often have appalling facilities.[48] In 1974–1975, blacks in Amsterdam were all referred to a housing association—aptly named "Our Interest" and operating under the slogan "We don't discriminate" —which was soon fully booked with Surinamese.[49]

There is a modern Dutch myth that: "You only have to be a Turk or a Surinamese to get a place in a flash."[50] Whites themselves feel discriminated against. Consciously or unconsciously, the suggestion is that they should have precedence. This is extended to mean that every time a house does *not* go to a white applicant, it is an instance of injustice; once all the whites have been provided with housing, the second-class citizens can have what's left. Though perhaps not meant as crudely as stated here, there is an undercurrent of tension behind comments one often hears in the Netherlands, like ". . . those Turks coming to live next door, while my daughter has been on the waiting list for such a long time." (Would they react the same way to a Dutch family coming to live next door?)

Few forms of institutional racism have been the subject of as much discussion as the white-oriented educational system. A relatively large number of publications have appeared concerning bicultural education, bilingual education, and the recent and growing efforts in intercultural education.[51] The racism present in educational materials was mentioned earlier; black as well as white pupils are exposed to this material. Little research has yet been done on the relationships between white and black students.[52] An important form of discrimination originates with teachers and advisors, with the result that black students are not able to make as much use as white students of opportunities for self-development. Although fundamental research is lacking in this area, there are indications that students from ethnic groups are often placed in classes below their intellectual level.[53] There is probably more to this than "language skill inferiority" or a problem in fitting in with the Eurocentric educational system, which are explanations that have been offered in official reports.[54]

Discrimination in housing and in education does not stand by itself. The same patterns of hostility and rejection occur in other institutions, such as in encounters with the police.

"May I see your driver's license and registration?"
"Sorry, I don't have them on me."
"Well then, do you have any other ID?"
"Yes, my passport." The passport is presented to the officer. As it turns out, the holder is an American.
"So, a false passport!"
"Come on, you can see it's my own photo!"
"Now don't go opening your big mouth so wide."

This was the beginning of a long and unpleasant experience for a black American who had been living in the Netherlands for many years. It wasn't until his white father-in-law was called in that the police changed their tone. The man, in the meantime, had been detained as a criminal.

Police action often clearly demonstrates the difference between institutional racism through *discriminatory formal exercise of one's function* on the one hand and *informal exercise of the function* on the other. Formal duties include the rules, responsibilities, and other official aspects of a given office. The informal side has to do with *how* those duties are executed. Checking drivers, for example, is one of the formal duties of the police. Discrimination exists if black drivers are stopped disproportionately more often than whites. Research indicates more frequent checking of blacks in traffic or in "suspect situations."[55] The designation "suspect" in such cases is, of course, at the discretion of the police. (In Britain, they refer to these as "sus" cases.[56]) Young black men and boys in particular often fall victim to policemen who harass them. Their skin color alone seems to give cause for suspicion.

Many whites find a polite, quite friendly officer facing them at the car door or behind the desk at the police station. Being nice is not obligatory, "it's just part of the job." There is also no reason *not* to be nice. This politeness and friendliness — an informal part of the fulfillment of police duties — is experienced less often by blacks, however. This is not only true of their experience with police, but also with representatives of other institutions. The police do, however, have the power to channel racism into concrete (physical) discrimination, in the form of removal of freedoms, violence, unwarranted brutality, etc. The fact that one must go to the police to *make* a charge of discrimination complicates matters still further. Blacks who do press charges are frequently faced with disappointment or humiliation. To ask for justice from an institution that itself functions in a racist manner is a pointless venture.

The effect of institutional racism is that blacks cannot take much (or any) advantage of resources and services supposedly available to the general public.

Through the examples above, I have attempted to show that a racist society is characterized by institutions that function in racist ways. Institutional racism is practiced by individual whites who, by means of their office, treat blacks adversely relative to whites.[57] By systematically putting blacks at a disadvantage and by denying them equal societal opportunities, these individuals emphasize the fact that racism is the collective problem of whites.

Individual Racism

Since racism is by definition a group problem, the concept of individual racism may be somewhat confusing. To begin with, an understanding of individual racism reveals how the ideology of white superiority and the rejection of blacks is assimilated into the opinions and attitudes of individuals. In that sense, individual racism corresponds to racial/ethnic prejudice.[58] In addition, it involves discrimination, specifically in the areas of private relationships (neighborhoods, acquaintances, choice of friendships) and informal contact (people on the street or in stores).

There is a gray area in the division between institutional and individual racism, however.[59] Ignoring a black colleague by never inviting her for a drink after work, or by excluding her from other types of contact among colleagues, is a form of individual racism. It is certainly an individual's right to decide whether to get to know a particular colleague better. But the informal exclusion of that black colleague can interfere with her performance in the organization and reduce the chances of her complete acceptance in the work climate. In this sense, such an attitude can also exemplify institutional racism.

This convergence of individual and institutional racism is again apparent, for example, in the cases of Dutch employers who would allegedly hire blacks "if it were a matter of personal opinion," but say they must take into consideration the protests (individual racism) of the white work team;[60] a "good working climate" must be maintained. On first examination, the employer seems not to have acted upon racist considerations. If it were up to him or her, after all, the black would have received equal treatment.[61] He is motivated only by commercial goals: The bad working climate that could supposedly be caused by taking blacks into the white work team would result in a loss of income.

It is, however, the employer's own choice when he accepts the racism of others. And the flaw in his argument becomes even clearer if we distinguish between *active* and *passive racism*. *Active racism*, or at least active discrimination, refers to all acts that—consciously or unconsciously—emerge directly from the motivation to exclude or to inferiorize blacks because they are black. *Passive racism* is complicity with someone else's racism. Laughing at a humiliating joke about "how many blacks does it take . . ." ("but it's such a *good* one") and "not hearing" others' racist comments are passively racist acts.[62]

We should not underestimate how often passive racism actually occurs. It is extremely symptomatic of a climate in which prejudice and discrimination are viewed as unfriendly or rude, but *not* as racist. This makes it all right not to object to people who are so "rude" as to ignore a black colleague. Similarly, being served by a black in a restaurant is acceptable, but sharing a table with one is not.

An extension of individual racism is *collective racism:* the organized or semi-organized racism of, for example, a community that rejects the idea of black neighbors, young whites who assault black pedestrians, or meetings that incite hatred against "foreigners." The nature of collective racism—by preference public and often rough—makes this the form of racism that overshadows all the others.[63] This is not only true of the Dutch situation. In the United States as well, open and violent action against blacks has long been the only officially acknowledged form of racism.[64] Yet the extremism of a small group can only be "extreme" in relation to the more moderate racism of a much larger group.

Various studies have shown that individual racism is widespread in Dutch society. The farther from home the contact with ethnic minorities is, and thus the greater the social distance, the higher the level of acceptance among the general Dutch population.[65] According to the Social and Cultural Report of 1982, 75% of the white Dutch population stated they would accept Surinamese and guest workers as colleagues. The same percentage said they would accept children from these groups as classmates for their own children. The "tolerance" of neighbors of a different racial/ethnic origin is lower. Only 45% claimed to have no objections at all.[66] Lagendijk's figures (also 1982) offer a less optimistic picture: 35–52% of the Dutch proved to be prejudiced against colleagues of color and 50–62% were prejudiced against neighbors of color.[67]

These differences in the measurements of prejudice demonstrate that determining the extent of racism is no easy task. An important factor to consider here is that most whites are well aware of the norm that prejudice toward other ethnic groups is "wrong." This issue preoccupied various American researchers in the social psychology of race relations, so they introduced "unobtrusive" measures of racial bias in behavior among black and white Americans. This means that the target persons did not know that specific aspects of their behavior were being observed by researchers. Some of the experiments showed that whites tended to be more aggressive toward black targets, and less helpful to a black person in need than to a white.[68]

In answering survey questions, the desire to come across as "nice" (unprejudiced) can also eclipse negative feelings. As a result, a more positive image is projected than is the reality. Other research results indicate, however, that even when white Americans make positive attitudinal statements about a black person, the underlying affective tone may suggest the opposite feeling.[69] Conversely, a high degree of prejudice, for instance against the idea of a black marrying into the family, can prove to be less severe than expected once the situation actually comes to pass. We can conclude, then, that although measurements of prejudice do say something about whether the climate of opinion is more or less favorable for the appearance of discrimination, they say little about the question of whether and to what extent discrimination actually takes place.

Sociologists, and specifically social psychologists, have occupied themselves for years with the question of the relationship between prejudice and discrimination. They believed that insight into the kind of prejudice that people have against ethnic groups would have a predictive value with respect to their behavior toward such groups.[70] No such definitive relationship between prejudice and discrimination has been found. But it *has* become clear that the existence of prejudice in whites is fertile breeding ground for discrimination when the opportunity arises (i.e., when whites come into contact with blacks). Prejudice usually stimulates and provokes discrimination, and vice versa.[71] For example, the prejudiced belief that black students are stupid can cause a teacher to give them less attention (a form of discrimination). Less attention can result in the students' "falling behind" and consequent low achievement in comparison to white students. Conclusion number one: Black students don't do as well. Conclusion number two: "See—they're dumb." This connection between prejudice and discrimination can be viewed as a "self-fulfilling prophecy."

If whites were to keep their prejudice against blacks to themselves, the problem of racism would remain limited to whites. But the ideology stating that whites can be treated as superior and blacks as inferior is translated into action by discrimination.

We have seen that discrimination toward ethnic groups takes on an institutional form through direct or indirect discriminatory regulations. An important part of both institutional and individual discrimination, however, is what takes place during actual interaction between whites and blacks. How often do white people actually come into contact with people from different ethnic groups?

In the Netherlands, about 95% of the regional population is white. In the larger cities, this percentage varies from 80–90%. Some 55–75% of the Dutch claim never to come into contact with ethnic groups, 20–25% have contact with them "occasionally," and only 10–20% have "daily or regular" contact with citizens of color. The amount of contact with Indonesian Dutch is slightly higher. Still, almost half of the Dutch—48%—"never" have anything to do with this group.[72] These numbers do not differentiate between types of contact, such as in the workplace, at school, while shopping, or between neighbors.

Beyond from the 1988 census data,[73] I do not have corresponding statistics for black-white interactions in the U.S. It is likely that in the major metropolitan areas the number of whites who come into contact with blacks in public situations, at work, or in school is greater than in the Netherlands. Given the historical and current racial segregation of U.S. neighborhoods, however, *extended* interracial contact may actually be less frequent than in the Netherlands.

Naturally the situation is different for individuals belonging to ethnic groups, who are only a small percentage of the population and may be dispersed over the city or region. Although no statistics are known, it is clear that they do come into daily contact with whites: from the baker to the postal worker, from colleagues to managers, from classmates to school deans, from movie ushers to social workers and doctors.

This frequent and extensive everyday contact with whites makes blacks, more than whites, "experts" on the way whites behave toward blacks. This experience is based on contact with whites of various backgrounds: young and old, men and women, acquaintances and strangers, and so on. Therefore, in varying situations and with a varied group of whites, blacks are constantly aware of the ways in which whites actively express a belief in white superiority.

For blacks, racism is the everyday reality. It can be expected to occur in many forms in their daily contact with whites.[74]

Changing Terminology

Up to this point I have alternated between the terms "black" and "ethnic group." The need for one "correct" designation for all the different groups sharing an oppressed position and the experience of racism is a discussion in itself. I have already stated that the concept of "race" is a myth and that at most we can speak of racial types. By this we mean certain stereotypes of what biologists and physical anthropologists of the previous century called the Mongolian, Caucasian, and Negroid "races." The first two terms were soon abandoned in favor of the geographic group designations European, Amerindian or Native American, or Asian. Strangely enough, the term *neger* (Negro) has persisted to this day in the Netherlands. In Dutch newspapers, you still read of *negermeisjes* and *negerkinderen* ["girl-Negroes" and "child-Negroes"], but never of "women-Caucasians" or "child-Caucasians."

In the U.S., whites have always been called "white," but people from Africa were not always called "black." The Africans were brought over to the American continent as "Negroes." A decade later the term "colored" was introduced. A change occurred once again with the rise of the black movement in the 1960s. People refused to be called "Negro" or "colored," terms which were, after all, invented by the white oppressors. In the 1960s blacks chose to be called "blacks." The latest terms are Afro-American and African-American.[75]

It is no coincidence that the terminology used for and about the oppressed group, and not the oppressors, is changing. This is also related to the "degradation" of a given term. The word "Negro" was rejected not merely because it was a "white" term. Over the years, the word became almost synonymous with the humiliation, oppression, and racism experienced by blacks. It had acquired the stigma of an offensive, dirty word, at least if spoken by a white. For the same reasons, the term "guest worker" [*gastarbeider* in Dutch, or *gastarbeiter* in German] is being used less and less. The word "guest" in "guest workers" sounds almost cynical in light of the structural discrimination and the many prejudices against Mediterranean workers such as Turks and Moroccans in Northern Europe. People now prefer to speak of "migrant workers."

The term "black" has never stood literally for black skin color. It symbolizes the oppression of "non-whites" by the white ideology of "racial purity," and at once puts brown, gold-colored, and beige-colored people together in the same category. Neither does the term "white" stand for a skin color that is literally white. Most white people are pinkish or sallow. The Dutch prefer to call themselves *blanke*, a term with decidedly positive connotations in their language. Notice that the Afrikaners of South Africa also call themselves *blanken*. In the United States, the term black has always been applied only to African-Americans. In discussions in American feminist circles, it has been remarked that while Chicanas and Japanese women, for example, feel a solidarity with African-American women based on their common experience of white racism, they do not identify with the term "black." Consequently, they have begun to use the umbrella term "women of color" to refer to women from oppressed ethnic groups.

What is the situation now in the Netherlands? A debate over terminology has never actually taken place. Many white Dutch continue to hold firmly to the use of the denigrating word *neger*. Within the black community, however, this is changing. It will be apparent from the interviews with Surinamese women that some of them still use the term *neger* (translated here as "Negro"), as did the Dutch colonists so many years ago. Others refer to themselves by turns as "dark," "brown," "black," and similar descriptions. In publications and other public media, terms such as "ethnic minorities," "ethnic groups," "blacks," "foreigners," "migrants," "aliens," "colored people," or "immigrants" frequently alternate.

The problem is mainly political. How do we find a name that reflects the shared experience of racism, while at the same time offering emotional identification? "Ethnic minorities" is a political-academic designation for ethnic groups who have less power and fewer means to power than the "ethnic majority." In the Netherlands, the term "ethnic minorities" is applied to Surinamese, Turks, Moluccans, Moroccans, and other ethnic groups which have fewer opportunities and rights as a result of their origins. For the same reason, Americans or Germans in the Netherlands are not regarded as ethnic minorities, for example. While they do form a numerical "minority," socioeconomically speaking they are not identifiable as an oppressed group.

The word combination "ethnic minority," however, is a rather unfortunate one, as it implies that certain groups are "minor" because of their background. As a result, some confusion over the meaning of "minority" in its political and its racist sense is often unavoidable. Therefore many people prefer to speak of "ethnic groups."

The word "ethnic" also causes trouble. The group in power is likely to generalize ethnocentrically about the cultures of "ethnic groups." They do so partly because these groups seem to form small units. These are then defined as "different" by the ruling group, which considers itself the norm and therefore "normal." We can thus see why in the Netherlands (and in countries such as Britain and the U.S. as well) the term "ethnic" is equated with "culturally different from the dominant norm group," or even "exotic."

In relation to the American situation, we have already discussed the problem of the emotional reaction to the reference "black" for people of non-African origin, such as Chicanas and Japanese, corresponding to Moluccans, Chinese, Turks, or Hindus in the Netherlands, for example. On this basis, the Turkish women's newspaper in the Netherlands rejected the use of the terms "black" and "white" during a discussion on racism held at the first feminist congress in November 1982.[76] Julia da Lima, a Moluccan woman, argues for the black/white terminology in *Voor racisten ben je niet wit en daarom niet goed* [for racists you're not white and therefore not good].[77] The same is true of Lya Djadoenath and others in *Zwarte mensen in Londen: Verslag van een oriëntatiereis* [black people in London: report of an orientation journey].[78]

More inclusive terms, such as "foreigners" or "migrants," literally remove the groups concerned from access to the rights that ordinarily apply to citizens, suggesting only a temporary stay in the country. The word "aliens" is quite clinical; it also makes no distinction between people of differing origins. For example, people in the Netherlands of American and Turkish descent are both not originally Dutch, yet each group has a very different position in the society. To add to the confusion, in the U.S. "alien" is used to refer to non-citizens. In earlier Dutch publications I used the term *gekleurd*,[79] a less preferable translation of the phrase "of color." At the time I felt it sounded strange to speak of people "of color." The term was, however, different from the English/American "colored," which would be the equivalent of *kleurling* in Dutch and in Afrikaans. This designation has been abandoned in political discussions, and rightly so, considering that white South Africans have always spoken of "blacks" on the one hand and "coloreds" *(kleurlingen)*—people of mixed origin—on the other.

Terms such as "black," "of color," and "ethnic (minority) group" will be mixed together throughout this book. In fact, stretching the language even further, I find designations like "colorful" (as opposed to white or colorless) also very beautiful. "What's in a name?" Quite true. The recurrent stuttering heard when whites (*and* blacks!) talk about an "uh . . . dark person" or "uh . . . black woman" or "uh . . . Turk, but she might have been Moroccan," and so on, makes one think twice. The "logic" behind the great majority of the world's people calling themselves "black" because a small group tries their best to be "pure white" provides much food for thought.

Everyday Racism

In a previous section we distinguished between cultural, institutional, and individual racism. These interrelated types of racism determine to a great extent the social position and experiences of people of color in a society. To gain further insight into the meaning of racism in black people's experience, I now introduce the concept of *everyday racism*. By this I mean the various types and expressions of racism experienced by ethnic groups in everyday contact with members of the more powerful (white) group. Everyday racism is, thus, racism from the point of view of people of color, defined by those who experience it.

Little research has been done on the mechanisms of everyday racism. One reason for this may be that the majority of researchers are white and do not take on racism as their central research issue. Many researchers do not recognize racism as a problem, or they avoid it in interviews with the ethnic groups they "research."[80] In addition, black people frequently indicate that it is not easy to talk about racism with white people because whites do not "really understand." Since many white researchers lack true insight into the experience of racism, black subjects often find themselves confronted with the defensive attitudes of white researchers. In addition, blacks often feel it impolite or unkind to express criticism of the researcher's own white peers, which is what ultimately happens if the racism of whites is brought up in the context of the research.[81]

Another possible explanation has more to do with theories of how to combat racism. During the 1960s and 1970s in particular, it was unilaterally believed that prejudice and discrimination would disappear if whites were better informed of the norms, values, and lifestyles of ethnic groups. The misconception here was that racism was purely a result of whites being misinformed about ethnic groups. It should be clear by now that, although being misinformed has a catalytic effect, it cannot be seen as the essential problem. The idea of better distribution of information caught on, however. Both American and British sociologists have launched full-scale research into "ethnicity": examining the norms, values, interests, customs, religion, culture, and the everyday way of life of ethnic groups.[82]

A similar trend is observable in the Netherlands. The Dutch "minority" policy, outlined in the 1983 Summary of the Policy Document on Minorities, is also based on the incorrect assumption that the reduction of prejudice is a matter of providing "better" information about "minorities," instead of education about prejudice itself and about the function of racism in the society. (I referred above to the tenacity of prejudice and the sociohistorical foundation of this.) Participating in ethnic cultural events and recognizing other ways in which ethnic groups enrich the society is in and of itself a positive thing, to be sure. But whites must be open to it. Racism, the idea that the white culture is superior, acts against this. It is thus only wishful thinking to believe that information alone could combat racism in a fundamental way—unless that information makes the problem of racism itself visible and clear.

A great danger in limiting ourselves to academic research on "ethnicity" and the "nature" of ethnic groups is that this information can be abused to give culturally deterministic explanations of the oppression. If racism and discrimination are disregarded as fundamental causes of a considerable amount of black-white inequality, sociocultural factors in the ethnic groups themselves might be cited to "prove" that these groups have only themselves to blame for their current position. This is a form of scientific racism, also referred to as "blaming the victim." An infamous example of this is the Moynihan report (1965), which explained the oppressed position of black Americans by their so-called incomplete family structure and particularly by the role of the black woman in the family. It is also interesting to note that the literature has always shown much more interest in the "abnormal" family structure of black working-class families than in the "adjusted" black middle-class family.[83]

We recognize racism most easily when it is expressed in outward and direct ways. Experience has shown that whites often consciously or unconsciously conceal their own racist intentions in their contact with blacks.[84] This in turn can make it difficult for blacks to point to discriminatory treatment in a given situation.[85] By the same token, research into racism occurring in everyday interaction is an arduous task. Accordingly, most of the research that has appeared on racism has been limited to the most visible acts of discrimination. Researchers have identified discrimination in the job application process and in the distribution of housing, for instance.[86] But what takes place throughout the rest of the day—at work, in the neighborhood, or in the stairwell of a building—has remained unexplored. These everyday, constantly recurring experiences of humiliation can be extremely offensive and can have far-reaching effects on black people.[87]

In the United States, the period of open hatred and discrimination against blacks—before they gained equal civil rights in 1964—has gradually given way to a situation in which racism has become increasingly covert. Covert racism has been called the "modern" racism of the United States.[88] In a certain sense, the racism in the Netherlands has become more blatant and abusive, in comparison to the covert racism in the United States; but here too the long-term trend seems to be concealment of prejudice and discrimination.[89] Thus, for example, a Dutch person will say, "Those people are still a lot happier in their own country," rather than, "They ought to go back where they came from." (Notice too the dissociation and distancing inherent in the phrase "those people," an expression often used for ethnic groups.) Covert racism demands of blacks that they examine the behavior of whites closely, with a critical eye.

Covert racism does not necessarily imply that the underlying racist feelings are being concealed intentionally. In a racist society, public morality and the accepted norms may actually condemn racism. But the concepts of white superiority and the rejection of blacks will already have established themselves to such an extent that instead of being exceptional, they become "normal." From the point of view of people of color, it is possible to sense the presence of racism and, through various observations and insights, to make it almost tangible. But even then it may be difficult to make any concrete accusations because the racism is usually denied. "I didn't mean it that way" is a standard response, reflecting this denial.

The results of extensive research done in Britain on racism against black job applicants were revealing on this issue. It was observed that, within a company, "the true extent of discrimination in promotion may be as great as that of discrimination in recruitment, but it cannot be assessed by means of objective tests, because it is not possible to control what happens inside an organization."[90]

This in itself points to an essential problem: It is very difficult to determine "objectively" the nature of everyday interaction between whites and blacks.[91] While the importance of developing a scientific understanding of racism—and especially subtle racism—has been stressed by researchers,[92] attempts to describe subtle prejudices and discrimination are infrequent.[93] A variety of studies have shown that those who are discriminated against appear to have more insight into discrimination mechanisms than those who discriminate.[94] This rather broad conclusion confirms the notion that blacks have a certain amount of expertise about racism through extensive experience with whites. The latter, conversely, are often hardly aware of the racism in their own attitudes and behavior.[95]

Blacks can also be "unaware" of the racism they experience.[96] (This is more true of the Dutch situation than the American, but still occurs in the U.S. despite considerable progress.) To realize that you are being treated with hostility, unfriendliness, condescension, or aggression by whites is the first step. To make the connection that this stems from your skin color or ethnic origins is the next, often very difficult, step. There is a great tendency to think that you "must have provoked it." This comes from a very natural disbelief in the coarseness and abusiveness of other people. And it certainly isn't easy to acknowledge your own experience of discrimination when it appears, as it does in the Netherlands, that your family, friends, classmates, or colleagues have no trouble with it. *Nobody talks about it*—and if you do, people accuse you of "airing your dirty laundry."

It is revealing to consider a frequent point of confusion in this regard: that *being* discriminated against is the same as *feeling* discriminated against. The implication is that discrimination doesn't exist if you refuse to *feel* discriminated against. If you don't feel the discrimination, then you need not have any trouble with it, according to this logic. Being troubled by discrimination, after all, is like *having problems*, and having problems can be seen as being *powerless*. It is clear that when one considers the experience of discrimination a sign of personal weakness (i.e., having problems), one will be tempted to suppress this awareness and pretend that there is nothing wrong. This attitude is often expressed as: "You just make it harder for yourself if you start noticing all the discrimination. You have to rise above it."

Keeping silent about racism, however, does not make it go away. Everyday racism is not the personal problem of blacks. It is a massive societal problem. "Rising above it" can therefore only mean *constantly* drawing attention to racism and challenging it.

Why Only Black Women Speak Out in This Book

In this book I have chosen to present black women's opinions of and insights into the problem of racism, because they have seldom been consulted on this issue. The study of black women's experience is linked to recent developments in the field of women's studies [97] (the note provides a brief bibliography). Because of their experience of various forms of oppression and their political interest in such studies, women of color can give important, more subtle theoretical content to the study of women's oppression and feminism.

Furthermore, their experiences reveal that white women's

racism is often very similar to the sexism against which white women have fought so hard. In this respect, white women may find that they can both recognize and learn from black women's experiences and insights. In a unique study on ethnocentricism done at Dutch high schools, it was found that white girls appear to be less ethnocentric in their opinions than white boys. The researchers theorized that the girls' own "emancipation struggles" had taught them to be more open to the similar efforts of ethnic groups. In contrast, boys are confronted with both the new feminist consciousness of the girls and the civil rights consciousness and actions of citizens of color. White boys (men) thus find their privileged position—positive discrimination—as *men* and as *white*, coming under attack.[98]

Although history has shown that different forms of oppression strengthen each other,[99] this does not necessarily mean that one oppressed group will identify with another oppressed group. White women have often adopted a *political* position in solidarity with blacks as the oppressed group, as in American history.[100] That did not mean, however, that the white women were anti-racist in their *everyday contact* with black women, or that they tried to be.[101] The commonly held opinion that women, as a result of their experience with sexism, are more receptive to resistance against racism than men, must therefore be taken with a grain of salt. Also, people are more inclined to have egalitarian attitudes when it concerns matters that have little bearing on their own life. Thus whites, whether in the Netherlands, Britain, or the U.S., who speak out or demonstrate against apartheid in South Africa, are not necessarily anti-racist when it comes to contacts with blacks in their own country.

Black women are faced with oppression on the basis of their gender (sexism), their racial/ethnic origin (racism), and—in most cases—on the basis of their class as well (classism). These different forms of oppression converge in black women's experience. Black women cannot be divided into "black," "female," and "economically exploited" groups. Being both women and black, they may meet with different forms of sexism than do white women, or perhaps the same kinds but to a greater extent. Since they are not only black, but also women, they may encounter different forms of racism than do black men. And, in their relationships with white men, the racism they are confronted with can be closely tied in with sexism.

In this book, some women will be explicit about the impact of class and gender factors on their daily lives. Others will ignore them. All of them, however, expose in their stories the pervasiveness of racism, experienced personally or lived vicariously through their identification with other blacks. These everyday realities are described and analyzed in the following two chapters.

CHAPTER II

*

Surinamese Women Tell of Their Daily Experiences with Whites

Some Background on Racism in the Netherlands

The Netherlands is a multi-ethnic society with a complicated history. Before entering into the Surinamese interviews, I want to sketch for the American reader the political and historical context in which these women live. Over the centuries, the Netherlands has come to include various ethnic groups. The most important period in this trend was during the years after World War II. As a result of political tensions following the independence of Indonesia, an estimated 250,000 Indonesian Dutch and 12,000 Moluccans emigrated to the Netherlands during the 1950s. The latter group has since grown to approximately 32,000.[102] In the 1960s and 1970s, Dutch companies brought in laborers from the Mediterranean area to carry out unskilled work. This group consisted mainly of Spaniards, Italians, Yugoslavs, Turks, Moroccans, Portuguese, and Cape Verdians. At first it was primarily men who came; later their wives and children joined them. All told, the number of immigrants from the Mediterranean area totals about 325,000.[103]

During the same period, Dutch citizens of Surinamese and Antillian descent were settling in the Netherlands. In the beginning, most of these were recruited laborers, students, and small business owners who saw better futures for their children. Their motivation changed with the announcement of Surinam's independence in 1975. Fearing political unrest and insecure about the future, a great many Surinamese chose to settle in the Netherlands and retain Dutch citizenship.

Before 1975, the Surinamese held Dutch passports and therefore had the same legal rights as Dutch natives. Though centuries of colonialism had made Surinam a permanent part of the Dutch economy, the job market, educational opportunities, and social security system in the Netherlands offered more to individual Surinamese than they could possibly have in Surinam. In a nutshell, the Surinamese are "here" because the Dutch were over "there," exploiting Surinam's resources and making its population dependent on developments in the Netherlands.

In the second half of the 1980s, there were about 55,000 Antillians and 190,000 Surinamese living in the Netherlands.[104] A small number of political refugees from Chile, Bolivia, Vietnam, and other countries have also emigrated. In total, 5–6% of the Dutch population is of foreign descent.[105] However, in the big cities such as Amsterdam, ethnic groups formed about 20% of the population in 1990. It is expected that by the year 2000, about half of the population of Amsterdam will be non-white.

During the 1950s, the Dutch policy with respect to the Indonesian Dutch was one of *assimilation*. Assimilation is also referred to as the "melting pot idea," the belief that society is a culturally homogenous unit into which immigrants must be completely absorbed.[106] From the standpoint of the immigrants, assimilation means having to give up many of their norms, values, and habits. It is extremely difficult for a "minority group" with little or no political power to keep their cultural identity in the face of great pressure from the dominant group. This requirement of complete conformity asks as its price the group's absolute rejection of their own culture, as though it were inferior.

Little is known yet about the influence of the assimilation policy on the well-being of the Indonesian Dutch in the Netherlands. An opinion heard more and more frequently is that the assimilation process went quietly and that the Indonesian Dutch are now fully accepted by the native Dutch.[107] The fact that approximately one-third of the native Dutch polled in a 1983 survey[108] indicated that they would not want to have Indonesians as neighbors makes this assertion debatable, at the very least. For a gripping impression of the struggle for retention of the Indonesian culture under pressure from a Dutch environment that was frequently not understanding and even hostile, I refer the reader to the novel *Geen gewoon Indisch meisje* [No ordinary Indonesian girl] by Marion Bloem.[109]

The Dutch policy regarding the non-Dutch in the Netherlands has been different from their general policies. Initially it was assumed that their residence would be temporary. The government made a few provisions; for the rest, ethnic minorities received limited financial opportunities to set up their own organizations or social services.

The idea of cultural *tolerance* was characteristic of the 1960s and 1970s: a "charitable" tolerance of the temporary presence of ethnic groups. Over the years, Dutch tolerance has become a national myth. The myth of tolerance is problematic, because it confirms positive Dutch self-perceptions but says little about the real rights and opportunities of other ethnic groups. In a 1980 survey, for example, 69% of the Dutch actually stated that newcomers only have the right to keep "non-objectionable habits."[110]

By the end of the 1970s, the realization had grown that the Netherlands had acquired a number of new ethnic groups on a permanent basis. As indicated above, the multi-ethnic nature of the current Dutch population is especially conspicuous in the larger cities.

In recent years, government policy has focused on *integration* of these new citizens into the society. The Minorities Amendment of 1983 describes a "reorientation"[111] whereby the autonomous organization of ethnic minorities was to be gradually restricted in favor of their integration into the Dutch system. One difference between assimilation and integration, in theory at least, is that the integrationist view allows ethnic minorities to retain aspects of their own cultures.

The idea of integration is a positive starting point if it means that all ethnic groups will be equally represented at all levels and in all sectors of the society. In concrete terms, one could then take for granted, for example, that Surinamese women would become not only nurses for the elderly, but also directors of nursing homes.

A critical limitation of the Dutch concept of integration, however, is that it avoids the question of racism, viewing it as a "separate" issue. In this view, a few reforms such as adapted legislation, legal measures, information, and possibly an anti-discrimination institute[112] are considered sufficiently effective means of combating racism. This outlook determined the policy in the U.S. after the 1960s, and also applied in Britain; it now proves to be the view of the Dutch government as well.[113] It is expressed in the Minorities Amendment by the consistent use of terms such as "disadvantage" *(achterstelling)*, "discrimination" *(discriminatie)*, and "prejudice" *(vooroordeel)*. The word *racisme* is avoided, along with any recognition that Dutch society might need to address its own racism.[114]

Most of what is known about the historical development of Dutch racism against people of color is information on African slavery or colonial practices in the former Dutch East Indies. This information has only indirect reference to processes in Dutch society itself. It is not unlikely that there must have been *latent* racism for many years. In the end, the well-bred Dutch hospitality could not stand up to an actual confrontation with black people. A patronizing attitude gradually developed into racism.

After World War II, as I have said, the Dutch word *racisme* became taboo as an interpretation of the relationship of the Dutch with their fellow citizens of color.[115] Yet since 1982, when a representative of a racist party was elected to the Dutch Parliament, it has become painfully clear that the *existence* of racism in the Netherlands is no longer deniable.[116]

This recent awareness applies especially to Dutch whites. Most blacks, as might seem self-evident, already know from their day-to-day experience that racism exists in the Netherlands and that instances of racism are frequent and widespread. The hesitation of blacks to use the forbidden word, combined with whites' lack of understanding of its true meaning, have made discussion of the problem difficult, however. The result is that many forms of prejudice, aggression, and discrimination that blacks experience from whites are also difficult to discuss. A black reacting to such experiences is seen as hypersensitive, annoying, or small-minded. This becomes clear when we realize that, in general, the Dutch only recognize racism in its most blatant and open forms, those ringing of social Darwinism. As a result, one cannot speak of racism because Dutch whites might construe this as an accusation of violent or fascistic tendencies. They want to dissociate themselves from these tendencies, and rightly so.[117] An opinion heard quite often is that something "may well be discrimination, but you don't have to call it outright *racism.*"

The danger lies not in the word, but in its practice. One of the most basic errors made is this claim that the designation "racist" should be reserved for people who openly exhibit hate, aggression, and hostility toward blacks. This unbalanced attention granted to what is actually a small extremist group hollows out the meaning of racism. Prejudice and discrimination toward blacks do not occur primarily as isolated, obvious incidents. Whites regularly idealize and favor themselves as a group. The obvious *positive* discrimination by whites toward themselves is a mirror image of their systematic *negative* discrimination toward blacks. Racism is thus a *group problem:* the problem of whites as a group oppressing blacks.[118]

Consciously or unconsciously, every white person in Dutch society takes direct or indirect advantage of his or her privileged position in relation to black citizens. Positive discrimination toward whites—i.e., taking for granted human rights for whites, but not, or to a lesser degree, for blacks—occurs everywhere in the society. The word "rights" as it is used here does not refer to the judicial meaning, but rather to acceptance, respect, and other forms of recognition of the dignity of blacks as people. Whites can reject blacks and treat them as inferiors because whites as a group hold the positions and power that make racism possible in the society. Consequently, more often than not, blacks in the Netherlands hold the lowest social positions and only limited social status.

It is clear that this collective subordination of blacks cannot be the doings of a small extremist group or any political splinter group. A sensible discussion of the problem of racism is therefore only possible with the acknowledgment that the society as a whole is racist by nature.[119] We need to be able to say that the Netherlands is a racist society. This means that racism is not a characteristic of a specific kind of individual with an authoritarian personality, for example, or of a specific group, such as people in working-class communities.[120]

The assertion that most Dutch are racist is likely to make Dutch whites indignant. After all, who would gladly let themselves be called racist? This is not to say that the Dutch in general are openly in agreement that people with a darker skin color are inferior and must be treated as such. The notion that Dutch whites, because of their skin color and "culture," are superior to other peoples, and on that basis should also be able to exercise power and control over them, is a colonial inheritance. It has been passed on implicitly from generation to generation. Feelings of superiority are included so naturally in the socialization of Dutch whites, in their upbringing, their education, the media, politics, labor relations—in short, in the entire organization and functioning of the society—that many whites do not recognize the racism in their attitudes and behavior toward blacks.

In the interviews that make up the rest of this chapter, 14 Surinamese women express this paradox in lively detail. Their stories illustrate both this reluctance to speak openly about racism and the pervasive reality of racism's presence in Dutch society.

"Personally, I Don't Have Much Trouble with Discrimination"

Discrimination is not a pleasant subject for an interview with someone you hardly know. I had previously met only 2 of the 14 women interviewed here. I became acquainted with the others through women I had already interviewed.

This section introduces the women. Each gives her general opinion of discrimination in the Netherlands and describes how she has experienced it. The names of the women interviewed as well as certain background data have been changed in the interests of anonymity. Quotations have been edited without changing the original tone or meaning.

Shirley V. is 24. She has been living in the Netherlands for 11 years and has a 2-year-old daughter. The only previous contact I had with her was on the telephone, arranging our appointment.

A friendly-looking young woman opens the door. "No, it's no problem—I was expecting you already," she says, in response to my apology for coming somewhat early, thinking it would take longer to get from the west end of town to her ground floor apartment on the east side.

During the interview she sits calmly across from me. In contrast to her lively little daughter, who plays near us, Shirley sometimes gives the impression of being drained of life. She gave up her job as a geriatric nurse when she became pregnant and had to stay in the hospital for several months with complications. Since then she has had little desire to do anything. Her appetite and her general state of health keep "going downhill," she feels. She tells me that she used to spend a lot of time in the company of Dutch people. That has changed, however: "Now I spend more time with Surinamese, because that became so annoying. Everywhere I went I heard *a sma disi e doe lik' wan patata* [she acts like a Hollander—*patata*, literally "potato," is a term of ridicule used by Surinamese to refer to the Dutch, for whom potatoes are a staple food]. So, you know, you start to think, why not just stick with your own people?"

Social pressure not to become "Dutchified" is not the only reason Shirley spends more time with Surinamese now. "When you're in completely Dutch company, you just don't feel like yourself. You feel more at home with Surinamese people."

What would you say is the difference?

"Maybe the way they treat you. Yes, they just treat you differently. But how exactly, I couldn't say. They think differently and they act differently. Don't they?" She looks at me inquisitively. "I feel better with Surinamese. I have more fun."

Do you perhaps feel more accepted?

"I don't know. I don't often have trouble with the Dutch. I haven't really had bad experiences with them. You're in *their* country, so, 'when in Rome . . . . ' You have to take what you can get. You have to take it. And I'm pretty easygoing. What I can't do, I can't do, that's all."

Her next comment emphasizes the belief that as a black it is your own fault if you have unpleasant experiences with whites. "I'm no troublemaker. But those Surinamese boys, they really. . . . At least, the ones who just recently came to the Netherlands. They've actually made a mess of it for us. It didn't used to be this way for us. Things that used to just be overlooked by the Dutch now start them off on a barrage of swearing: Damn nigger this and damn nigger that."

In one respect she feels that the Dutch have become less tolerant because "people [Surinamese] ruined it for themselves." But at the same time, she says, "They lump us all together in the same category: All Surinamese are bad. But not everyone steals, and not everyone is on heroin. Not everyone is a pickpocket." She adds, "They [Surinamese] always say that those *patatas* discriminate against us. But sometimes they [the Surinamese] ask for it. Inside they just keep thinking or suspecting that they're being discriminated against. Look, if you're already worried about it, you'll always go around thinking 'those people don't like me.' I just don't think you can go around being prejudiced."

The above reveals a complex aggregate of ideas about the Dutch, the Surinamese, and discrimination in the Netherlands. There's no smoke without fire, she feels, responding to the increased intolerance among the Dutch. "They may have had negative experiences with Negroes." But, "not all Surinamese are bad," and personally, "I haven't had *really* bad experiences with Dutch people." In her view, this is due not only to her own flexible attitude but also to her belief that feeling discriminated against is a self-fulfilling prophecy. Once "you start worrying about it," you'll also start feeling discriminated against. Finally, she prefers to keep her comments about Dutch people neutral or positive. This is revealed in a parenthetical remark. In mentioning that she feels better around Surinamese, she adds, "Surinamese say that Dutch people are two-faced. But really, who isn't?"

The opinions and experiences of several other women will shed light on the implications of the idea that Dutch people are "two-faced." Concerning her own group, Shirley points out the small scale of the Surinamese community, where everyone knows everyone else and "tells everything to each other."

Carla R. lives with her cousin in a three-room apartment. She is 23 and has lived in the Netherlands for only three years. Her cousin, with whom she grew up, came earlier and began working as a nurse. With her help, Carla was able get work immediately as a geriatric nurse. In addition to this work, she now attends night school at the School of Social Work.

When I phone just before the appointment to let her know I am coming, there is no answer. After a moment's hesitation I decide to cycle over anyway. It's not far, and she'd impressed me as friendly and helpful when, a few days before, we spoke on the phone for the first time. Sure enough, she is at home when I arrive. She just hadn't heard the phone ringing.

Carla sits beside me on the sofa during the interview. She is well-spoken and talks calmly. She also gives the impression of knowing just what she wants.

Her experience is that "you encounter discrimination almost everywhere. Even in Surinam I had to face it. At school, the *soeurs* [sisters; the name given to white nuns in Surinam] often discriminate against 'Negroes.' The light-skinned or the whites were sent to the A-track class, and the dark-skinned often went to the B. The dark-skinned were frequently sent to the Ulo and the others to the Mulo. (For an explanation of these terms, see note 121.) It was also a question of how much money your family had, and that whole bit. I didn't experience racism right away when I came here, so I can't say it has influenced me in any particular way. Of course the Dutch discriminate, but I wouldn't say I've really had *much* trouble with it."

Carla has a great deal of contact with whites in her work at a nursing home. Commenting on her contact with her colleagues there, she says, "I've never had any problem with those whites. They would probably like to come and visit here sometime, but maybe I don't give them the opportunity. I mean, well, you wouldn't want to read them wrong. Somehow or other they are never really straight with you, however friendly they seem. They're really two-faced. They never did anything to me, but in general everyone knows that the Dutch are real slimeballs. So you just have to watch out a bit around them."

Carla's mistrust of the Dutch is echoed and elaborated further by *Laila O.* "When Dutch people are talking about certain unpleasant characteristics of Surinamese, I feel as if it's directed right at me. You can often hear them thinking, you know? They don't say it, but you feel that they are thinking about it. But never toward me. These people are prejudiced against color."

Laila is the only woman whom I speak with at her work. She is a consultant with a life insurance company. We talk together in an attractive canal-house office. At first she sits at the edge of her chair, her back rigidly upright. During the course of the interview she leans back, relaxing.

She has been in the Netherlands for eight years. At 26, she already has come far in the career she had planned for herself.

Do Dutch people ever ask you why you are here?

"Yes, but I don't like it when they do; I think it's personal. I mean, if it's someone I talk to often or someone I know through my work or circle of friends, it's no problem. But if I'm standing in the bakery, I don't like being asked that kind of question."

Do you feel threatened by the question?
"Yes, I get the feeling that they just want me to leave. And they don't even know me.
"Dutch people stick their noses into everything. Too curious, probably. In general, I'm quite happy, though. They say that I'm always laughing. That's, of course, ridiculous. If I happen to be a bit quiet the next moment, busy with other things, for example, they say, 'God, you're so quiet. Are you angry about something? Sulky, maybe?' Now, that's just stupid. You can't be the same every day."

Ester U. raises similar points to Laila's, such as mistrust and an uneasy feeling because of all the questions she is asked by the Dutch.
"In the beginning, when I first came here, it was quite difficult because of all those things they said. They asked you the craziest things. It usually made me angry, because it doesn't stop at 'What did you come here to do?' They always ask more: 'Do they have TV in Surinam? Do the people there wear shoes? Do you have beds in Surinam?' It's a strange culture. I just don't get it. I've been through a lot with these Dutch. They're *mean*, you know. I always say, you better look out for them. They'll laugh along with you and say all kinds of nice things. But afterwards! You shouldn't think that when someone says of you, 'What a nice girl she is,' that they mean it. They're not all that way, but most of them are."

Ester is 22 and has been in the Netherlands for 12 years. She recently moved to a modern apartment with her boyfriend, Jan. She does not "really" feel herself to be Surinamese anymore, and from her clothing—jeans with a comfortable, loose sweater—she hardly differs from many of her Dutch peers.
"It used to be worse," she says. "They couldn't do things with you because you were black. I experienced a lot of racism back then. I mean really *a lot*. We had a friend, a Dutch boy. At the time we lived in the Bijlmer [a modern housing project on the outskirts of Amsterdam]. He wasn't allowed to be with us because we were black. And if he came anyway, he wasn't given supper at home, or he was given nothing but oatmeal. Then he would slip away and be with us again. That's the kind of thing I experienced. Or people pushing ahead of you when you're shopping. They say something like, 'Oh, she just has to wait.'

"Eventually I just adjusted to the whole way of life of the Dutch. How they think, everything. You have to. Otherwise you fall apart here."

I met Ester for the first time on the day of the interview. As we talked, she lay on the couch in her home. She says she is tired, constantly sleepy. She is sure that she has been infected with a disease afflicting several of the elderly patients where she works. For the time being she has had to give up her job as a nurse. The doctor there claims he can't find anything wrong; he prescribes medication, but can't see any reason for her to stay at home.

"My boyfriend—he's Dutch—is very angry about it. Just yesterday he said, 'Maybe because you're a Surinamese woman they think you don't want to work. I'm coming with you on Friday. I'll tell that man once and for all what's going on and how awful you feel.'"

Ester sees complete adaptation as a way to avoid being discriminated against. Yet she has not been entirely spared from discrimination, as we will see later. It is significant, however, that she neither explicitly denies nor acknowledges having met with racism. Statements such as, "I used to get upset about all those things. Now I just don't pay any mind," are typical of Ester's attitude.

Mavis W. is one of the women I had met previously, at a party given by a mutual acquaintance, but we had never really talked. Mavis is 27 and has been in the Netherlands for 20 years. She gives the impression of being a strong and yet warm person. The interview goes on for quite a long time. Occasionally we are interrupted by the sounds of her newborn baby.

Mavis is one of the few Surinamese women I interviewed who told me that she expected to experience discrimination as a black woman. She had been in the Netherlands since childhood, and her mother had intuitively prepared her for it. "I've always been lucky with Dutch people, you know. But my mother used to tell me, 'Well, there are some things that are not so nice. You will— whether or not you want to—experience it someday yourself.'"

You were saying that the Dutch sometimes see you as different from other Surinamese.

"Yes. When they are talking about Surinamese, they say, 'I don't mean *you*, of course! You're totally different.' And then I say,

I'm not different at all. I am a Surinamese woman. I've been living
here a long time, but I will never feel like a Dutch woman. And
just as someone can complain about those Surinamese kids in the
tram who seem so suspicious, it's the same story with Dutch kids.
They're hanging out all over the place, too. I mean, when you just
walk through the city and see what some of them do! That kind
of person can be found everywhere in the world. We just happen
to be a minority, so we stand out. Whatever happens, a foreigner
did it. And I often say that to them. If it sinks in, then they say,
'Yes, actually you're right.' But when something happens and
there are both Dutch and Surinamese kids there, I think they will
always point to the Surinamese first. I don't think they'll ever
learn. It's really awful. Very harmful, I think."

When you reverse the balance, it goes quite differently,
Mavis believes. She gives the example of a colleague who recently
went to Surinam for the first time. "Well, she really stared her
eyes out. She says, 'I never knew how hospitable Surinamese
people were. And so kind to foreigners.' She says, 'You can't say
the same for us.'"

Are you ever asked why you are here?

"Yes, sure, from time to time. I think it's a strange question.
The older you get, the more you think, why do they ask such a
question in the first place? There are so many kinds of people
here, after all. I don't ask them why they go to Canada or
Australia to live, do I? It would sound a little aggressive. Mostly
I wonder what business it is of theirs. You don't really realize
that you might not be wanted around, but that might be part of
it too. It's quite possible that it's behind that kind of comment,
'I don't understand why you didn't stay in Surinam; it's a lot
nicer there, isn't it?'"

Like Shirley and Ester, Mavis also indicates that it used to
be different. Shirley feels that the tolerance has decreased. Mavis
and Ester, however, feel that a certain kind of discrimination
occurs *more* often; we might present this as the issue of "Zwarte
Piet."

Zwarte Piet [Black Pete] is Santa's helper—or servant—in
the Dutch version of the Santa Claus legend and rituals reenacted
each year. He carries the sack of gifts and punishes the "bad"
children for Santa. He is presented as the stereotype of an "uncivilized African": broad lips, big gold earrings, a dumb clown-
like figure, speaking a kind of pidgin or uneducated Dutch.

It has been and often still is the tradition that whites dress up as Zwarte Piet for this holiday, using blackface makeup, painting big red lips over their own, and speaking broken Dutch. Mavis: "When I came here in 1961, there were some Surinamese here, but not many. At Christmas time it was terrible. They'd call you 'Zwarte Piet,' as a black child. One kid, a girl of about 15, made a comment like that to me. But I didn't get it. I said, 'What did you say?' Well, then she started calling me more names. I got angry. That was the only time that I had a real fight with a Dutch girl. It actually came to blows."

So she extended her idea of Zwarte Piet to the Surinamese.

"Yes. But on the whole, Dutch children aren't a problem. I think the really outlandish comments they make about foreigners they've picked up at home. So it was probably something she'd heard at home that made that girl suddenly shout 'Zwarte Piet' at me."

Except for the portrayals of Africans in pictures in missionary books, Zwarte Piet is probably the first black figure Dutch children are confronted with—clownish, but also frightening. Meeting with real black people, then, understandably results in an association with Zwarte Piet. This means that the black person is defined negatively and exotically in the child's mind right from the start.

Helen E. is 25 and came to the Netherlands ten years ago. She is a strikingly beautiful woman and talks very enthusiastically about all kinds of experiences. "I *never* feel discriminated against. Maybe it's just the way I am. I don't believe you have to be white to be somebody. I feel great about my brown color. If they can feel like they're better, well, I can feel I'm *much* better! You have to be a little self-assured, don't you, or you start getting offended by every little thing."

In essence she is saying that it's your own fault—you attract the unpleasant experiences that come your way. As the interview questions touch on potentially negative kinds of contact with the Dutch, she states repeatedly that she doesn't remember experiencing any of those sorts of things, at least not personally.

Yet she does seem to experience a more general feeling of insecurity in Dutch society. "There will always be a tendency for people to offend you. They would like to see you break down in one way or another.

"Surinamese often get grouped together in the same category. But that's the same everywhere. A small group ruined it for the rest of the pack. I came to Holland with an all-white group. When I arrived in Holland I looked for my Surinamese friends. We look for each other because we know who we're up against—those whites."

Joan N. is in agreement with Helen about the superiority complex of whites. "They're always thinking that they are better, those whites. But not to me; I know what they're worth."

Joan is 27 and has been in the Netherlands for ten years. She works as a typist at a health insurance company, but is at home today because she is covered with scratches and bruises as a result of a nasty automobile accident. She can hardly sit, heroically suppressing the pain that can plainly be read on her face. She won't hear of a postponement. It is a Wednesday afternoon, and from time to time her seven-year-old son bursts in with a question or to show us what he is doing.

"Hearing those Dutch talking the way they do about things does make me feel unwanted," says Joan. "Who wouldn't! I think they'd like all those foreigners *out*. Some would, anyway. The people who know us Surinamese don't have such views about us. But if they don't know us, then they think something like, what are those people doing here, anyway? As though we're too much for them. It's not as if I feel that I personally am 'too much.' I don't really meet with much discrimination myself. I don't have much of a problem with it. I'm a sharp cookie, and they can't get me down."

From the above it would appear that while Joan may recognize that foreigners are unwanted, she also considers herself an exception to this. She resolves this discrepancy by pointing out that though you may *be* unwanted, you need not *feel* that way. Elsewhere in the interview she hints that "this discrimination every now and then" is one of the things she doesn't like about the Netherlands. But she won't let herself be put down, as she says, so it doesn't really bother her that much. With this she reveals how she deals with discrimination (by keeping "sharp"), but not the ways she is confronted with it. This will become clear shortly.

Ilse V. is a no-nonsense woman of 23. She has been living in the Netherlands for eight years. She is the seventh woman I interview, and the first one to say that she is often seen as a "typical Surinamese" by Dutch people. They consider her aggressive and sharp-tongued. She re-creates certain events with such a vivid and apt choice of words that, despite the serious nature of the subject, on several occasions we find ourselves doubled over with laughter as we sit next to each other on the sofa. Once the interview is over, she immediately phones a friend to urge her to be interviewed as well. When this friend does not at once react with enthusiasm, Ilse lets me know, with a "just between us" gesture of the hand, "Don't you worry, I'll take care of it for you." Like the other women who offered a referral, she keeps firmly to her promise "not to tell her anything about the interview."

"Listen," says Ilse. "Those Hollanders just *lay it on thick.* When you're face to face with them, it's, 'Oh, what a dear girl you are!' Then after a few days go by, you hear how So-and-so said this and that about you.

"The young people don't discriminate as badly as the older ones. For the older generation, we're still intruders." Later this opinion proves to be closely related to her work as a nurse in a home for the elderly.

When asked whether she has encountered discrimination herself, her answer proves very revealing. "I have never really had trouble with them discriminating or anything. When people are talking about it, I always ask them, 'What do you mean?' Because I've never really consciously experienced it. Okay, in the tram I have, but that's more common. And then I answer back, too. As soon as they begin to generalize, I don't like it. If one Surinamese did something, talk about that Surinamese, but don't start generalizing all of a sudden. Because not all of us are like that."

The combination of "I've never really consciously experienced it" and "Okay, in the tram I have" suggests that she associates discrimination with big, public deeds, against which one is more or less defenseless. Notice also the casualness with which, "Okay, in the tram I have," is followed by, "and then I answer back."

Rita A. lives in a one-room walk-up. She is 21 and has been in the Netherlands only two-and-a-half years. She is friendly, but at first comes across as passive and reserved. This changes when the tape is switched off at the end of the interview. She is the only woman who was visibly uncomfortable in the presence of a running tape recorder, I realize in retrospect.

Rita claims not to have had any unpleasant experiences with the Dutch.

Is that because of you, because you have been lucky, for example, or is it the attitude of other Surinamese that causes them to be discriminated against?

"I think it's partly luck. It may also have to do with the attitude, but partly not. I mean, I am not the only Surinamese here. I think it's just a few Surinamese who have spoiled it for the others. People only see that small group. Then they start to think, 'Everything black can go to hell, as far as I'm concerned. They should just beat it and go back to their own country.'"

Rita, like several others, speaks mistrustfully of the Dutch. "I know they're two-faced, saying one thing and doing another. So of course you just do the same to them."

Linda N. addresses this subject, saying, "Not all whites are bad. They say white is 'pure,' but it's not pure to me. Because they're two-faced. They have a good laugh with you, but if you don't watch out, the next thing you know they'll be getting you into a whole lot of trouble."

Linda is 22 and has been in the Netherlands for eight years. We talk together in a large room in the office of a Surinamese organization. Her daughter of 18 months is playing in a day-care center elsewhere. She is easygoing, though at first a bit shy because she isn't sure she will "be able to give the right answers," as she puts it. It becomes an absorbing conversation, with moments of anger on my part, in response to the racist manner in which she has been treated. But more on this later.

Linda: "Sometimes Dutch people ask you, 'What did you come here for?' They always ask that same damn thing. Maybe we're a problem for them. I have heard that they ask that question because there are a lot of blacks in high-ranking positions—blacks who just go to school and find work—while there are whites who don't get a job."

Olga K. is 24 and has been in the Netherlands for seven years. She talks for several hours about her work as a nurse, about day-to-day experiences while shopping, and about the agony of trying to find a better place to live than her noisy 9-by-12 boarding house room.

You arrived at Schiphol Airport. And then?

"Well, it was February," says Olga. "Co-old! It was terribly cold. The family here thought we would be coming a day later, so nobody came to pick us up. We got into a taxi. Cold, I tell you. The driver was nice. It was dark, so you couldn't see anything. When we got there, we had forgotten some of our things in the taxi. All the special candy we'd brought for my little cousins. We left it all in the taxi.

"In the beginning I liked it here. It was a little hard, because you had to adjust to things. I make friends easily, so it wasn't as hard for me. In nursing you do notice discrimination taking place. And in shops, too, particularly."

As with almost all of the women, *Lita L.* gives the impression of being older than her 23 years. She has been in the Netherlands seven years. Most of that time she has worked as a typist or receptionist. She is Laila's cousin. Laila had said, "You should talk with Lita, too. She is completely different from me. A real housewife."

Lita: "Although they don't discriminate against *me*, personally, I know for sure that those Hollanders do discriminate. I don't have any problems with it in my own neighborhood. Maybe it's because I don't notice it. Sometimes people can be unfriendly, but so can I." This last comment is characteristic of the image that she sketches of herself—on her guard, defensive, and "aggressive" in her attitude toward the Dutch.

Myra E. seems to be just the opposite, though even she denies having experienced any discrimination. She is 30 and has been living in the Netherlands for ten years. The interview comes at an inopportune time; her mind is elsewhere as there are some difficulties in the family. She does not allow me to go, however, because she has already had to postpone a previous appointment, which she says is very much against her nature. Myra is a very kind woman, but it seems that she has put up a wall around herself that only allows the passage of messages in which everything regarding contact with Dutch people is just fine.

"Since the very first day that I set foot in the Netherlands, I have *never* noticed that I was being discriminated against," she says. "Everywhere I go, I am always accepted. Maybe it has to do with the way I act or something. When my husband and I went out, we were always admitted everywhere."

The interview turns out to be quite brief. I do not wish to impose any further. But as if she too is disappointed that the circumstances were inconvenient, she phones me that evening. She speaks of her younger cousin who feels ashamed of her Surinamese background whenever she sees "those boys hanging out in the back of the tram. That [feeling] certainly can't be good."

Myra echoes the stereotypical image of adjustment that is upheld in Surinamese circles. "My neighbors know exactly when one of us has a birthday. The whole street knows me because I'm always dropping by." Lita, on the other hand, claims to have "no Dutch friends" and does "not want anything to do with those Hollanders." Yet both of the women deny experiencing any discrimination.

Carmila U. is the fourteenth and last woman heard from here. She is 28 years old and has spent the greatest part of her life—25 years—in the Netherlands. Carmila is the younger sister of a good friend of mine. We had met each other once before.

"I don't actually have any problems with it, with real discrimination. If you are open and just talk to the people, then I don't think you have much trouble with them."

But ultimately you would like to go back to Surinam?

"I just don't see it working out for me here anymore. The Dutch mentality has changed a lot in the last ten years. People used to be much more tolerant than they are now. And, well, I don't like the climate either. It is *so* cold. And then the hectic life. I have managed to handle myself in such a way that I think, if you [Dutch] treat me well, then I'll do the same to you. It's just that I've gotten a little tougher.

"I wouldn't like to live here until I die, but I wouldn't say I really feel unwelcome, either. So it's not that I feel uncomfortable. It's just that I don't see any future for me here. It's going downhill; minorities here are still only seen as scapegoats of the society. They get the blame for the unemployment situation and the housing shortage. Yet they are in fact the ones who have to take all the dirty jobs. Surinamese are not accepted here. They are constantly reminded that they are *colored*."

Summary

Almost all of the women indicated an awareness that prejudice
and discrimination do occur in the Netherlands. Yet they believe
that they *personally* are hardly affected by it. In other words,
initially they do not have an entirely negative view of their
personal experiences with Dutch people. This is true of those who
have lived in the Netherlands for short as well as long periods.

Particularly striking is the virtual absence of knowledge
about racism. They notice discrimination and prejudice, but they
do not have a comprehensive or theoretical framework for explaining these experiences. This is obviously a result both of the
Dutch taboo on the open discussion of racism and of the general
denial of racism by the majority group. Therefore, the women
resort to the common belief that a small group of Surinamese
"ruined it for the rest."

The women mainly associate Surinamese *men* with this. The
association is made indirectly, for example by referring to drugs,
heroin, or pickpockets—i.e., the criminal scene, a scene that has
traditionally been more the territory of men than of women,
regardless of their origins. When we consider that the prejudicial
reporting practices of the Dutch media, in particular the daily
newspapers, are largely responsible for this image of male Surinamese[122] as criminals, their reference to the offending group
becomes somewhat understandable.

In contrast to many Dutch, the Surinamese women do not
apply the idea of "the criminal Surinamese" to the entire Surinamese group. They appear to want to distinguish themselves
clearly from that particular group, yet at the same time they say
that the problem lies more in the *making of generalizations* about a
small group than in the group itself. If we were to generalize
similarly about the proportionally equal, but numerically much
greater, group of Dutch "criminals,"[123] it would be mighty frightening to mix with the Dutch.

About half of the women indicate that they do not trust
Dutch people. Despite the lack of opportunity to gain knowledge
about racism through the educational system or through the
media, the Surinamese women have come to question Dutch
behavior. In this regard, they repeatedly state that Dutch people
are "two-faced": not saying what they mean and not meaning
what they say.

This mistrust is also apparent from the various answers to my question: *How do you feel about Dutch people trying to tan themselves?*

Shirley: "They call us names, swearing, 'Brown this, nigger that,' but they themselves wait for the sun every day of the summer just so they can lie in it and get a bit of color!"

Carla: "You often hear them saying, 'You don't need to get a tan. You're nice and brown.' But I don't think that's really what they mean. I think they're looking for something completely different than the dark skin we've got. They don't want to be so pale, so absolutely white. But I sincerely doubt they'd really want to be as dark as we are."

Mavis: "They are always complaining about people with a different skin color. But they themselves feel awful about being so pale."

Ilse: "One day you're black and they swear at you for it, and the next day they are jealous because they want to be brown themselves."

Rita: "I don't think they're happy with their color. But when they say, 'What a beautiful brown color you have,' I'm not sure they really mean it."

These opinions seem to suggest both mistrust and bafflement. Or, as Ilse says, referring to this question, "I just don't get those Hollanders when it comes to that."

This equivocal attitude about darker skin color is typical of how the Dutch behave toward black people. The repeated observation that Dutch people are two-faced could also be interpreted as meaning that the Dutch do not admit their true feelings.

This brings up the women's abundantly evident tendency to say that they themselves experience little or no discrimination. Phrases like "not really," "not that often," or "not much trouble with it," are characteristic. These expressions come across as just as *vague* and *intangible* as the many forms of everyday racism with which the women clearly are confronted.

Because this racism frequently appears in an implicit form, involving seemingly trivial injustices, it is understandable that the women do not respond with blunt answers like, "Yes, I am often discriminated against." This would require keeping track of numerous, often minor, painful incidents that are either tolerated or pushed aside because they cannot be substantiated.

In addition, the women seem to want to assure others that they don't want to "whine and complain" or "make a big deal of it." In one sense they are remarkably tolerant of the Dutch, but this can, of course, also be seen as a form of self-protection. If one is constantly burdened with an awareness of all kinds of injustices and painful incidents, it isn't easy to go on. Which also explains comments such as, "I don't let it bother me anymore," or, "You can't let yourself be offended by every little thing."

Further on it will become clear that discrimination is not caused by a particular attitude on the part of the "victim" herself. We will see that all the women—regardless of their degree of adjustment, the duration of their stay in the country, the kind of education they have had, or whether their appearance is more or less beautiful, light or very dark—have met with prejudice and discrimination.

In the following accounts of concrete forms of everyday racism we shall see that the experiences are seldom described in terms of racism, discrimination, and prejudice. The ingredients of these, however, are repeatedly mentioned: attitudes and acts that disadvantage the women in comparison to whites. Situations arise involving contact with the Dutch in seeking housing, with neighbors and work associates, in educational circles, in shops, on the trams [streetcars], in discotheques, and with people on the street. Although on the surface these would seem to be isolated events, it will become clear that they are systematically recurring expressions of racism.

After surveying all of the examples given of prejudice and discriminatory treatment by whites, I found they could be classified into three categories. I call these the three main forms of racism:

Inferiorization
Social or spatial distancing
Social or physical aggression

These are not mutually exclusive categories; their forms often overlap.[124] I will elaborate on this during the following exploration of the experience of racism.

Housing and Neighbors

After living with her oldest sister for a while, *Rita* gets a room as a boarder in the nursing home where she is a trainee nurse. The girls live together in one wing of the building.

Rita: "There is always a kind of deathly silence in the air here. Like a convent. No boys can live here. And visitors cannot stay overnight. At 11:00 P.M. they just have to leave. You're not allowed to have your own telephone, either. Everyone has given this place a different name, like 'Virgin Village.' I'm the only Surinamese girl here."

Do you ever socialize with the other girls?

"After our evening shift, sometimes we drink a beer together, watch TV, that kind of thing. Because being alone here is the worst. Sometimes you can almost see the walls closing in on you. But what can you do? Nothing. It is unbelievably hard to find a place to live."

Rita expects the difficulties of finding other housing to be greater for her, as a black woman, than for Dutch people. As a result she feels the necessity to make extra efforts. "I'm planning to put some ads in the paper next month. It's an expensive way to do it, for sure. But, well, if you're a foreigner you have no choice. It's all a question of luck."

Will you mention in the ad that you are a Surinamese woman?

"I don't know yet, but I think so. Because imagine that someone does have something for you, and they find out you're a foreign girl. Then they'll just say, 'Hey, sorry, it's already rented out.' Or these days they just give it to you straight: 'Since you're a foreigner, we've decided not to rent it out after all.' And in some ads it's also clear: 'No foreigners,' or, 'Foreigners may apply.' You come across all that in the papers. And you gradually get used to it."

This kind of blatant discrimination is not strictly legal, but there are few chances to successfully fight the cases in the courts.

Ilse confirms that the Dutch will sometimes state explicitly that they do not want to take in any foreigners as tenants. "Those landlords discriminate, not the G.D.H. [the municipal housing service, which acts as a housing agent in the public sector]. I know people who were offered a house and went to see it. The landlord said, 'No, I don't want any foreigners.' What do you do then? The G.D.H. can't do anything about it."

Linda's experience with the G.D.H. is different. She believes they do discriminate. She lives in a rather large room but, now that she has a child, is looking for two separate rooms. She pays 350 Dutch guilders per month, which she can hardly manage on her minimal income. Recently she was contacted by the G.D.H.

"I was offered a house, but I didn't want it," she explains. "Much too expensive. I don't get that much money. I would have to pay almost 500 guilders and live in the Bijlmer. [The Bijlmer, a modern housing project on the outskirts of Amsterdam, is a relatively unattractive place to live. It has a reputation of being poorly maintained and having higher crime rates than most of Amsterdam.] They try to put everyone there so that it will eventually become a slum. That's what it looks like already. There aren't many whites there anymore. Really, they want to chuck all the blacks in one corner. Now they've taken away my *urgentiebewijs* [certificate of need], but I am going to fight for it. I said to them, 'I won't take it. Nobody can force me to live there.' Because even if they force me into it, how am I supposed to live then? I said that, too."

Olga tells a similar story. She was also told repeatedly that she should go to the Bijlmer if she wanted an apartment. "But I'd told them right from the start that I didn't want the Bijlmer. I said, That's all you tell Surinamese and Turks, 'Yes, you can get a house: Bijlmer.' It's too expensive for me. Usually when I go to the G.D.H., I see a lot of foreigners. Especially Turks. And pitiful! 'Amsterdam-North or the Bijlmer—that's it!' But when you hear those prices!"

As if to prove that discrimination is not always just a question of discriminatory policy rules, but also of the unfair application of fair policy rules, Olga goes on to tell of a civil servant at the G.D.H. who abuses his position to express his own prejudices. "Every time I go, they have a new excuse, even though it's my turn. The guy says, 'By the end of the month I'll have a place for you.' I say, 'Yes, you can get me off easily that way. But I don't want the Bijlmer. You can't force me to live there.' I mean, no one wants to go to the Bijlmer. So the guy says, 'Yes, but you people love to hang around together, don't you?'"

Notice the phrase, "hang around together." Aside from the prejudice already implied in this statement, a comment like, "You like to be together in the same neighborhood," would have been far less offensive.

The reason Olga so urgently wants another apartment is that she and her partner cannot manage anymore in a 9-by-12 room, with a double bed taking up almost half the space. The building is also extremely noisy and damp. From the outside you would never suspect that the two narrow floors upstairs are a boarding house with some 30 rooms—many with dividing walls of hardboard.

But Olga is very enthusiastic about the landlord, an older man. "He's a really nice man. I pay 400 guilders, but gladly. If I'm bored I can go down and sit with him. Or he calls me up. He's lonely."

Did he ever want more from you than to just sit together?

"No. I don't give him any reason to, either. I think he considers me his child. In the beginning, I couldn't get along with him. I thought, maybe he doesn't like Surinamese. Because he had said to me, 'You are the last Surinamese woman I'm taking in.' I said, 'Why do you discriminate like that?' He said, 'Just come inside and see.' He had a list with photos of only Surinamese girls. I asked where it came from. He said, 'They are my grandchildren.' All of his children are married to Surinamese."

Not Fitting In

The presence of a black woman in a white family, does not in itself guarantee that the family—even the white husband—will be free of racism, unfortunately. *Mavis's* experience illustrates this clearly. "Someone had placed an ad in the paper," she related. "They were going away for two years, I think, and wanted to rent out their home temporarily. I thought, I'll go over and see it. It was a dark girl. Not Surinamese; I think she might have come from Trinidad. She was married to a Dutchman. Well, we had a nice talk, about what my family was like, and that kind of thing. She thought it would work out fine. She said, 'Come by again after my husband has been home.' When I came back to see her, I could have cried. Really cried. Her husband didn't like the idea of a foreigner living in his house."

Her own husband?

"Yes. She said her husband wasn't sure at first, and so she had said something like, 'Really, she's such a nice lady, a nice person.' But he talked to his brother and the rest of his family anyway. And you know what that's like, with the parents and so on. Like, 'Hmm, you better not do it.' And you know what made up the man's mind? His mother—the girl's mother-in-law, in other words. She lived in a modern housing project and there were a few Surinamese families living there. A lot of cars passed by there on the weekend, making noise and parking outside the house. The mother assumed, 'Maybe she acts sweet now, but later she'll make a mess of it.' Well, it was really awful. But I said to that girl, I feel worse for you than for me. He's *your* husband. And you're colored too. You even have a child together! I feel sorry for you that your husband talks like that, along with your mother-in-law and your brother-in-law."

Two-faced

Mavis, as I noted in the previous section, grew up believing that she would be discriminated against. But the ways in which it occurred, and especially its inexplicit quality, came as a blow to her. In the following example, she reveals that discrimination can not only be shocking but can also bring on great indignation and anger. And yet, she carefully analyzes the whole situation before coming to the conclusion that she is discriminated against because she is black.

"I called up a housing agency. Perhaps since I speak Dutch so well, people don't think right away when I call, oh, she's from Surinam. But the moment I arrive and say, 'You remember, it's about that house; I called you earlier,' the woman says, 'Are you sure you spoke to *me*?' It really put me off. The agency is on Beethoven Street [a well-known street in a chic area of Amsterdam], so you can just imagine . . . . I said, 'Yes, I'm sure I spoke to you. It was your voice.' There were two men and one woman, so I couldn't have been mistaken about it. I think to myself, well, I get it. I say, 'Just forget it,' because I don't want to make a scene. They'd just get on their high horse, giving me an endless story about their house.

"So I left. I went home, and oh . . . I had never experienced that. I knew that people discriminated, but *this*, this kind of thing I hadn't ever experienced. I think to myself, look what a Judas she is. That woman even dared say to me, 'Are you sure you spoke to me?' I was so mad; I have never used a housing agency since. I felt really awful. I couldn't understand how someone could be so two-faced. You think, maybe I'm just crazy. And at that moment you can yell as much as you want, but it doesn't make any difference. The only thing you can do is act like it's nothing and leave. I mean, if someone swears at you, you know how to react. But not in this situation." This feeling of helplessness can cause one to avoid such situations out of self-protection. For Mavis, this means specifically that, out of fear of being discriminated against underhandedly, she resolves never again to make use of a housing agency. Her already slim chances in the housing market become even more limited as a result.

Earlier I mentioned that the majority of Dutch people surveyed indicated not wanting to have neighbors from other ethnic groups. What actually takes place when a black woman moves in next door?

Most of the women claim to have little or no contact with their neighbors. A few do not know their neighbors at all; others will exchange greetings if they meet in passing. Myra has a very good relationship with her neighbors and Ester often stops in to have coffee with the neighbor upstairs. Shirley is the only one who lives next door to a Surinamese family. Only in the summer do they occasionally chat over the backyard fence. Helen lives next door to an older couple, and Linda to an older woman. They describe them as people who want to offer a bit of protection to such young Surinamese "girls." Helen considers this very kind of her neighbors. Linda has mixed feelings about it, saying, "The lady next door says, 'You're still so young. I'll keep an eye out for you. You mustn't be angry with me.' She said I should come to her the minute something's wrong, any time. But she is constantly gossiping. So I know what will happen if I go to her—she'll have something to gab about. The previous tenant also said to me, 'Watch out, she gossips.'"

Joan's upstairs neighbor sometimes sits for Joan's son, and in exchange Joan takes care of the cats when her neighbor is away for a weekend. "We see each other when we need each other. A knock on the door. But we don't come by each time and have coffee together. That's not my style."

How do you think she likes having a Surinamese woman as her neighbor?

"I think she likes it. I'm also the kind of person who, if I've cooked something good, and there's a little extra, I'll run upstairs with a plate of it when she comes home. That kind of thing. She likes that. She wouldn't immediately think of bringing something down to me, but that's not really necessary anyway. After all, I can also cook Dutch meals myself. And I think of how she's all alone . . . . "

Breaking Social Rules

The women experience racism of various forms in contact with white neighbors. *Lita* tells of a young couple from whom she and her Surinamese boyfriend rented an attic apartment. The landlady in particular had an ambivalent attitude toward blacks. On the one hand, she seemed to see Lita and Glenn as a positive exception. On the other hand, she thought that every black man wanted to "do it" with a white woman. She therefore disregarded certain rules of decorum that are observed with respect to white tenants.

Lita: "It was a really beautiful room. She had actually wanted to rent it for just 50 guilders, but we paid 100. If we felt like playing records, we could use their stereo system. We could watch TV at their place too. Everything was high-class. It was really fantastic. But you have to realize that my husband—at the time still my boyfriend—really bought them off. The woman was always in need of money. And so it was, 'Here you are,' and then they were nice to us again. Or I cooked something, and then they would come and join us for dinner. And the Dutch always like Surinamese food, you know.

"We liked the man, but not that woman. What was so typical was that she always went for my boyfriend's friends. Every time a friend of his was coming over, she went to make up her face. Put something nice on, you know. Once when I was away, she came and sat naked on my boyfriend's bed. She said to him, 'Please forgive me, but I'm like this sometimes,' and that kind of thing. And of course my boyfriend acted as if she were sitting next to him fully clothed. He doesn't go for *patatas*. I mean, if it had been a Surinamese girl, I might think, hey, wait a minute there . . . . But I didn't have to be afraid of that patata. Actually she didn't want anything to do with 'blackies,' she always used to say. But that contradicts everything she did, doesn't it? Making herself up every time for those blackies."

Ilse also had to deal with a neighbor who ignored certain proprieties with her as a black woman.

"Those neighbors from downstairs are real sweethearts, I don't deny that. I can always go to them. But the kind of things they think they can get away with sometimes! Recently I had my house full of people. My brothers, everyone was here. But I was lying in bed. The guy knocked on the door and my daughter opened it. Before you know it, he's standing right in my bedroom."

Disheartened, she adds, "A Surinamese would never do that. I was so angry. I can't stand that kind of thing. You just don't *do* things like that! I wouldn't dream of going into *their* bedroom."

From the above examples we can see that when certain white people behave in a racist manner in specific situations, the women do not immediately interpret *all* their behavior in terms of racism.

Moreover, it is evident that everyday racism can be expressed in seemingly trivial annoyances, such as impoliteness. *Mavis*, too, gave examples of "minor" social aggression against black neighbors: "You only see the neighbors from downstairs if there's a crisis. It could drive you crazy. If something is wrong, a clogged drain, for instance, she's here right away. When we first came to live here—it was awful! The smallest little thing and it was always: 'Miss, something's happened. Could you just come and take a look? I don't know where it's coming from. It must be coming from your place.' Well, there was sometimes nothing at all wrong in our place. I remember saying to my mother, 'Mom, if a Dutch family had been living here, she *never* would have done this to them.' Because they wouldn't stand for it. But she thinks, ugh, Surinamese, I'll just do it, I don't care. Whenever I have a problem, I'll just come and ring their bell. But she's learned to cut it out. Once my mother got terribly upset with her, though she doesn't usually get angry easily. Now that woman hasn't come with her complaints for a few years."

Mavis does not see this neighbor's behavior as an isolated case. She connects this experience to other signals, such as the atmosphere in the neighborhood as a whole. "It's written on their faces that they probably don't like it at all, having a foreigner as a neighbor. Some of them, people who have been living here since they were young, don't like it one bit. And this area here, it's supposed to be 'high class.' But if I look at those people, I think, where do they get that idea?"

Mavis is the only woman who has lived in expensive neighborhoods. "We used to live on P.C. Hooft Street [a fashionable shopping street in Amsterdam]. That was worse than here. Terrible.

The neighbors on the first floor were nice, but that's probably because the woman was a foreigner herself. She was from Norway. But directly below us, on the second floor, was a Dutch couple. Well, you can't believe the kind of things they said to us! My brother was still a little boy then. You heard the toot-toot of his little toy car. The walls are thin in those houses, so you could probably hear him playing in the daytime. That man had the nerve to pick up the phone and give me a lot of flak."

It was clearly a painful experience and Mavis does not at first repeat what actually came across the telephone line.

It may be an upsetting question, but what exactly did he say then?

" 'What a ruckus! What do you think, you think you're living in the jungle?' They must think that Surinam is a jungle. You get that kind of comment all the time."

But they say that upper-class people don't discriminate.

"Listen, we've lived almost everywhere in Amsterdam— West, East, South. But those are actually the people who gave me the hardest time."

Work Situations I: Patients and Clients

More than half of the women work or have worked in the health care field. This is not surprising in view of the fact that Surinamese nurses were hired and migrated to work in Dutch hospitals as far back as the 1950s.[125] This continued until around 1970. Then the country's "own" labor reserve began to increase. The entrance of men into this traditionally female work situation played a significant role as well. Men—the newcomers—soon began to move more swiftly up the ladder to managerial positions. It is not unlikely that these developments, unfavorable to women, had their heaviest impact on black nurses. Specific data on this is not available. *Olga*, herself a nurse, is the only one who talks about a Surinamese head nurse. The others implicitly confirm *Linda's* observation: "I work for a temp agency. I visit several nursing homes by turns. The head nurses in the wards are mostly Dutch, but the rest are generally Surinamese."

The women interviewed have all held low-level positions in the health care sector, as geriatric nurses-in-training or as home helpers. Moreover, they are more often temps than permanent employees. The position of temps in the health care field is not a bed of roses; as stand-ins, they are often relegated to the least pleasant tasks and are not always accepted as equals on the work team.

Olga: "They treat you as a temp, no matter who you are, you know. You just have to work, work, work, and keep your mouth shut. And that's just not possible, because you see a lot as a temp; you see people being teased or work being done poorly."

Ester, a geriatric nurse, comments on this: "When you're a temp, they use you as a kind of girl Friday. For instance, if someone has just had an inopportune bowel movement and the permanent nurses don't feel like cleaning it up, they send you, 'by the way,' to the patient, saying, 'Could you see how Mrs. So-and-so is doing?' You go there and see it, and you clean it up. That kind of thing. They abuse you a lot as a temp, especially if you don't dare to say anything. But I've got a ready tongue."

The work done by these women is mainly service-oriented and domestic in nature: aiding elderly, chronic, and long-term patients in the activities they cannot manage themselves.

Ester and several other women believe that the Dutch "girls" do not do the work well. "It is the only possibility for 17- or 18-year-old girls to earn money while they study. Not that I'm so much older, but they have absolutely no idea of what to do. And they put that kind of person into nursing. The patients suffer because of it. These girls have no patience, and they get to cursing at them. If the people say, 'I need to go to the bathroom,' they just let them wait as long as possible—'I have no time.' You notice these things especially if you come in as a temp. For example, they don't wash the people well. They're all in such a rush. 'Well, we have to be finished by 10:30 A.M. for the coffee break.' And so they go like that, whoosh-bang, through the whole ward. They have no time for the people. Yes, often there is no staff around either; but I mean, if everyone cooperates a little bit, everything *can* get done. But each one is lazier than the next. So how are you supposed to get the work done? They're too damned lazy to do anything. Just want to earn a fast buck. Sitting around the whole day smoking cigarettes, then running through the ward. You might think they work their hides off, but actually they don't want to do a thing! Sure, one of them may work hard. But I think it's a crime."

Olga talks about this issue: "We were taught that we should let these people do everything they are still able to do. But the

Dutch girls don't do that. They want to be through as soon as possible for the coffee break. I mean, I've never paid any attention to coffee breaks. I had a Surinamese head nurse—what a blessing! Never coffee at 10:00 A.M. If someone had said, 'It's ten o'clock, coffee!' and we had to have 20 people washed, well, it's just impossible, the people wouldn't get clean. Some patients prefer to be washed by us because of this. We take our time with them. 'And now you put your bra on yourself.' 'Yeah, but I can't.' 'Well, just try, I'll wait for you.' And then she tries to do it, in peace and calm. And after a while she learns to dress herself again. Then you say, 'I never knew you could still do so *much*.' And the woman says, 'But those Dutch girls go so fast. I've had a container of powder here for a year already, but it never gets used.' See, I wash those people the way I would wash myself. The ones who aren't senile like to be washed by a Surinamese. They say we always give them those pretty hairdos, so that they look like a lady. Not just a rubber band, but nicely done up. They like that."

All this suggests that Surinamese women choose for the well-being of the patient, at the cost of their own coffee break if necessary. The Dutch, in contrast, will not budge from their right to a break. Almost all the health care workers interviewed commented that Surinamese women make concessions regarding their rights. One wonders if this motivates employers to hire greater numbers of Surinamese women in these lower level jobs.

Olga expresses in very characteristic terms why she is so patient with the elderly people: "I think of my own grandmother. She isn't here anymore, but I think, what if she were still in the Netherlands and she were to come into a home like this one. In one sense, I'd rather sit with my co-nurses during the coffee break. But if I have to help these people, I can't do that. Because I feel for them all."

Working with elderly, often senile people takes a great deal of resilience, Olga explains. "Sometimes you get slapped. They'll spit in your face. So if you don't have much patience you shouldn't do this kind of work."

Yet she has quite a few good feelings about the work, as well. "Working with the ones who aren't crazy, only physically handicapped, is fun. They spoil you. And you learn a lot from them, too. I've learned to crochet and knit."

A negative image of Surinamese

All of the women working in the health care sector have had to face racism in their contact with clients or patients.

Joan worked for a while as a home helper for people with protracted illnesses and visited several Dutch people in their homes on a regular basis.

What was their feeling about getting help from a Surinamese woman?

"In the beginning they really wait to see 'what's this one going to be like?' But once they get to know you, it's fine."

Were they also interested in Surinam?

"Yes, they'd ask about it. But I always find it strange, the image people have of Surinam. Always so negative."

How does that come across?

"Simply from the stories they tell. But you know, it's not so strange, considering the Surinamese programs they show on television. Those huts and shacks. They think there's nothing else but that. So you talk to them about these things and then you hear, 'Surinamese are loud. They make a whole lot of noise.' I think they still know very little about Surinam. Nothing except the poverty, the misery, the aggressive side, mainly the negative things. It sometimes actually felt good to talk with them about it."

Rita, a nurse-in-training, has had similar experiences. "They think of Surinamese in such inferior terms, like, 'Those people live in trees.' That kind of disgusting thing."

A black nurse? No thanks.

Prejudice seems to occur not only at the level of ideas, but also at the level of instinctive emotional response to the person. Myra, a geriatric nurse, brings up the issue that some white people do not want to be helped by a black nurse. It appears that the painfulness of this kind of situation makes it difficult for her to put into words exactly what takes place. "For instance, you haven't done a thing to the person; he just sees you and he's got it in for you," Myra says. "And then he doesn't want to see you at all. 'You don't have to help me. Send So-and-so.' Or, 'No need for you to come.' Or then they say, 'The one with the frizzy hair,' etc."

Linda, who works in the same home, adds: "Some of them hate black people. They just say right out, 'You've got to go.' It's all right up to there, you know, but I can't stand it when they start calling us names. 'Damn Surinamese this, damn Surinamese that.' Then I'm ready to quit."

Ilse is a nurse-in-training in a ward for the senile. Like the other women, she does not let it upset her when patients hit her and abuse her verbally. "If they don't get what they want, they just hit you," she says. "And sometimes they just keep swearing at you without end. I'm prepared to put up with it if they're senile, because they can't help it."

Do they do that with everyone?

"They make no exceptions."

Olga concurs with her in this. "If you ask me, the senile ones don't ever like to be helped." Surinamese nurses are confronted with more than just the usual problems of working with senile people, however.

"Some senile people know quite well what they are doing, I want you to know. They may be very crazy, but they still know that you're a 'nigger' and 'black,'" says Ilse. "You get abused for it at times, as well. 'Go back to your own country. Go back to the jungle,' and that kind of thing."

When I ask Olga how the patients react to being helped by a Surinamese woman, she cries out spontaneously: "Those senile ones—Oh! Well! You get called all kinds of filth. With one of them, I came in with the washbowl—they're not well in the mind, so you don't blame them—but then I get: 'Go away, you with those big eyes,' and, 'Stinking Surinamese girl, filthy whore.' And it went on and on like that. If a Surinamese woman comes in—some of them, anyway, though not always—they really come down on her like a ton of bricks.

"No matter how senile they are, they say, 'Go back to your country.' That is the first thing they say. One of them packed everything away when you had to wash her, saying, 'You're the dirtiest, just look at your skin.' So I say that it isn't because I haven't washed. So I hear, 'Stinker, go catch typhus.' Then as you're coming in, another one starts in on you with, 'Murder, murder! Filthy murderer!' at first glance. It's hard with senile people. But the people who aren't insane do accept us. Not all of them. Some of them say, 'I do not want to be helped by you. Your voice is too loud, you sound so hard.'"

These examples bring to mind the images of blacks in, for example, children's books, as I mentioned earlier. Blacks as ugly, dirty characters who make noise, speak in sing-song tones, and have big, rolling eyeballs. In short, people who are strange and frightening.

Some of the women relate similar experiences in bitter anecdotes. *Carla,* a geriatric nurse, is angry and indignant about the many gross insults she has had to bear as a black woman who cares for white patients.

Have you ever met with discrimination?

"Yes, from the residents. I have an example. I had to help an old man who had lost all contact with the outside world. It went all right for a while, but one day he felt better. Then he discovered that I was black. I went to him to wash him. He looks at me and says, 'Go away, you'—it was a Jewish home—'You Negroes eat up all the Jewish bread.' I said to him, 'We eat Jewish bread, but we also clean up Jewish shit!' and I left. You can't really blame someone like that, but I am human too, after all. So I try to steer clear of him."

Ester has also experienced people who don't want to be helped by a black nurse. This is sometimes expressed openly. "They just say it to you, 'I'd rather not, I don't want to be washed by a black nurse.'"

How do you react at such moments?

"I say, 'Then we won't. Then you can just sit there.' I say, 'Even if there isn't one other staff member present on the ward, you won't get help from me.' I just let her sit there. Even if she has to go to the toilet, then she can just piss in her pants."

The conversation moves on to Ester's experience with another woman who would not accept help from a black nurse, but who would not say this directly. From the way in which Ester talks about this, it is apparent that it was after careful thought that she came to the conclusion that the woman had a racist attitude. Her judgment is based on systematic observations and on conferring with others. This not only makes her view plausible but simultaneously emphasizes how much extra attention it requires of her to see through hidden forms of racism. "That patient didn't want to be helped by a black nurse," says Ester. "Not at all if she was going to bed. You could bring her to the toilet, but not to bed. For instance, I was working the evening shift with three Surinamese nurses. Yes, one of us had to bring her to bed. So she always took the one with the lightest skin color.

"She had no other options. She's used to going to bed at 7:00 P.M., you know. But when there are three Surinamese nurses, she waits until the lightest comes along. She grabs you with, 'Nurse, will you bring me to bed soon?' And if you say, 'Why don't you ask that nurse?' she says, 'No, I prefer that you do it.' But everyone knew she was like that. If I sometimes worked with whites, they always said to me, 'Could you just bring her to bed, you can hear her screaming.' She sure screams! It was awful."

Then Ester's tone becomes one of indignation. "Yet in the morning she would allow you to bring her to the toilet. You're good enough for that. But you know what kind of people these are? These are the people who used to have a very high-class life-style. You know, with a servant and all that business. That's the kind of people that usually do this. You're good enough to do *this* kind of thing, but *that* you don't have to bother with."

Other women had to deal with this same tendency. *Rita* comments, "My sister worked for a while in home X. The old people there really saw blacks as their servants." Olga gives an example: "I say, 'You have to put your shoes on,' and she says, 'No, that's your job, isn't it? That's why I hired you.' She really thinks you are one of her servants."

Ilse describes a woman who expressed racist feelings of superiority by trying to put Ilse "in her place" as a black. "She used to be a nurse herself, in Indonesia. When I say that it's time to get out of bed, it's, 'Shut your mouth. In your country you can't even sit next to a white, and now you come here with your big mouth. In your country you don't have anything to say.' She just keeps going on about me coming from Indonesia and I can't get it into her head that that is not where I come from. To her, all dark people are Indonesians. Then she tears into you, 'Go back to your own country.'"

With one exception, Joan, all the women talked of encountering racism in patients or clients in convalescent and nursing homes. White patients abuse the black nurses, refuse to be washed by them, try to belittle them, or treat them as servants. Most of the colleagues and supervisors take a passive attitude toward these injustices. As a consequence, combating racism remains the responsibility of the black nurse.

What happens when the Surinamese nurse is caring for a patient in the patient's own home, and the patient displays racism by making it clear that she would rather have no help at all? Ester prefaces her description of this experience with the conclusion, "I don't work in people's homes anymore."

Was your experience very unpleasant?

"Yes. You go to their homes, and suppose you have to work from 9:00 A.M. to noon, and at 11:15 or 11:30 they send you away, saying, 'You're finished, it's summer, nice weather, go on out, enjoy yourself in the park.' So you go away and five minutes later they phone your boss. 'That girl who was here this morning left early.' But they sent you away themselves! So I say, 'No, I can't go, I'm supposed to work until noon. If I finish early I'll stay a bit longer and chat, if necessary.' But, no, they send you away. And once you've gone, they phone the main office."

Why do they do that?

"I think they want to get rid of you. Purely because you're dark-skinned. Once I got very angry with a woman. I got there in the morning, and she offered me a cup of coffee. I said, 'No, I have to get to work right away,' because I had to do her and then someone else. She says, 'No, just come and eat a little orange.' So I say, ' Well, I'll tell you what. I'm already busy here, so I'll just finish this, and then I'll come sit a minute and have the orange.' She says, 'OK.' I finished the work I had been doing. I went to sit down for the orange. She says, ' What are you doing?' I say, ' We agreed that I would eat that orange when I was finished, didn't we?' 'No, get to work. Where do you get the nerve to sit down?'

"One time she came down on me. 'Just go away,' she said, 'go away.' It was still much too early. Around 10:30 A.M. So I just left. So of course she phoned the main office right away."

Being accused of theft

When asked why the patient wanted to get rid of her, *Ester* answers that it did not only have to do with her being "dark-skinned." "Maybe they think you would steal from them or something."

Later, in the discussion of shopping situations, we will look more closely at the racist idea that all Surinamese steal, and the effect this has on individual women. Here Ester gives an example of how the client's expectation that she would steal was not merely offensive but also had serious consequences.

"I worked as a home helper. One woman had a gold necklace with a pendant she had left on the table. As it later turned out, her daughter-in-law had just been there and had put the necklace somewhere else. But the woman didn't know this. I came in in the morning to help her. After I left, she looked all over for the necklace. Gone. I was blamed for it! Fired. I got a letter saying that I need not go to work because I had taken the necklace from the woman and that I must come within 24 hours or she would call the police. But I was visiting a friend, so my mother had opened the mail. And she said, 'No, that's not possible, Ester doesn't do such things.' She wanted to go to the police. I said, 'No, I'll just go to these people and tell them I don't have that necklace.' It caused a whole commotion. A few weeks later I got a letter with apologies, saying that the necklace had been found. But I still lost the job. That's the kind of thing they do."

Carla also tells of an unjustified accusation of theft. It took place in a nursing home where she had been working for several years. When she describes it, she gives the impression of being less concerned about the fact that she, as a Surinamese, was offended, than about the possible negative consequences for other Surinamese. She brings up a complex problem. The prejudiced belief that she would steal because she is Surinamese leads to an actual accusation. She knows that the accusation is unjust, but other whites who happen to hear it do not. For them, it is a confirmation of an already prevailing prejudice. She thus relates her personal experience directly to the situation of other blacks and even feels responsible for it.

Carla: "In general I got on well with the residents, except for one man. He liked everyone, but if he couldn't find his newspapers or a few pills, it was always me who had taken them. It was really rotten. Then you get in the elevator with him and he talks about it. The people start thinking, oh, see that, another Surinamese. I went to the ward supervisor, who gave him hell for it. But he wouldn't get it out of his head. I asked him, 'Did you see me do it? It could be one of the others, couldn't it?' And he said, 'No, they are all darlings, but she did it.'"

Racist sexism

Black nurses are not only blacks, but also women. Sexism and racism are all too likely to go hand in hand in black women's relationships with white men.

Have you ever had the experience that male patients sexually assaulted or hassled you?

Ester: "In a convalescent home it doesn't happen much. But in a home for the elderly, those men can sure get hot! I have experienced that. Very old men, 92 and thereabouts. When you put them in the bath and that thing jumps straight up, you know, then they come out with, 'Nurse, would you do it if I pay?' But I never let it bother me. I pretend not to see it."

Most Surinamese women do not readily show embarrassment; after all, they don't blush. This has some consequences.

Carla: "There was a man everyone was afraid to wash— because the Dutch girls, especially, turn red, you know. I thought, oh, what the hell, since I don't turn red. He may have a hard-on, but he is asking to be washed. He can't do it himself, and so he can become very dirty. Well, the bath is filled and his lordship goes and lies down sumptuously in the bath like so, with his willie sticking up. Just in order to embarrass those girls. Well, he didn't embarrass me, but those Dutch girls didn't dare wash him. I say, 'If you don't pay any attention, he'll forget the whole thing. But if he sees that he is making an impression on you, then he'll go on and do more.' I have never had any trouble with him. But all those Dutch girls complain about him. And they turn beet red, right up to the ears. The man really gets a kick out of it."

But it doesn't stop there.

Carla: "We have a few residents who really don't give a damn. Sometimes when you come into their rooms, they start getting undressed. Or they try to pick you up by promising you money. They try it out because they've heard that Surinamese girls are pretty cheap or something, that you can get them in bed for ten bucks. I mean, if someone likes you, he can give you a kiss once in a while, nothing wrong with that. But there's one man who keeps trying to kiss you on the mouth, and I think that's going a little too far."

Do you find it annoying?

"I hate it! Once I went all the way to the ward supervisor. I had to help a man wash—he lives with his wife in a double room. Well, I went to wash him and he kept doing this to me, feeling my hips a bit. I thought, maybe he can't talk and he wants to make me understand something. But that wasn't the case. He was taking a lot of liberties. Just at the moment that I bent down to wash him, I got a wet kiss on my neck. At first I didn't say anything to his wife, but I did go to the permanent staff of the ward. It set off a whole scene with his wife. Of course that wasn't my intention, but I thought, I'll just tell. Because if you don't, they might just say something later, like, 'She enjoyed it.'"

Or is it sexist racism?

In the examples above, the accent has been on sexism. Racist overtones are also present in the prejudice that Surinamese women are "cheaper" than their Dutch peers, and therefore can be approached sexually with fewer scruples. The following are clear examples of sexism, but this aspect seems to become overshadowed by the racist prejudice at its foundation.

Carla: "Once we were making jokes in the kitchen with a male nurse. He played at molesting us, and we played along, calling out, 'Help, we're being raped!' We were laughing ourselves sick. Then that man came in—the same one who believed I had stolen his newspaper and so on. When we left, do you know what he said to the male nurse? 'You should do it with them, with those blackies.'"

So he meant more or less that if the male nurse had taken you . . .

"That it would have been good, yes. He hates blacks."

When asked whether she ever has trouble with male patients, *Olga* answers, "Yes, often. Often if they are senile, you find yourself suddenly being grabbed. There was also one who wasn't senile. He always used to give me a slap from behind, saying 'You're nice and big, aren't you?' He did that every day: 'Nice and big, a real piece.' I said, 'You better keep your hands off me.' But he wouldn't. Then he began saying, 'Yes, a nice chick. If I had seen you earlier, boy, wouldn't we have had some set of kids. Big woman. Pity I didn't see you earlier.'"

This proves to be a stereotypical racist attitude toward Olga as a black woman, when we examine the way in which she connects this experience with the behavior of other white men in the ward.

Are there often comments made like "a nice piece of Surinamese ass," or things to that effect?

"Yes, you hear that often. Even when you're just bathing them. The men, especially. Particularly if they think that we are big in the behind. 'Oh, you girls are so big, boy oh boy,' you know. They make jokes."

Olga is not seen as an individual, but as one of them ("you girls") who are so big in the behind.

Summary

As illustrated in the impressions of everyday racism above, these women have to contend with more than just tough working conditions as nurses. They are confronted with a variety of reactions from their clients and patients that make it glaringly clear that they are unwanted and inferior and that they can be treated as such.

A certain pattern begins to reveal itself. Forms of racism that have already been mentioned in the women's experiences in the housing market and relations with their neighbors are echoed in their work experience. The tendency of some whites to maintain *social distance* from blacks led to their refusal to rent to them or act as their housing agent. Similarly, at work several white patients did not want to be helped by a black nurse.

When the black woman nevertheless came into the vicinity of whites in the living situation, for example, *social aggression* was expressed in the form of harassment of the Surinamese neighbor or in brutally racist remarks on the telephone. In the workplace, women were abused verbally, sent away, or slapped (the overt nature of the racism was sometimes due to the senility of the patients).

Finally, the idea that whites are superior resulted in various forms of *inferiorization* of the women. This arose in the home, where certain rules of propriety were not considered applicable to blacks, and in the workplace, where the women were treated as servants and their honesty was doubted. When the prejudiced belief that Surinamese steal causes white clients to send black nurses away, it is not only a question of *inferiorization*, but the creation of *social distance* as well. Thus we see that the three principal forms of racism are not mutually exclusive; they overlap each other.

Work Situations II: Supervisors and Coworkers

This section concerns not only the women's experiences in nursing homes but also in administrative jobs. Recent opinion polls indicate that about one-third of the Dutch openly declare themselves against having a Surinamese colleague and supportive of preferential treatment of Dutch workers over ethnic minorities in the matter of promotions.[126] The question of whether Surinamese are accepted in management positions was not even posed in these polls.

What does it mean, in everyday practice, to work in a climate in which whites distance themselves from their black colleagues or otherwise exhibit prejudice and discrimination? As we have seen in the women's contact with patients and clients, this is not merely a matter of certain racist people who act in a consistently racist manner. When you work with people who are socialized within a racist society, the latent racism may surface at any time. The women's experience bears this out. The threat of racism, the tendency for whites to deny their own racism, and the myth that blacks are "hypersensitive" with regard to racism—an issue that I have not, as yet, addressed directly —all result in situations in which things are not always as they appear.

Carla gives a moving description of this. She is one of the few women who spontaneously brought up the subject of discrimination during our talk. The following discussion came at the very beginning of our interview.

Like most of the other women, Carla shows a definite reticence about making "sharp" statements at an early stage in the interview. She describes her activities in the nursing home and the nature of the cooperation with her coworkers.

Are there aspects of your work that are not so pleasant?

"Sometimes what happens with coworkers. Often you're working with someone, and you can't understand each other. Or you may feel that you're doing too much, you know. Sometimes I just try to give the idea, I don't think the same way you do."

Can you give an example?

"Suppose I'm working with you today. You do this side of the corridor, I do the other. You know that I'll help you when I finish. So you don't get a damn thing done. You think, she'll help me in a minute, anyway. Then they start abusing that a little. And if you try to say something about it, you just get the same old story. 'I didn't mean it like that,' they say. And then they start in on topics like discrimination. They think that we Negroes feel left out, whereas that isn't true in my case. They're glad to bring that up—'You Negroes always feel discriminated against'—when I don't have an inferiority complex at all, or anything like that. So that's not at all what I meant."

Let us read between the lines for a moment. First, Carla indicates that she has a different attitude toward work than certain others. She is not too lazy to do more than the tasks actually assigned her, while others, she feels, are. And she doesn't like this. To illustrate her meaning, she begins with a hypothetical situation: "Suppose I . . . and you . . . ." Halfway through her explanation, she is no longer saying "I" and "you," but "I" and "they." "They" are her white coworkers. She then says that "they" are "abusing . . . a little" her habit of jumping in to help others when she has finished her own work.

Carla does not interpret this as a form of discrimination, and stands by the statement that it is a question of differing attitudes toward work. But, she goes on, if she were to say anything, "they" would interpret it as an accusation of racism. Her response would be, "That's not how it was meant." What *was* meant remains unsaid.

In any case, Carla believes that she should not think that she is left out as a black. She indicates that she in no way feels left out—"That isn't true in my case." It is possible, however, that by this she also means: I don't think in terms of "we Negroes who feel left out/discriminated against." For to feel discriminated against as a black is associated with having an inferiority complex. And since having an inferiority complex implies that the problem lies in Carla herself—in other words, it is her own fault that she feels abused—she is not likely to want to or allow herself to feel discriminated against. It therefore seems as if she is being tricked by comments such as, "You Negroes always feel discriminated against." She also remarks that those coworkers are "glad to have the chance to bring it up." The question remains: Does she feel "tricked," and does she not like the argument of feeling discriminated against because she has the sense that she's being "summed up" in that one idea? Or does she not want to hear that argument because she *does* feel discriminated against, but doesn't have (or want to have) an inferiority complex, and thus also doesn't want her coworkers to use the argument in order to say behind her back, "We know what's wrong with her, she just has an inferiority complex, a bad attitude."

In any case, Carla has been well and truly gagged. What she would probably like to say to her coworkers is something like, "I think everyone should work equally hard here. If I usually give you a hand when I finish early, it doesn't mean you should anticipate it and automatically count on leaving a part of your work for me." Yet she does not express this dissatisfaction. *Because she is black*, she expects the "reproach" that "you Negroes always feel discriminated against."

Olga describes an experience similar to Carla's. She, too, does not interpret the situation clearly in terms of racism. She sighs, saying, "As a temp, you're sent from pillar to post. That's not much fun. I did learn a good deal working as a temp in the different homes. But those *Dutch*, uh-uh, I didn't like that part of it much."

The following experience contributed to Olga's decision to reject an offer of permanent employment at a certain home.

"You see, I worked there during the summer as a temp. But everyone wanted to get a nice tan, so they called in sick. Well, at a certain point there were just four of us left [four Surinamese]. Two were on the night shift. Before leaving in the morning they washed the people in one room. That covers ten people. We had 22 more to do. There were two of us Surinamese girls there and the ward supervisor. He was in the kitchen. So there were two of us for the whole ward. We're in there working, and a coordinator keeps coming by to see how far we've gotten. She sees that it's already 10:30. On her ward they're already finished, but she'd never send help to us. We just have to manage somehow. But our own ward supervisor, he was also to blame. Because we were done except for one room. And what's he doing? Just sitting in his office with a pot of coffee.

"The other girl says, 'Well, Olga, we're almost through, but there's one more room with six people.' It's a light one; two of the men only need to be given a basin of water, since they take care of themselves. But four of them do have to be washed, two for each of us. So I say, 'But where's Rob?' She says, 'Well, he's in his office drinking coffee.' I say, 'When it's so busy!' And when it is busy in that home, it's not busy just one day, but every day. You can't keep up with it. I say, 'I'm not going to take it anymore, you know.' Every time he sees that we're almost finished, he sits down. Yet if he could just keep at it a little longer, we could all be through earlier. We could all go drink coffee together. I went to him. I said, 'I don't like the fact that you do this.' He said, 'Yes, but you'll manage.'"

Not being allowed to speak Surinamese

All the women working in nursing homes say that they have several or "many" Surinamese coworkers. When asked if they speak to each other in Sranan Tongo (Surinamese), they answer somewhat differently. One feels that that would be unkind to her Dutch coworkers. Others, such as *Rita* and *Olga,* "choose the right moment" to speak Sranan Tongo with other Surinamese: when they are alone or when they are together at a separate table during the coffee break. Several women bring up the intolerance of their Dutch coworkers when they hear the women speaking Sranan Tongo.

Rita: "I never experienced it myself; I've heard from other Surinamese women that they [the Dutch] simply say directly, 'What are you carrying on about?' and that kind of thing."

Ilse says that it is officially forbidden for her to speak in Surinamese at work. She is completely against this, and she explains why. "One time a Dutch man came up to me, an old man. 'I have something for you,' he says. I think to myself, what can he have for me? I don't even know him. He brings me to meet his wife. A Surinamese woman, from the ward below us. 'This is my wife. Will you look in on her once in a while?' So once in a while I go downstairs. You know, she understands what you say; she also knows what she herself wants to say, but she can't put the words together. The only thing I could understand well was *mi goedoe, mi pikin* [my dear, my child]. She can still speak Surinamese, you know, but Dutch, no. I also helped her once when I had to work downstairs; I bathed her. She liked that so much! And then I spoke Surinamese with her. But it's not allowed if anyone else is present."

Why not?

"We just aren't allowed to speak Surinamese. They consider it rude because they don't know what we're saying. That really annoys me sometimes. You don't have to understand everything we say! [For a very similar U.S. story, see note 127.]

"There was also a Surinamese man among us, for instance. He was blind. You couldn't really have much contact with him unless you sat close to him and spoke to him in Surinamese. Well, I did. If he sat outside, and I was also outside with my group, I spoke Surinamese with him. He absolutely loved it. And then I always had to promise I would come back tomorrow." Now showing her outrage, Ilse continues, "If you can just do that small favor for those people. I mean, you know they're not going to live long. When they reach us, they're on their last legs—most of them never leave again. So why can't you give them that little bit of attention? And if it has to be in their language, I'll do it. There was also an Indonesian woman, and the doctor spoke to her in good Indonesian while I was there. I couldn't understand that either. I didn't say anything about it, because you don't know what effect it will have on the patient."

Yet it's so strange that they won't allow it.

"They think it's impolite. But if they speak a Dutch dialect, I don't understand them either."

Being seen as stupid

This reverse situation—that as a Surinamese you cannot understand certain Dutch people because of their regional accent—is also interpreted to the disadvantage of the Surinamese. When the Dutch do not understand the Surinamese language, the Surinamese person is considered impolite. When the Surinamese do not understand a Dutch dialect, that does not imply that the Dutch speaker is being impolite, but that the Surinamese must be stupid.

Joan talks about this. She worked in nursing for a short period. At a certain point she couldn't handle it anymore. Her strong identification with the clients caused her to feel personally responsible for their problems. In retrospect, she says, she is simply not suited for that sort of work.

Speaking about the teamwork that existed among her coworkers then, she says, "It was a lot of fun. But what often happened was that things took a while to sink in. For instance, if someone said something to you, especially just after your coming to the Netherlands, it took a while before you understood what they actually meant. That isn't so strange. Actually I think it's quite normal. Yet they saw it as a kind of stupidity. If they were to go to Surinam and I were to speak a few words of Surinamese with them, I wonder what they would do? They don't usually think of that. So I did have problems in that respect, yes. Sometimes I had the feeling they thought I was stupid then. But that changed as they got to know you."

The question of language also plays a role in Joan's present work environment, as a typist at a health insurance company.

When asked how her Dutch colleagues regard her, she says, "For a Surinamese woman, they think I am quite gutsy. Compared to the women they know, maybe, because I don't think Surinamese women are dumb. I think they've got a lot of spunk. But compared to the kind they come across—or the kind they can easily cut down, let me put it that way—they think I'm pretty gutsy and rash. It's just a question of thinking they're better.

"I'll give you an example. We Surinamese often say, 'You going?' A guy comes up to me at some point and says, 'You don't say it like that. It is, "Are you going?"' I say, 'But you understand me, don't you? You do know what I mean?' I say, 'Actually you should be amazed at how well I speak Dutch. It isn't even my own language.' They forget that very easily. They immediately want us to be the way *they* want. Well, that's not necessary."

Excessive control and harassment by supervisors

Objections to the use of Sranan Tongo when Dutch people are also present have to do with more than so-called impoliteness. Sranan Tongo is something vital that the Surinamese share with each other—an expression of community spirit. The whites present may experience this as exclusion and thus as a loss of control. This is important for an understanding of the racism behind their intolerance of conversations in Surinamese or their actual prohibition of it. The possibility of losing control over blacks plays a big role, particularly if the blacks emphasize their group consciousness in certain situations. Thus, leaving one black person alone and ignoring her or him seems to pose no problem. (This becomes particularly important in the discussion on education.) However, when blacks themselves choose not to be in the white group, and instead want to join other blacks, it suddenly becomes an issue.

In regard to this, *Carla* discusses the coffee break in the home where she and other Surinamese women are working. "Sometimes during the coffee break the Dutch girls make remarks about this. The blacks often sit at one table and the whites believe there's a kind of partisan politics going on. Whereas you're not thinking that way at all—you just like So-and-so and you want to sit with them over coffee." *Olga* illustrates this with the following example. Speaking about a night shift head nurse, D., she says: "She was really a bitch. I sat with three Surinamese girls in the group. If anyone did anything to Magda or to me, you could count on the other one to say something about it. And D. knew that. But she still wouldn't leave us alone."

Olga goes on further about her experiences with the head nurse, D. Her own observations, supported by the opinions and experiences of other Surinamese women, expose a range of "little" harassments through which D. displayed racism. It was not because she was head nurse that D. felt superior to Olga and other Surinamese, but because she was white. This is in part apparent from the fact that she involved other white nurses in controlling and denigrating Olga. Bit by bit, it becomes clear how D. used her position of power to try to prevent Olga from obtaining certification, creating an atmosphere that made it harder for Olga or other Surinamese women to succeed in their work. [Olga, like other nurses interviewed, worked as part of her training. Class hours alternated with a large number of practical work hours in convalescent and nursing homes.]

Olga: "I would rather be in school for a year than work. I have never found my work enjoyable. You begin as a group of 20 in the training. Then you are divided among a number of homes. I feel very abused; nursing is really hard, you know. It's there that you notice the discrimination. Openly, too. Most Surinamese girls in nursing work extremely hard. Harder than the Dutch girls. The director of the school where we studied has even said as much. But the Dutch girls can't accept that. And then if they're in with one head nurse or another, they say things like, 'That Olga has a big mouth.' That's how the harassment begins, with the spreading of all kinds of stories."

Olga then concentrates her example on D. "D. didn't like the way I dealt with the patients. She thought I was sleeping, not doing rounds, letting patients sleep in their urine, deliberately dropping them, and more of that bullshit. But my own ward supervisor said, 'No, I can't believe that of Olga.' D. wanted to get rid of me. That was obvious. If I hadn't hung in there, I wouldn't have gotten certified."

What did she do?

"I was at the end of my first year. At that point there are certain things you can do, and other things you are not yet supposed to. I could distribute medicines by then, for instance. But D. didn't want me to. She wouldn't let me have the responsibility. There was a Dutch girl, working on a different ward, who was not supposed to distribute medicines yet. But D. wanted to send for that girl to distribute the pills for me. I said, 'Sorry, D., I learned it, I know how to do it, I'll do it myself. If you think I'm not doing it right, then *you* can come check, but not a girl who has only been in the school for half a year.' She always wanted me to apologize to her, offer her my apologies."

Here Olga links her Surinamese background with D.'s racism. "She never trusted you. All of the Surinamese girls had to deal with this. If you were working under her in the night shift, she would sneak into the rooms after you had finished your round, while you were in the kitchen buttering bread for the next morning, for instance. She'd wake the people up again. Lights back on. Went around feeling to see if they were dry. She just didn't trust you. One day I spoke to her about it. Well, she thought I had a lot of nerve, to do that. Who am *I*, to tell *her* . . . . I said, 'If you don't want to believe I've done my work, then you should sit with me and we'll do it together.' "

In other situations as well, Olga described D. behaving differently toward nurses of color.

"The two of us were working together. She had to train me. She comes out with, 'Are you engaged?' You know, she starts interrogating you. Some girls tell her their whole life story. I'm really not into that. Like, 'Are you married? Do you have a boyfriend? Why did you come to Holland?' That was typical D. She did it to every foreign girl. She did it whether you were Surinamese or Moroccan. So she took me aside too, to ask questions. When she asked if I was engaged, I asked her if *she* was married. After that she never asked me anything again. She thinks I'm fresh. Since that day she hasn't liked me.

"Once in a while it goes like this: She has a friend who works in the daytime, and that woman starts keeping extra close watch on you. Then I hear that I laugh too much. I say, 'What difference does that make? The patients are senile, should I sit and look grumpy or something? Then they'll become aggressive.' I say to her, 'You are the only one who says that, so it isn't true. The others might not dare say it, but I certainly can laugh. I mean, I'm not going to laugh while I'm giving someone an injection. But those senile people are just nice and fun to be with. So why can't I laugh with them? Otherwise I can't get to know them.' "

Fresh, doesn't do her work, laughs too much, irresponsible: prejudices that are often used against blacks. D.'s racism did not stop at all the harassment and provocative comments, however.

Olga: "As ward supervisor, it's part of your job to evaluate the students: how she works at night, in the daytime, and in the evening. Well, in the daytime I was 'excellent.' But at night, I wasn't even worth a C. It was very annoying. In spite of all this, I had the support of a Surinamese woman, the coordinating head nurse. I had said to her, 'I'm leaving. I'm moving on. I quit! I can't take it anymore.' She said, 'You're crazy to leave. You still need your certification.'"

Olga was not the only Surinamese woman who had such a feeling of despair that she was driven to consider quitting. Though *Ester* did not mention it herself in our interview, Olga, who is Ester's friend, says, "Look at Ester, for example. She doesn't have her certification now. She couldn't take it. It was the harassment and criticism, you know. But I thought, I love this work, I *have* to get certification. It *was* difficult. Sometimes I came home crying. Crying! And my mother said, 'Child, you're not going anymore. This is the last time, because *if mie lóésoe go drape!!'* [Freely translated: If I go and see her, she'll remember it for a long time!] She thought that she could just go and talk to her, just like you would in Surinam. I said, 'No, if you go, I'll lose my job completely.' So she never went. But she couldn't see why I had to take all that."

Olga learned to systematically observe the behavior of head night nurse D. and other white colleagues. The realization that D. wasn't difficult only with *her*, and the support she received from the Surinamese head nurse, kept her going. However, it is not easy to observe the behavior of whites so closely and to pinpoint the subtle ways they behave differently toward you as a black colleague.

Consider, for example, *Joan's* experience. "After two and a half years of family care, I had to quit. When I came home, I always went around with the people's problems on my mind. Then I applied for work at a bank. I was hired, but again immediately discriminated against."

Can you talk a bit about it?

"Well, there were really nasty things. I had never worked in an office before. They started checking up on my typing speed. And checking to see that I came early, you know. Because the man didn't like me. If he said something . . . well, I was still in my trial period, but I wasn't going to just put up with everything. I'm not the kind to do that. I come to *work*. And that's *all*."

What was so unpleasant? Could you talk about exactly what he did or said?

"It was always vague things. I wouldn't just go and make a complaint against someone like that, for instance. You wouldn't know what to say. He was always taking digs at you. He also thought my typing speed wasn't fast enough after the first month. I could do 45 words a minute, so with another month I'd have been able to reach 90. But I just didn't get the chance. And then always being checked up on to see if I came on time. And I am always right on time, because I know they get you with that kind of thing."

This statement illustrates clearly that Joan, as a black woman, had to be more alert because she would be checked more closely. In other words, what would be acceptable for white workers would not be tolerated in her case.

Joan: "Then I called up the personnel office and told them what was going on. The man in the personnel office sensed what I meant and said, 'The best thing for you to do is quit. I will see to it that you are paid for the full two months.' I left. Then I got a nice letter: 'In view of the quality and quantity of Miss Joan's . . . .' With that I was laid off. I started getting unemployment benefits for two months, March to May. That was really awful. It was a very bad time. I was terribly ashamed of myself. Every week I had to go to the unemployment office to fill out a form. I hated having to do that. Stupid, isn't it, actually."

And how did they treat you at the unemployment office?

"There were two civil servants. One nice man. By chance he was often the one I spoke to. He understood my situation.

"Then I applied for work at a different bank. I was taken on, and went to work there. They also just kept breathing down my neck. Then I was asked to come in and talk to the managers. I told them, 'I can also just go back on unemployment, but the idea doesn't thrill me. I just feel unhappy.' They placed me in a department where there were nine Surinamese and just two Dutch. There was also a Surinamese heading the department. Actually, looking back on it, it was through them that I regained my self-confidence."

Both Joan and Olga indicate several times during their interviews that they do not just let themselves be told what to do all the time. Joan: "I always know how to answer them. I know how to fight for myself." Olga: "I have one advantage. If I don't like something, I just tell you. That's that." Both come into situations in which they are confronted with racism. It is expressed through excessive control over their work and attempts to discredit them, to make them feel insecure. Olga could test her experiences against those of other Surinamese women. Joan could not; she was the only black. Having no specific evidence to prove that she was being discriminated against, she was forced to give up her job. Olga, too, had moments of great doubt.

It is clear that everyday discrimination, even when it seems to be a question of "little" harassments, can have far-reaching effects, and that being discriminated against is not a question of *letting* oneself be discriminated against. In both cases, whites abused their position of power, a position that allowed them to negatively evaluate a black employee's work, to express their prejudice against blacks.

If that specific power is removed from their position or role, they find other ways to express their prejudice. *Olga* speaks further about head nurse D. When Olga did not have to be evaluated by D. anymore, the relationship changed.

Olga: "When I was in my second year, I thought, lady, now you can go to hell. The second year you can do everything on your own. At that time I was often on the night shift with D., but she called in sick repeatedly. She was sick whenever she had to do the night shift with me. And I wouldn't talk to her anymore either."

The emphasis on Olga's experiences with D. might give the impression that she was just unfortunate in being assigned to that particular woman. But once certified, Olga still met with racism at work from other Dutch nurses.

Disrespected as a supervisor

Olga is now in a management position herself and trains novice nurses. "I was accepted by the heads of staff, but I had troubles with the trainees. For instance, when I work with the residents, I want the room to be straightened up at the same time. Another nurse may not do that. So I say, 'You don't have to do it, but if you're working with me I will adjust to you and you also have to adjust to me.'"

Did they not like the fact that you, as a Surinamese, made the rules?

"There were always a few who didn't like it. But it didn't come from above. It came from the students themselves."
How could you tell?
"First, they don't want to work with you. They're assigned to work with you and they walk away. They hang out in the kitchen, and by then you might have already washed two patients. One even used to stay in the bathroom. Meanwhile you keep working, thinking she'll come. Finally they come into the room and then they don't speak to you."

This kind of "minor" sabotage was not the only expression of racism Olga encountered, and as a result she never found her work really enjoyable, though she consciously and enthusiastically chose a career in nursing. "Those students could be really rough. Really tough. Take for example the time I worked on a ward where the people were not senile. While one of the students is working with me in the room, he begins to talk to a patient. 'So, what do you think of all those Surinamese in the country these days?' Well, such a patient says just what she thinks, of course: 'They should stay in their own country.' I mean, you just don't do that kind of thing while I'm working with you, do you? That was deliberate."

In order not to be accused of racism, the student found a way to make someone else express out loud what he was probably thinking to himself: Send them back, so I don't have to work with them.

Discriminatory remarks

Many forms of racism are expressed in language aimed at a black who is present: humiliating remarks, accusations, swearing, and the like. These comments may in fact be spoken not directly *to*, but *about* blacks, present or absent. Most of the women are confronted with frequent comments about "Surinamese" or "foreigners." The white speakers then use a typical argument in order not to be accused of racism by the Surinamese present: "I didn't mean *you*." This often just makes things worse.

Laila gives an example. She is a consultant at a life insurance company. She describes what occurs during the coffee break, when people tend to gather into several small groups in the cafeteria. The following example concerns someone from the mail room.

Laila: "He lives in the Bijlmer. He was talking about Surinamese, that 'those Surinamese' are always hanging around the garage. 'They even stole my battery.' He didn't see it happen, but he already knows, Surinamese did it. How can he be so sure! I was so angry. I'm sitting right there and he just says that so calmly. I got up and left. He comes up to me later, saying, 'I didn't mean it personally.' I say, 'That's possible, but you shouldn't pass judgment on things you don't know.' And then you get the fact that old men always think they know better. 'I wasn't talking about you. *You're* good,' he says. So I say, 'I don't want you to say that. There are *plenty* who are good.'"

Laila then reaches the heart of the matter, defining what it means to her. "Maybe since you happen to know me personally, you think I'm 'good.' Isn't that how it is? That's often how people think. You are one of the good ones. What a lot of bunk. Since they know you, you're one of the good ones and someone they don't know is a bad one. I really detest that."

The prejudice against Surinamese is thus kept alive and Laila is but an exception to the rule. In this case, she heard it expressed directly; on other occasions she must assume "it wasn't intended personally," so that whites can speak contemptuously of blacks in her presence without embarrassment. What is so striking is that the customary social rules are suddenly no longer heeded—not to speak of others with disrespect and certainly not if you know that someone present has some affinity with them.

In relation to this, Laila also talks of one of her closer colleagues. "A client phoned, and at some point this colleague of mine was talking about a room rental service. He was asked who the rooms were rented out to. 'Well,' he said, 'Turks, Moroccans, Sambos, you know.' I was shocked. I didn't say a word. Wrong of me, of course. I should have said immediately that I didn't like it."

Laila is not the only woman who describes situations in which she is literally struck dumb by the coarse way racism is displayed. *Joan,* who now works as a typist, comments that her Dutch colleagues speak negatively about Surinamese.

What do they say?

"That everything having to do with Surinamese involves hashish, for instance. That Surinamese are hash dealers. That's the direction it usually takes. And theft? It's always the fault of the Surinamese. Just look at the newspapers: that's where they find it. Over and over you see little articles about Surinamese doing this and Surinamese doing that. And you hear the comments: 'Those Surinamese again. Why don't they cut that guy's throat?' And: 'They'll come in here and steal the whole kit and caboodle. Haven't they gotten enough by now?' When it's a Surinamese, right away they print, 'So-and-so, a Surinamese . . . .' But when it's a Dutch man, then they say something like, 'Mr. O.' and mention no nationality. Sometimes you're absolutely speechless at the things that go on."

Such events cause the women to keep on their guard against the people concerned. Racist comments that are passed off as being about someone other than the Surinamese person present are nevertheless experienced as offensive.

Helen tells of a situation involving a Pakistani man who had come into the travel agency where she works as a secretary. After not being successfully understood by Helen's white coworkers, the man turned to her and repeated his request. "But he expressed himself in such a strange way that I couldn't understand him either. When I asked him to explain, he suddenly got angry and began to shout. I got angry too. When he left, the others said, 'Oh, it's not just that Pakistani. There are a lot of other people who think they can come in here and do what they like.' Well, I felt immediately that they were referring to Surinamese. And I said so. Surinamese are very often all lumped together."

Joan indicates that she sometimes finds herself in a dilemma in such situations. The racism is felt intuitively, but one doesn't always succeed in reacting directly to it. As she puts it, if it's written in the newspaper, you cannot deny that a Surinamese did behave wrongly. "On the one hand, sometimes I am ashamed of it, too. On the other hand, it pisses me off, because Surinamese aren't the only ones who do these things. If they would only keep that in mind. That's what I think it's all about."

For a Surinamese, then, merely reading the paper becomes a confrontation with discrimination. The nationality of the offending Surinamese is mentioned, as a rule, while that of the offending Dutch person is not. When the newspapers repeatedly stress that it was not a Dutch person but a Surinamese who went too far, it has the effect of encouraging generalizations about Surinamese people.

When the discussion moves to the topic of generalizations, *Ilse* reacts immediately. It upsets her greatly when whites lump all

Surinamese together. Although in other situations, such as on the streetcar, she responds quickly and sharply to racist comments about "foreigners," at work she tries to be tolerant toward a white nurse who expresses racism. The rage that shows behind Ilse's manner of speaking about these events reveals how difficult it is for her to overlook the racism.

Ilse: "At work they say I'm aggressive, but I don't give a damn. I can't stand it when they start generalizing. I really don't like it. If a Surinamese has done something to you, then talk about that Surinamese. But don't immediately start generalizing, because they aren't all like that. There's also a girl at work who says, 'I don't like one single foreigner,' but she is always getting herself humped by Negroes! Now that she has a Dutch boyfriend, those Negroes suddenly aren't any good anymore. I can't stand it. I just happen to know about it. I haven't said anything to her yet, but if she goes so far that I can't take it anymore, I'll say it."

Blacks should have no ambitions

Laila, an insurance consultant, relates the following story. "It was funny. When Ruben [the man with whom she lives] had to do his military service, I had nothing to do in the evenings. So I took a correspondence course to get my license in the insurance business. Two of my colleagues didn't like the idea." Laughing, she continues, "Well, that's ridiculous. Then one of them began asking, 'Can I borrow your course books?' And he passes the course. Fine for him. The other one now wants to have his license too, and I say, 'You don't even let me have that much.' And they say, 'Well, how else do you think we could continue to work with you?'

"But since then I've talked it over with Ruben. Should I work toward a degree too? He isn't so degree-minded. He says, 'You don't have to make a career, you know.' I said, 'In some ways you're right, but God, you never know how things will be later. Maybe I'll need a career when I'm 40. I don't think I'd make the perfect housewife. I have to have the feeling that I'm still important. I like that.'"

Although related casually and straightforwardly, the issues Laila raises are significant ones. To begin with, the behavior of her white male colleagues who cannot accept, because of their pride, that the only one with a license would be the only woman among them. Or might the consideration have been: We can't allow the only black among us to have the highest qualifications. In other words, is it a question of sexism or racism? Or both? Laila draws a connection to her own Surinamese boyfriend. He too raises objections to her ambitions. She implies that she felt her colleagues' comments were directed at her not as a black, but as a woman. The fact remains that a double prejudice may be at work, in view of her relationship as a black woman to white men. The prejudice is against both blacks and women, that they must be either stupid or less qualified in comparison to whites and men.

In *Joan's* case, the intentions are more obvious. Here is a situation in which her male boss tries to discourage her.

Joan: "I'm taking a course in business correspondence. My boss's sister is taking the same course. I said, ' I'm taking such and such a course.' And he says, 'Oh, my sister is in it too. What gave you the idea to do such a thing? Do you think you can handle it?' And I think to myself, because it 's a Surinamese, she's not supposed to be able to do it."

Joan's objectifying phrasing—referring to herself in the third person with "it's a Surinamese" and "she's not supposed to be able to do it"—highlights bitingly the basic characteristic of racial/ethnic prejudice. Although the boss knows Joan personally, he still sees her as one among the whole group of Surinamese, with the characteristic attribute of being less intelligent. Which can lead to a situation like the following one.

Joan: "One day I came into work feeling very cheerful. I said to them, 'Hi everybody, I got an A!' I had been afraid to begin the course at first, you see. I thought it would be difficult to do because it had been such a long time since I was a student. So I said, 'Hey everybody, an A!' And the boss says to me, 'An A? You? Sure it wasn't an F?'"

On the surface these seem to be trivial incidents, unkind remarks, sideswipes. Though Joan herself does not explicitly say so, we cannot ignore the relationship between these incidents (which are, after all, characteristic expressions of the boss's judgmental attitude) and the fact that Joan does not want to take advantage of certain opportunities within the company. "You can apply for a course and it will be paid for by the company. I never applied. I just didn't want to. That way I wouldn't have to owe anyone anything."

Joan's boss could be even more abusive in his racism. Explaining her resistance to taking on more responsibility within the company, she says, "Once I had a talk with him. I wanted to work half-days, since my son had always been in day-care. But I was one of their hard workers, so they felt very bad about my having succeeded in arranging a financial supplement to my income so that I could work fewer hours. Suddenly he began to swear at me. 'If you had kept your legs together, we never would have had this problem!' In other words, if I hadn't had a child, I wouldn't have had to work half-days. When that happens, I wonder if they would have said the same thing to a white woman."

The boss was abusing his power to humiliate Joan. At that moment she could do nothing about her powerlessness or her anger about it. Considering this, it is understandable that she then concludes rather triumphantly: "But not long afterward, his own wife became pregnant. Well, he has had a hard time bringing that child into the world. I thought to myself, you want to say something to *me* about children? *You* just try it."

Summary

We now have an impression of racism in everyday interactions with colleagues, supervisors, and other people in work situations. In many cases, the everyday racism the women experience is combined with elements of everyday sexism. The situational context of their job determines, to a large extent, the specific forms of racism they face in their work life. With the exception of Laila, whose education places her in a different position in the job market, all of the women are in jobs involving a strict hierarchy; they occupy the least-skilled clerical and nursing positions. Their experiences of racism are inextricably bound up with typical manifestations of class oppression, such as overwork, heavy physical labor, poor working conditions, little job satisfaction, authoritative bosses, and strict supervision of their performance on the job.

Most of the examples given above illustrate how the idea that white people are superior is expressed through the *inferioriza-tion* of the Surinamese women: treating them like servants, considering them stupid, anxiously controlling their work, or forbidding them to speak Surinamese. There are also examples of ways in which whites create *social distance* from the women—such as refusing to give assistance at work, not wanting to work with

them, and not wanting to work in a position under them—
although to a certain extent these, too, are related to attitudes
of superiority. Not only contempt, but also *social aggression* is
expressed through vicious remarks about the supposed sexual
morals of the Surinamese woman and by uttering racist remarks
in her presence.

In Chapter I, I said that rigidity is a significant characteristic
of racial/ethnic prejudice. Prejudiced people do not want to hear
arguments other than those confirming their prejudice. They do
not thank people for presenting more subtle information; on the
contrary, a prejudiced person often resists information deliberately. Thus, a person's prejudice that blacks are stupid keeps him
or her from accepting contrary evidence. We have seen that the
intelligence and ambition of the women (as well as their challenging of the inferior position assigned to them) are not appreciated.

In the discussion of the next topic, education, we find that
the tendency to see black students as less intelligent, and to
actually sabotage their efforts, typifies the experiences of the
women in the Dutch educational system.

Education

The Dutch educational system differs in fundamental ways from
that of the United States. When students reach about 12 years of
age, they are sorted according to an estimation of their ability and
channeled into different "tracks"—types of high schools. This
decision is made on the basis of the teacher's and parents'
judgment of the child's potential, intelligence, and motivation.

The "lowest" track is the LBO, leading to less skilled trades,
and the percentage of children of immigrant minorities in LBO is
somewhat higher than that of Dutch children. The next level is
the MAVO, which is preparatory to specialized vocational/tech-
nical schools for administrative jobs, technical occupations, and
agriculture. The next level is the HAVO, which is generally
preparatory to specialized vocational/technical schools that are
closer to the American college level. Finally, there is the VWO,
which prepares students for entrance to universities. Once tracked
into a school, the student can transfer to a higher level, but this
usually involves repeating a year of school. One consequence of

this system is that the initial sorting process largely determines the individual's future educational and vocational opportunities.

Due to Dutch colonialism, the educational system in Surinam was a copy of the Dutch system. This included using the Dutch curriculum as well as the Dutch language in which it was taught. Most of the women interviewed received part of their education in Surinam and finished further schooling in the Netherlands.

Joan, having completed secondary school in Surinam, has taken other courses since coming to the Netherlands. Linda, Lita, Shirley, Laila, and Helen have all attended secondary school programs in the Netherlands. Ilse, Ester, Rita, and Olga have attended nursing school to train as nurse's aides, and Myra to train in the care of the elderly. Mavis has her diploma from a Dutch teacher's college, and Carmila is presently in teacher's college. Carla is studying social work.

It was easier for some women than for others to make the transition to white Dutch schools, after attending Surinamese schools where they were surrounded by other brown faces.

Lita says that this transition went quite smoothly for her. "I came here during the Dutch summer vacation. In September I went right to school, to the MAVO. It was fun, a nice school; I fit right in. There were a lot of Surinamese at the school, which made a big difference. My sister was at the same school, too, so we shared everything. Having someone you can talk to really makes a difference."

Lita insists repeatedly that she had no trouble at school. Yet it is evident that she had a defensive attitude from the start. "I really had no problem, sitting here in the middle of all the whiteys. I just had a big mouth. Swearing. Letting them feel that I could stand up to any one of them. At some point they even began to respect me. I acted like I was a karate kid, you know. Performed all kinds of stunts. Those kids could talk tough, but they didn't dare do a thing. No, I had no problems."

Linda was in the sixth grade when she came to the Netherlands and was placed in the LBO. She too found it supportive to have another Surinamese girl in the class. "At first I was the only Surinamese girl in the class. But since you keep changing groups for the different courses, you come into contact with other people. Then a girl came who said that she knew me from Surinam. Now we're really good friends. It's not that I couldn't fit in with the whites, but it was more fun to be with people from my own country. Especially when you're sitting together and telling stories in your own language. You can't tell them to the whites. You'd have to start translating again."

Helen mentions similar things, such as loneliness as the only black, and cultural differences. She had been in a very large school; an enormous contrast to the small school in Surinam where everyone knew everyone. "Little children entering at the elementary school level can still adjust. But once you're a teen, it's harder to pick certain things up and to forget certain scenes as you knew them."

What did you miss?

"I don't remember anymore. I don't remember what it was that made me feel so out of place. It was a hell of a bad time for me. The school was so big, and there was so little contact. I didn't know those kids and they didn't know me. Right through to the end of the year I didn't know anyone at all. I hung around with one Surinamese boy who was also at that school. We used to talk together at the breaks. But everything was so impersonal.

"When I first came here, there weren't so many Surinamese at school. You just feel it; you're a foreigner, you know? I did have a Dutch girlfriend, but you couldn't really be 'friends.' There was contact, but not the kind of contact I'd known with Surinamese friends. It just wasn't there. I've still never had that with a Dutch girl. You know, we know each other, we know what we like about each other and what we can expect of each other.

"Maybe I'm not open [to whites], or maybe they just don't attract me. I really do make the assumption you have to be interesting to me if we're to hit it off together. Because at some point I could talk to you about our culture, but then I find out you don't know anything about it. And then come all the inhibitions, all the collisions. And it's all over."

Laila, too, found the atmosphere in her MAVO school impersonal. She felt uncomfortable. "You had to fend for yourself. No one got involved with anyone else's problems; the problems aren't ever supposed to exist, or they don't see them. And you don't talk about them. That was the feeling. Very impersonal."

What do you think your classmates thought of you?

"Probably that I was the quiet type, didn't say much. But you know, if I don't feel comfortable, I'm not going to talk, either. That's a little upsetting. They may not have known what to think of me."

Carla started social work school as soon as she arrived in the Netherlands. She became so isolated in the program that she dropped out at an early stage.

Carla: "I was practically the only dark one. To be honest, I didn't feel at all comfortable. People spoke to you, but not in a way that you really had contact. At some point I couldn't take it any more.

"It's not that you were being actively discriminated against, but if you were sitting in the recreation room, no one bothered about you. Your classmates might say hello while waiting together for the tram, but there still wasn't really any good communication. You felt something was missing. You felt: There's something wrong, I don't belong here. They were all white girls. There was good contact, but it wasn't as if I could walk up to one of them outside class and tell them about my job or say, 'Something wild happened to me today'—you couldn't do that with them. There was always a certain distance. You just felt it. So I quit, I left."

It is interesting to note that though the experience Carla is describing implies the essential character of racial/ethnic discrimination—being treated differently by whites because they regard you as a member of the "other" ethnic group—she expressly denies having been discriminated against. A possible explanation for this contradiction is that Carla associates discrimination with concrete actions. She did *feel* she was being excluded, but this feeling arose not from active *deeds*, but precisely from their omission. This also explains her sense that "something was missing" and that "no one bothered about you."

Carla lost a year, having to repeat a school term because of being unable to function at this school. Other Surinamese women also effectively lost school terms, for example by having been placed in a track that was beneath their intellectual level.

Rita had already completed a few years of teacher's college in Surinam. Once in the Netherlands, she decided to go into nursing, however. She ended up at the lowest level of this kind of education, training to be a nurse's aide. Her training was basically in care-giving, rather than nursing. Aides are allowed to *take care* of the patients—washing, feeding, cleaning beds, assisting with dressing, etc.—but they are not allowed to medicate.

Rita: "There's nothing very special about the training. It was easy for me, since my level was much higher. So I was in effect downgraded. That's why I would like to try to get a bit higher up."

Similarly, when *Lita* came to the Netherlands she was placed in the second year of MAVO, which provided no challenge for her.

Lita: "Everything was terribly easy. I always got the highest grades. My second-year report card was excellent; my lowest grade was a B–." She was promoted to the third-year class. Her abilities continued to be underestimated. The school officials even tried to keep her from taking the final exams, convinced that she wouldn't be able to pass them.

"In the third year I was cutting classes constantly. None of the teachers believed I would pass the exams. They'd tell me, 'If I were you, I'd just leave it for now and begin all over again next year.' They didn't want me to take even one. I said to them, 'Give me a chance. You know that if you don't allow me to take them, I'll always hold it against you.' After a lot of talk back and forth, they finally let me do it. And sure enough, I passed. They just didn't want to believe it. When I went to receive my diploma, they stood there with such surprised faces, as if to say, now how did she manage to pull that off?"

Nonetheless, the school officials resisted promoting Lita to the fourth year. "They wanted me to repeat the third year, and I didn't want to. So I quit school."

Lita was accepted into the fourth year at another school. There she was "all alone," as she describes it. Moreover, since she had already lost a year she was relatively "old" for the fourth year, at 17. "At a certain point you begin to feel you're an adult. You don't gab so much anymore; you become calmer. Then I really didn't feel like being in school anymore."

Neither Rita nor Lita identified their intelligence being underestimated as a form of racism. Yet the experiences they describe cannot be seen independently from other illustrations of the prejudice that Surinamese girls at school are "stupid."

Negative reactions to high grades

The educational setting lends itself well to a close examination of the idea: If they would only adjust, they wouldn't be discriminated against. In practice, the notion of adjustment often implies that ethnic groups should adapt themselves to a model that was

created without their participation. Thus, the message of "adjustment" is: Just participate in school, where no special provisions
will be made for you.

At the same time, another form of "just participating" is
frowned upon, that is, when the participant proves to be as
bright and motivated as others in the class. Apparently, *that*
much adjustment is unnecessary. In reality, of course, intelligence is not a matter of adjustment. What does require adjustment is the white's image of black students. He or she must learn
that black students are not, by definition, less bright. But prejudices die hard.

Helen discusses this. "My classmates sometimes found it
very strange that I could get high grades too."

How could you tell?

"You could just tell, from certain things. For instance, you'd
be sitting with a couple of friends in geography class. You'd
gotten a high grade and they hadn't. They look at you with
amazement, and the next thing you know, they're saying you
spend all day studying. Yes, I could tell simply from their conversations."

Were these Dutch girls?

"Yes. They felt uneasy about it. They expected very little
from you as a Surinamese girl."

When I ask *Rita* whether her Dutch classmates seemed
surprised at the ease with which she handled school material, she
answers, "I don't know if it surprised them. But I think the
students around me had a lot of contact with Surinamese. So
when it came to the prejudice that Surinamese are stupid and that
kind of thing ... they just *knew* Surinamese weren't stupid. But
now I'm working with a girl from Surinam. She's also training as
a nurse. In her group they do discriminate. She hasn't told me
exactly what happens. But you know, they envy us when we get
such high grades."

Olga agrees. "They thought, Jesus, she doesn't understand
Dutch. While I was the one who got the best grades. They thought
that was a little strange; how is it possible? Some were jealous,
sure."

Though Olga is talking about the prejudiced attitudes of
white students, she claims not to have experienced any discrimination. "I've never had to deal with the idea that maybe I'm
being discriminated against. Never. If I didn't understand some-

thing, I just asked someone, "Could you explain that for me?" I didn't specifically look for a Surinamese girl to explain it."

Not being taken seriously

Several other women also mentioned that when they needed help, their classmates were very accommodating.

Mavis, referring to her classmates at a teacher's college, says, "They'd do anything for me. Even when I was sick for a month, they'd bring me my assignments every day. They kept me in touch about everything."

Ilse has had a similar experience with the Dutch students at nursing school. "I've never felt discriminated against. At the moment, I'm the only Surinamese in the group. Well, I don't notice it a bit. I've never felt left out. They are always willing to help me. Last week, for instance, I hadn't been present in one of my courses for three days, but I was clocked in by someone every day. Nice. Sure, I had to get them a bag of salt licorice in return, but you'd expect that." [Ilse's sense of humor shows in her mention of salt licorice—*drop* in Dutch. *Drop* is an absolute Dutch passion, a fact that puzzles most foreigners—even non-Dutch Europeans—who usually don't like it at all. But *drop* is to the Dutch like catnip is to a cat.]

An unusual relationship seems to have arisen here: the Dutch women are the givers of help and the Surinamese woman is the receiver. Yet often the acceptance of a Surinamese woman as an equal does not come so easily. We have already heard *Carla* say that she ultimately left social work school because she was excluded in certain ways and could not function well there. When we consider the following additional information about the situation at that school, we see that her classmates gave her almost no chance to work with them as a full participant in the program.

Carla: "I don't know what they thought of themselves. In certain classes, if they noticed you doing something well, they might become afraid that you'd start bossing them around or something. If you were supposed to work on a project in a group, all of them got together with their friends, and at some point you were left out. No one said, 'Why don't you come join our group?' which might have happened among a group of us coloreds. 'Hey, you're not in a group yet, come with us.' No, here you had to work it out for yourself."

Carla's presence in a group was clearly not considered an asset. Neither was her intellectual contribution taken seriously. "My participation was always only minimal. They seemed to have much more to say than you had. Or if you did say something, it would have to be discussed longer before being accepted and put down on paper. At the school I'm attending now, I see none of that. I like the group I'm in now."

Helen's potential contribution to working groups in her secondary school was also usually disregarded. "In the beginning I didn't dare open my mouth. People just talked right past you. It was as if you weren't even there."

Receiving low grades

Since Dutch students tended to cling to the prejudice that girls from Surinam were incapable of achieving as much as themselves, they were often jealous when the performance of a Surinamese student contradicted their expectations. In some cases, the Surinamese student did not get the chance to show what she could do. She was simply ignored.

The same prejudice on the part of the teacher can have very serious consequences, because teachers are in a position of power. The practice of giving undeservedly low grades to Surinamese students is a form of institutional discrimination mentioned quite frequently.

Linda: "I've finished school now, but I sure hope they make it easier for the other Surinamese who go there. When I was a freshman in high school, I had a teacher for a Dutch course who always failed me. It came up a lot when he gave dictations. My Dutch girlfriend and I always used to get almost the same answers in a dictation. But all I saw on *my* paper was red marks, all the time. Everyone was afraid of that teacher—except me. I stand up for my rights. If I don't deserve an F, it shouldn't be written on my paper. I said to her, 'Hey, what's this?' Took the notebook from my friend to show it, too. 'Yes, uh, I must have seen it wrong. But it's still an F.'"

Linda suspects that she is failed just because she is black. The teacher, however, contends that her work is not satisfactory. The fact is, the teacher is in the position of power: first, as the teacher, the one who decides whether Linda is promoted to the next grade level; second, as an adult; and third, as an "insider" in Dutch society. Linda, in contrast, is a young black girl who has just arrived in the Netherlands. Linda experiences the situation as very unfair and is enraged by it. Driven up against her individual powerlessness within the school system, she channels her anger into a threat. Since she cannot tolerate the fact that this teacher is abusing her power, Linda lets her know that outside the school walls her institutional power is gone.

Linda: "I said to her, 'An F, huh? Just you wait 'til after school. You flunk me one more time, and you'll see what happens when you come outside. You better not count on ever seeing that moped of yours again.' Yeah, maybe I can't really fight it out that way, but if she fights me this way, I'm going to make sure I can fight back, even if it *is* some big white lady. I told her I knew where she lives. And I told her that it wouldn't matter to me whether she's got kids or not, or whether her husband was with her, or whatever. I'd come right up to her and give her one fine slap in the face, just like that."

This remained just a threat, which is all it was ever meant to be. Linda could find no other way to illustrate that the teacher could not succeed in humiliating her.

[There is also some sarcastic humor in *how* she threatens the teacher. In the Netherlands, where many people bicycle to school and work, a moped is considered a lazy, sissy way to travel; it has a social stigma attached. Linda is making fun of her teacher simply by mentioning the moped, thus taking away some of the teacher's power, symbolically.]

Previous incidents had already given Linda good reason to conclude that the teacher "just didn't like black." Comparing her experience with that of another student from Surinam, she continues, "That teacher had tried it out with another girl, a Hindustani girl. It got so bad that she had to go back to Surinam. That girl had always been a model student. But the teacher phoned her house and told all kinds of lies. And there are some stupid people who will believe anything a teacher says, whatever she says must be right. It's easier for them just to listen to those whites. So they called that girl names and wrote a lot of letters to her mother, who was still in Surinam. Finally her mother had her come back, when that wasn't called for at all."

Linda seems not only to be angry at what this teacher has done to *her*; she is also strongly affected by the experience of the Hindustani girl. "I felt badly for her. That's why, when it happened to me, I said, 'I'm not afraid. I'll take care of that discrimination.'"

In her junior year, Linda finally got a new teacher for her Dutch course. This teacher confirmed Linda's opinion of the first teacher. "The second teacher said to me, 'I don't understand why she always gave you a failing mark.' That second one was really kind. Just the first one was a bitch. An awful bitch."

Mavis had a similar experience with her Dutch teachers at teacher's college. She had done her entire elementary and secondary education in the Netherlands. She describes having received unjustifiably low grades in Dutch, as a result of the teachers' prejudice that a Surinamese could not master Dutch better than a native Dutch student.

Mavis: "I always wanted to go into teaching. But I had been in teacher training for a year, and it wasn't going well at all. I got into arguments with them. I couldn't get along with the Dutch instructor anymore. He always had something to say to me. Nothing was ever good enough for him. My dictations weren't good, and if he came to observe my internship teaching, you could forget it. So I left."

Mavis tells this story shortly after the interview has begun. She is vague about what happened and appears not to want to go into detail. It is a painful experience; I wait until later in the interview before asking further about it.

You were talking about a Dutch teacher who gave you trouble, at the teacher's college. Could you tell me a bit more about it?

"That was really horrendous. It was a Catholic college. Outrageously strict, I thought. You had to do your teaching internship in certain prescribed grades. Mine was in a second grade class. Well, according to that second grade teacher's standards, I did pretty well at it. She said I turned out to be very good. Then that Dutch teacher came to observe my teaching there. He had plenty of criticism. Wretched; it made me sick. You know, *once* wouldn't have been so bad. But when he went on and on, pointing out only negative things, I really didn't like it. I thought to myself, it'll pass . . . the next time he comes to observe, I'm sure I'll do better."

Mavis did not immediately infer that the instructor's reasons for discouraging her were racist. *It might be partly my own fault,* she seems to have thought. She tried even harder, to no avail. "He assumed that Surinamese students were simply no good in Dutch. You may have studied it for years in Surinam or here, but they don't care. They just assume that you can't possibly be better in Dutch than a Dutch person. I figured that out pretty early. It really made me sick, too. I really began to hate that guy. Dictations, *nothing* was good. I never did anything right. I thought, I'll fail Dutch, and I'll just have to repeat this year again. Well, then I left school. I never completed the program."

Carla lost a year of school because her classmates made it untenable for her to remain. Mavis, too, found herself forced to leave school so as not to have to deal with any more harassment from this teacher. To be sure, a stimulating attitude on the part of a teacher can contribute significantly to a student's motivation to learn. But since this is part of the *informal* responsibility of the teacher, it is hard to confront teachers with it on the level of their formal duties. As there was little of a specific nature that Mavis could say against this teacher, his discriminatory attitude could not be "proven." Only much later was the accuracy of her judgment confirmed—much too late for her to act upon it.

Mavis: "As I heard from others later, it turned out that he really *did* discriminate. There were two Hindustani girls who had continued in the program. Well, if they hadn't stood their ground, they'd have failed because of this man. But they filed a complaint. They went to the director and made a big thing of it—which is why they were ultimately able to pass."

Unfortunately, racial/ethnic prejudice is not merely a characteristic of certain individuals. Transferring to another school is therefore no guarantee that the problem will be over. Mavis was forced to face this fact after registering at another college.

Mavis: "I've graduated since then, but not without first repeating the Dutch exam. A Dutch instructor usually assumes that foreigners can't speak like native students. And you certainly notice it. The whole year long I was getting Bs, but on the exam I was given an F. Mighty strange. An F! I couldn't believe it. If I'd failed another subject as well, I might have been flunked out of the program."

What exactly was the situation here? The examination committee at the final exam included not the teacher she had studied with in her senior year, but the teacher from her freshman year. As Mavis speaks, her memories surface with increasing clarity. At first she says that she hardly understands it, because, as she puts it, "I had no trouble with her in the first year." So she seeks the

explanation elsewhere. "Maybe she had experienced that Surinamese students in previous years hadn't turned out well. And
maybe she just assumes, well, it'll be the same with Mavis. So she
doesn't even take the trouble to notice that what she counts as
correct on the paper of a Dutch girl should also be correct on my
paper. To tell you the truth, I don't know what's behind it. I never
used to have trouble with her. . . . But I guess, in her heart she
feels something like, no, as a Surinamese girl, she can't get such
a good grade."

Mavis begins to have doubts. She suspects that the teacher
was prejudiced in giving her an F. But in that case, wouldn't her
prejudice have been apparent during the first year? Is it possible
that the racism was so subtle at that time that Mavis does not
readily remember the experiences? When I suggest to her that it
can sometimes be difficult to discern discrimination in certain
comments or occurrences, and yet one can be left with a strange
feeling from the experience, it seems to provide some clarity.

Mavis: "Well, once when I turned in a lesson plan, she said,
'Well, it's passing.' Touch and go, you know? I said, 'Oh, yeah?
Is it only passing?' I said, 'If you ask me, it's a very good lesson.
You really should have been there. This is just on paper; you
didn't see how beautifully I carried it out.' Then she said, 'I don't
think it was *written* well enough.'" (In the interviews with African-
American women, this response proves to be a notoriously com-
mon excuse, used to mask racism against black students.)

The teacher then voices her prejudice explicitly. "Then she
went on: 'But that's all right, I've had much worse from Surinamese students.' At that point I looked at her, confused. I thought,
what? It didn't really sink in. Later I thought, what a thing to say.
Just because you've had trouble with one or another student
doesn't mean that I'm the same. She thinks they're all alike: All
Surinamese have trouble with Dutch. But it doesn't have to be
that way. But, you know, it was just at the end of the term, so I
didn't see her anymore. I went on to the second year and got
another teacher for Dutch. For the exam in the second year, I had
the first year teacher again as examiner. The second year teacher
always gave me good grades; everything went fine. So when I got
an F, I thought, that's not possible. I went to the director. I said to
him, 'I think something dishonest is going on.' He said, 'Don't
worry about it. You'll get to take the exam over again, and you'll
pass it without any problem.' Well, I got a C the second time."

Later Mavis hears other negative stories about this teacher's attitude toward blacks. "I heard that she had once gotten into an argument because she'd given too low a grade to Surinamese students."

Mavis was intuitively convinced that she would receive at least a passing grade on the exam. She was therefore extremely surprised to hear that she had failed. Filing a complaint with the director did not result in further investigation of the teacher's performance. Yet the director did come to the conclusion that something was wrong. "He said, 'We looked at your report cards and thought, this just isn't possible.'" The director was sympathetic: "He felt very upset about it." Yet—albeit in an understanding tone of voice—he looks for the fault in Mavis herself. "'You might have just been feeling a bit down. Maybe it just wasn't your day. I've seen to it that you get the chance for a re-examination.'"

Rough and rude treatment

One expression of racism is a white's disregard of customary courtesy and decency in his or her contact with blacks.

Linda encountered this at school. "They want to do certain things with you just to see how much they can get away with. Take my gym teacher, for instance. Once someone pushed me during a gym class when I had to jump a hurdle. The gym teacher said, 'You'll have to do the jump again, then.' I said, 'No, I'm not about to do that.' He said, 'You won't? Well, then,' and he grabbed me by the back of my neck."

Linda stammers out the story. "I told him, 'If you had just spoken to me nicely, I would have gone ahead and done it. But you start pushing me around! You could just say, "Would you step aside," couldn't you? You didn't have to get rough like that.' They think they're sort of superior to you just because you're of a different race. They say white is 'purity,' but they're not pure as far as I can see. They're just a bunch of leeches."

The notion that blacks are inferior was expressed explicitly by a white in *Rita's* social science class.

"I was sitting with a girl in the group, a Dutch girl. She *really* discriminated a lot. She'd lived in Africa a long time, and you could just read it on her face: She didn't like black. She hated black, in fact. This kind of thing can come up easily in these

classes—especially in a social science course. We were discussing
Third World issues and she was trying to prove that blacks are
inferior and that 'we whites are in charge.' If you'd heard the
things she said! There were plenty of things that made it plain as
day that she just shoved everything black into a corner and saw
it as a pile of shit. That's what she was like."

Other comments were evidently so harsh and rude that Rita
remains vague when I cautiously inquire further. It then becomes
clear that Rita and the only other Surinamese girl in the class had
received no support whatever from the other (white) students.
Neither did her own teacher take action. Everyone stood by and
watched; apparently no one had the need to distance themselves
from the racist statements being made.

Rita: "It came to a point where the other Surinamese girl
and I began swearing at her. Since there was a disagreement, the
group said, 'Let's quit this.' The teacher had no idea what to do."

Olga has always enjoyed school. When asked whether there
were any unpleasant aspects, she answers, "Now, let me think.
Well, sometimes people talked about Surinamese. I didn't like
that, because they treat us as if we are all alike. When they talked
about Surinamese—some of them did this, not all—they went
right after you, driving it in. If three Surinamese happened to
have arrived late, they would say, 'Surinamese always get here
late. They're all hanging out at the supermarket.' But it's only
three guys! I think, why don't you just go and talk to those three?
But no, it's 'all Surinamese.' Otherwise things were fine at
school."

Olga is actually receiving mixed messages. She has had
many positive experiences, but at the same time she is constantly
being reminded of current prejudices against Surinamese. The
confusion this creates proves to be significant, as seen in light of
the following comment.

*Were you ever seen as different from the other Surinamese at
school?*

Olga: "No one ever said it to me. They did say that they
thought I had good leadership qualities. Which is also why they
encouraged me to go to nursing school. But maybe they also
thought a Surinamese girl can't manage other people. That's
possible, too."

This reveals a double-bind in which Olga is trapped. Olga
suggests that she more readily expects Dutch people to under-

value her than to appreciate her capabilities. The fact that she has good leadership qualities is in itself positive. But "good" relative to whom? Is she being compared with her Dutch classmates or with a prejudiced concept of Surinamese girls?

Below I will take a closer look at the low expectations that whites have and express of Surinamese students. How does such an attitude encroach upon the educational career of an individual woman?

Thwarted ambitions

In this section, *Carmila* speaks at length, describing a significant part of her educational history in the Netherlands. To a greater extent than in the interviews with the other women, the interview with Carmila centered largely on one theme: her experiences in the educational system. Her story points out forms of racism that we will recognize from other women's accounts of school situations. Carmila's experience demonstrates how both the expectation of racism and its actual manifestations shaped her educational career.

Carmila constantly fought against her teachers' and classmates' prejudice that she was a slow learner and that her goal of pursuing a higher education was aiming too high. Relative to her white (male) classmates, she was confronted with greater barriers to progress, so that she always had to have extra energy available to resist intimidation. As you will have noticed, I add "male" in parentheses in the sentence above. The tendency to encourage women less—or even to actively discourage them—in their attempts to get a higher education is a familiar form of *sexism*, after all. Black women can sometimes distinguish, on the basis of circumstances and certain other "signs," whether they are being discriminated against for their sex or for being black. Carmila's experiences demonstrate that this distinction can be hard to make.

Carmila begins the interview full of enthusiasm. She is attending a teacher's college, where her majors are French and biology. At the time of our interview, she has just completed a student teaching internship at a vocational school.

"I have good contact with the students. I don't see students as just some kind of object into which you have to pump knowledge. Students are also people; you have to keep that in mind. So

I'm not the one to play the authoritarian teacher role. When I
finished my internship at another school, the students were really
sad to see me leave. They were really sad. And that really made
an impression on me. I couldn't believe it. Nowadays it's also
important to have a relationship with your classes based on
mutual trust."

*Were they open to having a relationship based on mutual trust
with you, as a Surinamese woman?*

"At first I thought they would reject me. But since I myself
was quite open to them and could get along well with them, it
didn't take long for us to develop a bond. I never noticed any
discrimination or anything."

Carmila goes on to discuss her courses, her educational
philosophy, and her desire to return to Surinam. She would like
to work in Surinam eventually. But there is also a negative
motivation behind her desire to leave. Having spent almost all
her life in the Netherlands, she wants to be in a less hostile
environment.

*You have said that the Dutch have become less tolerant. How can
you tell?*

"I've experienced it personally. I once wrote a paper in
French. Since I kept getting low grades on a certain part of the
grammar, I worked extra hard on that point with the help of
another Surinamese girl. Before handing in the paper, I had her
check it over. Then I typed it up and handed it in. The teacher
just tore it up under my nose. He said, 'It isn't your own work,'
since I'd always gotten poor grades. I was alone with him when
he said it, and I just stared. I couldn't quite believe that he'd just
torn it up. Later of course it sunk in. Then he said, 'You have to
rewrite it, but not at home—here, at the institute.' I said okay, but
I was really upset about it. There was also nobody you could go
to about it. That's an example of what I mean by not being
tolerant. He thought someone else had written it. I did think to
myself then, something about all this just isn't right, but I didn't
pursue it any further." Carmila wrote another paper at school,
and passed.

Relating this incident, she is reminded of a series of others.
Characteristically, she hesitates to make the link to racism when
describing her experiences. Instead she consistently speaks of
"intolerance." During the interview, the endless string of experiences with the same pattern—underestimation, denigration, teas-

ing, and undermining her efforts—seem to her like pieces of a puzzle to be fit together. Only late in the interview does she interpret the whole experience in terms of racism.

The same teacher who had torn up Carmila's paper also tried to use other means of convincing her that she wasn't good enough to be in teacher training. He continued expressing his discouraging opinions with such persistence that Carmila, fearing she would be expelled from the school, reconciled herself to transferring to a lower level of training.

Carmila: "I had done a year of second degree French. [The Dutch system of teacher certification is divided into first degree, second degree, and third degree, from highest to lowest. The "degree" determines the kinds of schools and the grade levels one is certified for.] But the whole section was falling somewhat behind in French lessons. That's quite normal, since the program is so heavy. I thought, even though I'm slightly behind, I'll try doing the second degree. Well, that teacher saw to it that I'd have to take exams to catch up that slight bit. I passed them, but before I took them he kept saying, 'Why don't you just do the third degree?' He kept saying that.

"He said it until I actually broke down and did it. I just figured that if I didn't, they could kick me right out. You never know. Or they could put you at a disadvantage by giving you low grades. Since I had a scholarship, I had no choice. I thought, okay, then it's third degree."

Was he intolerant toward you as a Surinamese woman, or was he an unkind man in general?

"He was only that way toward me. It's the only time I've ever been confronted with anything like that. But hell, when I look back on it, he was really just a pathetic character."

Isn't it frustrating for you to be doing third degree now?

"It *is* frustrating. Especially since they didn't place me in the third year of the third degree program. Instead, what did they do? They said, we're putting you into third degree—which is already one level lower—and then we're throwing you back into the second year. So in fact I lost *two* years."

Carmila does not use the word discrimination, but her example does describe its essence: negative treatment on racial grounds. She immediately goes on to tell of her experience with another teacher. Although she emphasizes her feeling of having been treated unfairly, she asserts it has nothing to do with the color of her skin. Yet even as she begins her account of what took place, almost without realizing it, she appends it to the sequence of discriminatory experiences.

"Recently I was given a warning since I've failed one exam three times already. I keep *just* missing the passing grade. Well, so you can't really say I haven't studied at all, can you?"

Did this involve that same man?

"No, this was another one. But they're chips off the same block, aren't they? They still won't allow me to do my last teaching internship. And that's purely because of that guy. I went to the head of the department, but, you know, no time for me, too busy. Then I went to the dean, thinking, I've had enough of this. I mean, I can't keep going on like this forever. I explained what was going on. She said, 'If it continues, go see the director.' And then the director *will* have to do something about it. What I found strange was the kind of grading scale that teacher had. If you got 125 points, you could get an A+. I had 80 points, and he failed me. That got me wondering. I wanted to see his grading scale explained in black and white, but they didn't have it. That's the kind of thing . . . . Look, as a colored, you can of course assume it's your skin color, but that's not my way. I don't want to draw an immediate link to myself; I want to think it over first. I had to write two letters and then give further explanations before I could file a request to retake the exam. I've been granted permission to retake it—orally. But my examiner will be that guy who tore up my paper, again! If they fail me now, you can bet I'll take action, sister! Because that's obviously just wrong."

Carmila refers again to the increased "intolerance" of the Dutch. Her explanation of the problems she encounters is that people won't accept that she, as a black woman, is in a high-level training program. She is referring specifically to prejudices among whites who are themselves highly educated. Just as Mavis indicated, in her response to the question about differing neighborhoods, Carmila too illustrates that prejudice and racism are prevalent in the "high classes" of society, despite the myth in the Netherlands that racism is only to be found in old neighborhoods and among the poorly educated.

"That's why I say the mentality has changed. You notice it when you're studying, if you try to aspire to something better. They usually expect you to be slow. Afterwards it turns out otherwise. I've even had the experience—and that was also in the

French course—of getting a text about minorities to test our pronunciation and speaking skills."

In her description of this incident, notice how Carmila reveals that she is confronted with prejudice often, and that her reaction—almost as a reflex—is one of self-protection. "Well, you get this text about minorities. But then I'm the kind of person who thinks, oh, here we go again. I decide to just switch it right off. Then they really begin to get you angry. So I let them come at me, and then I come back with all the arguments I've got. Because they start saying things like, 'Yeah, those people are stupid anyway,' and, 'What are they doing here? What do those people come here for?' and so on."

Thus, Carmila must not only attend to her French conversation skills, she must also be vigilant for discriminatory remarks about ethnic groups and always ready to react. This means she has a doubly tough exam to take. Furthermore, she runs the risk of being "trapped" if her defensive arguments are taken in a bad way politically by the examination board. Finally, she is so cornered that she can only react in blind rage, which nearly costs her her grades.

"Once they made me angry. *So* angry. They started saying things like what I just told you, that those people are stupid and all that. I listened, under fire, just taking it. All in French, mind you. It was during the time there was an invasion going on in the war between Iran and Iraq, and I said, 'I hope World War III comes soon and that they bomb Europe to the ground. Then there won't be anything left over.' And then the guy said, in French, 'I'm giving you an F.'"

Another teacher who happened to be present evidently felt this was going too far and came to Carmila's assistance. She turned the discussion to Carmila's background, which she had previously heard Carmila talk about enthusiastically. Carmila took this opportunity to express her pride in her origins, saying that the truth of the matter is that her family has a much higher status and earns greater respect in the Surinamese society than the families of teachers in Dutch society. This desperate last resort illustrates poignantly the effectiveness of the attempt to denigrate her.

"I thought, I'll show them I'm not afraid of them. Suddenly they had nothing more to say. It was actually a survival strategy."

Fortunately, the teacher's resolve to fail her remained no more than a threat. Carmila got a C in the end.

Carmila's experience with one of the internship advisors, described below, is a very clear example of the way in which both sexism and racism are at work in the oppression she encounters as a black woman. She relates the experience in the context of elaborating on her feeling that as a black woman she is continually trying to "survive" in her education.

"It's actually a battle. And at a certain point you have to win that battle, don't you, because the survivor is always a winner. That's why I think it's also good to experience that even if I fail an exam three times, I still know I'll pass it in the end. That they can't . . . um . . . well, they try to drive me crazy. Saying all kinds of nasty things, like that I can't do it, and all that. I had that in the biology course too.

"Look, some girls get their course credits filled in bed. So what happens? The guy tries to butter *me* up, too—Carmila this and Carmila that. Once he had his hand on my shoulder like this, and he's trying to give me a kiss. I say, 'You better forget that before you even start, or I'll give it to you where it hurts, man.' I mean, it's my body and I'm not into that kind of shit. That's probably what ultimately kept him from doing it.

"But then he was assigned to me as internship advisor. He gave me absolutely no attention, though he really is supposed to, you know. But all right, so I didn't get any attention. When you do an internship, you can really get to see what a Dutch person is like, let me tell you. They just dump you, if you want to know the truth. I thought to myself, I ain't gonna lick that man's boots. I'll just try to do it myself. I just have to learn it myself."

In contrast to her classmates, Carmila does not receive the guidance and instruction to which she is entitled. Therefore it comes as no surprise when her internship is later judged to be qualitatively poor. The scenario of the "self-fulfilling prophecy" is clearly visible. Unlike the others, she must manage without guidance. Then the prejudice that she is not good enough to complete an internship successfully can be confirmed. The blame is placed on her.

"They didn't pass me for the internship. In the post-internship conference they went so far—laying on so much negative criticism, really pulling me to pieces—that I couldn't take it anymore. I had worked so hard and looked forward to it so much. I burst into tears, and they made a point of it in the final evaluation conference. The teacher then began taking advantage of it, saying, 'You feel unhappy in front of the class. You're not suited for teaching. You'll never be able to teach well.' That's what it came down to.

"Then I said, 'I don't feel at *all* unhappy before the class. I feel quite natural. Things may go wrong, but that doesn't mean I feel unhappy.' What kind of nonsense is that? But then the other two teachers echoed this, saying again I was unhappy. So everyone was against me, 'the unhappy girl.' Then all of a sudden, 'Well, you didn't pass the internship.' I say, 'Well, great. What am I supposed to do now?' And then they proposed I do an additional internship."

Carmila explained the situation to her Education Theory teacher. She had once seen Carmila give a simulated lesson and had confidence in her ability. When she read the report of the final conference with Carmila, she knew immediately that there had to be something behind it.

"She said, 'No, it's just not possible. You just have to have somebody else. You have to have me.' And she brought it up in a meeting. That created a big mess. They gave her hell for it. Especially that man, you know, because he really didn't want me to pass. Deliberately. But she succeeded in becoming my internship advisor."

Having been given a different internship advisor, she was compelled to do the entire internship over again. In very little time she proved to work so well that the advisor gave her approval early, with complete conviction. After being informed that her advisor had seen enough, Carmila was allowed to terminate her internship early.

"With the first one, I didn't have any chance to be myself, to prove what I had to prove. Thanks to this teacher, I passed."

You have great perseverance. I think you're very courageous; it can't be easy when you keep hearing that you're really not suited to teaching.

"No, it isn't. But that's exactly what these people want to do, make you feel insecure. Reduce your self-respect to nothing. They just think you can't do it. I mean, if I hadn't experienced it myself, I would say, 'Oh, bullshit.' But I had already experienced it when I was in HAVO."

Although Carmila does not state it directly, she gives the impression of having a strong fear of exams. The fear of failing her geography and German courses, in which she did not do quite as well, obsessed her so much that she did fail those courses twice. She herself knows that this had nothing to do with her level of intelligence. The school dean made no attempt to find out what the trouble was. He had already drawn his conclusions.

"Twice I failed to get my HAVO diploma. But I don't give up so easy. I have a strong will, as far as that's concerned. I went to the school dean with my mother."

Carmila's way of showing that the dean was not receptive to what she had to say is very symbolic. She emphasizes parenthetically that, despite knowing better, he repeatedly pronounced her name incorrectly.

"The school dean said to my mother: '*Car*-mila' [The correct pronunciation is "Car-*mee*-la."]—yeah, that's what he called me —'*Car*mila should just find work in an office or a factory, since she really can't do HAVO. She's too slow for that.' My mother didn't say a word. But I stood up and said, 'You just listen to me. The fact that I failed twice in geography and German doesn't mean I can't do it. I'm leaving this school. And happily—because I know for sure that I'll pass at another school.'" Her words proved true.

After letting slip the fact that she made an A+, the highest grade in the class, on the French exam, Carmila modestly brushes off my admiration.

"It wasn't necessary... a D would have been enough. It's like this with me: I fight, I have to fight really hard. But it's precisely through that fight that I keep my spirits up, to keep going. And those people can tell me a thousand times that I'm no good for this, no good for that, but you have to go on fighting. You don't reach your goal just like that over here. I don't mean to say it's discrimination. It's more harassment. That's what I'd call it. Humiliating you, trying to reduce your self-respect bit by bit."

With this, Carmila indicates that she regards the problems sensibly and soberly, a position she has held throughout the interview. Until I finally ask:

Do you have the idea that this harassment also has something to do with the fact that you are a Surinamese woman?

She then says (with reproach in her voice), "I'm dead sure of it. I mean, if I was as white as those guys, I don't think I'd have had any problems. But I always tell myself, if you don't want to drown, you better keep your head above water. You have to know for yourself that you can do it, and you have to keep saying it to yourself. They'll always tell you you can't. I think you just have to stand up for yourself, be more independent. And I just ignore them, to tell you the truth. Even if I have to go to the queen, I'm going to get my degrees. I won't let them get in my way. I know where I'm going and I know the way to get there. I just think, you have to struggle to survive. If you don't do it, you get nowhere."

Summary

We now see that the three main forms of racism are also present in educational situations and recur there systematically. In the women's experiences as students, in particular, everyday racism means being confronted with whites' attempts to *inferiorize* them. The white's low expectations of them and surprised reactions to their scholastic achievements, for example, are evidence of their prejudice that the black woman cannot be bright. But it does not stop there. Whites also seek confirmation of this prejudice. The teachers, in particular, may go to all lengths to establish it: giving expressly low grades; communicating exclusively derogatory, destructive, and even scathing criticism; ignoring the black student; or "recommending" compulsory transfer to a lower certification level or a lower level educational program.

There are also attempts to create *social distance,* as seen in the behavior of white classmates who leave the Surinamese student to fend for herself, speak about her as if she isn't present, or exclude her from their activities. *Social aggression* appears in the form of a teacher's roughness and physical violence, classmates' jealousy when a Surinamese scores high on an exam, or harsh racist statements.

The ordeals of the women teach us that the experience of everyday racism is not confined to the particular moment discrimination is experienced. Their awareness of existing prejudices and of the relative unpredictability of when and by whom these prejudices may be expressed puts the women constantly on the alert for the possibility of being treated in a racist manner.

An *alert attitude toward potential racism* is thus another, indirect, aspect of the experience of everyday racism. Everyday racism, to the black woman, means continually experiencing the *threat* of the racist social climate, even if she is not actually discriminated against every single day. This is because whites— depending on the extent of their prejudice, the circumstances, and personal factors—sometimes will discriminate and sometimes will not. The precise moment when racism will motivate certain acts (or their omission) remains relatively unpredictable. Once a woman has encountered racism in a particular person, she will be more on her guard in his or her presence. She is quicker, then, to recognize subsequent acts of racism, from the same person or others. She applies this acquired knowledge to her judgment of experiences with whites in general.

Public Situations I: Shopping

Contact during shopping is generally of an anonymous nature. Customers in a shop are usually complete strangers to each other, and the same is true of the relationship of sales personnel to the customers, except in the case of small neighborhood stores patronized by a regular clientele. Several women have had positive experiences with shop owners or salespersons at small shops or market stands where they are regular patrons.

Referring to this, *Mavis* says: "I hardly ever go downtown. I usually stay in this neighborhood. The people here know me very well. If I haven't been in the shops for a while because I've been sick, they ask where I've been. And if I happen not to have brought enough money for what I need one time, I can always come by and pay the next day."

Ester has had similar experiences. "There's a Turkish grocery here and a Dutch greengrocer across the street. If I need some fresh parsley—but just a little bit, say—they give it to me free. And at the Turkish shop, if I'm short a few cents or a guilder, he says, 'Oh, just pay it tomorrow.' They're nice."

One of the first Dutch habits that Surinamese people must get used to when shopping involves their ideas of hygiene. The Surinamese is at first taken aback when she sees the woman in the bakery take a fresh loaf of bread from the rack for her with the same bare hand that, not a moment before, held the change for the previous customer. Another adjustment they must make concerns the implied rules and customs governing who is next in line to be helped.

Laila: "I think it's terrible when someone says to me, 'Hey, I was before you.' Sometimes I can be absent-minded and I forget who was standing in front of me. Then I say right away, 'I'm sorry, I guess I was daydreaming,' or something like that."

What disturbs Laila is not the customer's reminder in itself, but the way in which it is given, blaming her for deliberately pushing ahead. "I don't like it when someone thinks you do it on purpose. It's especially the way they say it, you know, that bothers me. I mean, if you say it another way, I think it's okay. But when they do it to me, I do the same thing back. You teach yourself to adapt, as the Dutch say."

Being snubbed

At the heart of aggressive reactions against black customers who, by accident, go before their turn is the prejudice that whites should take precedence. This often leads to discrimination on the part of the other customers present. *Ester* says that, when she was younger, she sometimes never got her turn. "They cut ahead and said, 'Oh, she can just wait.'"

Carla confirms this with her own experience. "Once I was standing in line at the supermarket, and a woman came over and got in line ahead of me. Two women, actually. I think they had been shopping together. But one of them came and stood right in front of me. I thought to myself, I won't say a word. When the customer in front of me was done, this woman pushed in front of me to pay. So the cashier asked who was first, and that woman looked at me really strangely. I said, 'I was first, wasn't I? You got in front of me, but I was ahead of you.' And I paid the cashier. Well, those bitches started swearing at me! 'That's it! What else can you expect from those darkies?' And I said, 'You just go on and say what you want. You can't hurt me. Justice will triumph!' I said, 'And who do you think you are, anyway, bitch!' I sure gave her a piece of my mind.

"They do it a lot at the post office, too. That kind of person tries to get in front of you when you're standing in line. Maybe even just to see if you'll notice. And if you don't say anything, they'll just go ahead of you, of course. If you do say something, you're told you're a goddamn nigger or negress. Well, I don't care. Sometimes I've said, 'Ma'am, you may go before me,' if they have a baby carriage, for instance. But the rest have to wait their turn. And I stick to that principle."

When I ask *Joan* about her experiences with other customers, she describes similar events: Whites indicating that, as a black, she should not think of being able to go before a Dutch person, and displaying hostility if she accidentally goes out of turn. "At the butcher shop, there's usually no real line. If you happen not to see someone else come in before you, and you start ordering meat, you hear, 'Hey, I was ahead of you.' So I say, 'Sorry, I didn't see you there. I can make mistakes sometimes, too, can't I?' But when someone like that begins shouting, I can't take it. Then I think, don't be such a pig, lady. It can happen that you make a mistake once, right? It doesn't have to mean they are discriminating, or anything. Maybe that's how I see it."

Once again, the problem as Joan experiences it is not that it was pointed out to her that it was not yet her turn, but the way this was expressed. As a consequence of being black, she is not allowed to make a mistake. The event is not of extraordinary significance in and of itself. But "small" things become much more unbearable when they are associated with myriad other signs of unkindness, hostility, or contempt. They form the links in a chain of prejudice and discrimination that the women must face continually. Joan therefore sees a relationship between her experiences with other customers and with the store personnel.

Joan: "Recently I had that kind of experience again. I was at the supermarket. I'm not tall, and I needed something I couldn't reach. So I asked one of the boys to get it for me. He pretended not to hear me. But there was another boy there, so I asked him, 'Could you reach that for me, because that gentleman doesn't really feel like doing it.' And 'that gentleman' then said to me, 'If you'd just asked a little more clearly!' I said, 'You mean I should get down on my knees before you'd get it for me? Go to hell, mister,' I said. 'I don't need it anymore, in that case. I'll look for another.' I thought that boy really had a lot of nerve. And I wonder, do they say that kind of thing to Dutch customers too? Maybe. But I'm quick with an answer."

Being watched carefully

Ignoring a Surinamese customer purely to deny her that little bit of kindness is the flip side of another form of discrimination: hurriedly asking what the black customer wants and trying to get finished with her quickly.

Rita: "It happens quite often that when they see a black come into their store they leave all the other customers standing there and come to help you first. Because, you know, they see a black and right away they think: They steal. Maybe they've had bad experiences in the past, so their mistrust comes up as soon as you come in. They come up to you fast, so you'll be able to go sooner. When I see it happening, I think, up yours, I don't need your stuff. When I see it, I leave the store immediately."

I ask *Linda* whether she feels that she has ever been watched more carefully because of being Surinamese. "Yes, when buying clothes. I really hate it when it happens. When you come into the store, they look at you as if to say: She's come to shoplift, no question about it. Then they leave the whites and come over to you. They don't realize the whites are ripping them off the whole time. Because sometimes I've watched *them* shoplifting. And I think, just go ahead and steal it, because they only see the black." To be constantly considered suspect infuriates her so much that she actually gets some satisfaction out of catching white customers in the act of shoplifting. If you hadn't kept leering over the blacks, you would have caught those whites stealing, she seems to say.

Browsing without buying anything when you go into a store becomes suspicious in the case of a black customer—while considered quite a normal "freedom" for whites. Linda: "If you haven't bought anything, they think you *must* have come to steal, right? It's so uncivilized. They're not going to point the finger at *me*! If they try, they'll be wishing that store was a lot bigger." Behind this tough "they-ain't-gonna-insult-me-so-easy" exterior is a pained indignation that Linda only intimates. To be treated as a suspect is painful. It ruins the pleasure of shopping.

"Someone suddenly comes up behind you with, 'Ahem!' [in a stern voice] 'Can I help you?' This all of a sudden, when they've been busy with someone else. And then they start scrutinizing you. At that point, I say, 'Who needs this? Let's get out of here.'"

Shirley, too, is prevented from shopping leisurely in a store. "As soon as you enter the store, you hear, 'Can I help you?' Maybe you just want to look around. I don't usually go into a shop with the immediate intention of buying, no matter what shop it is. So you say, 'No, I'd just like to look.' Then they do turn around, but they *still* keep an eye on you. *Why?* Let me take my time looking and picking things out. Don't tell me I can look, and then stand there secretly watching every move I make."

Lita describes a different way she has been underhandedly kept under surveillance. "Sometimes they watch me extra care-

fully, you know. Take the shop on the corner here. I don't know
what gets into them, but when I go to the back of the store,
someone always rushes along after me. Supposedly organizing
boxes on shelves, you know. Or at the supermarket or the V&D
[a Dutch department store similar to JC Penney], I can be busy in
a corner and someone always comes over to fix and unpack boxes
—supposedly. But I'm wise to their tricks."

Carla was asked to check her shopping bag at the entrance.
Yet she saw that other customers were allowed to pass through
without checking their bags. "I'd been shopping at the outdoor
market, and then I wanted to look at a pair of slacks in this store.
My bag wasn't very full, but I did have a lot of money in it. As I
walked to the back of the shop, I heard this man say, would I
please leave my bag at the front of the store? I asked, "Why? Am
I the only one who has to check my bag, or does everyone?
Because if I'm the only one, I'll just leave this store right now.
But if it's a rule here that everyone has to check their bag, okay.'
I say, 'I also have valuables in my bag. I have money in my bag.'

"So he says, 'Now, Miss, don't take it that way.' I say, 'If I
leave it there, how do I know you won't poke around in it?'"

The salesman then said to Carla that she should just forget
about it, but the harm was already done. When you are *a priori*
singled out as a potential thief, you don't feel much like staying.
"I ended up not buying anything after all. I looked around for a
minute and then just left."

What went through your mind when he said that to you?

"I thought, he must be out to get me, especially me. Because
I saw other people with shopping bags come in without being
asked to check them at the door. So he had it out for *me*. That's
also why I left."

Ester is by now so used to the inspection of bags that she
undergoes it as a matter of course. "They're always following at
your heels. Sometimes you get to the cashier and they ask you,
'May I take a look in your bag?' But I don't steal, that's what's
important."

Don't you get angry when they ask you to do that?

"No, I just open my bag. You see, if you come down on these
people, everybody in the store turns around to watch. Then they
really believe you stole something. But if you don't make a fuss
and instead just open up your bag with a smile .... I don't let
myself get worked up about those people."

Ester shows clearly the vicious cycle in which she is trapped. As a result of whites' racist assumption that black people steal, she is forced to open her bag repeatedly at the cashier. If she were to refuse, it might cause a commotion. This in turn, given the dominant prejudices, would probably lead the other customers—whites—to jump to the conclusion that she had indeed stolen something. So Ester chooses to accept this discriminatory treatment.

Ester: "When I tell my [Dutch] boyfriend about it, he gets more upset about it than I do." She *used* to get upset about it, as the next incident reveals. Her attitude seems to have changed over the years, however. "I don't get worked up about it anymore. You expect these things to happen. As a Surinamese, you *know* you'll always be pounced on. So you have to be prepared."

Ester has tried to turn the tables by embarrassing the store personnel. Like several other women, she notices that black customers are checked more carefully. "When you go into a store, they follow you around constantly. Especially if one of those security guards is there. I've turned to them and said, 'You might as well push my shopping cart for me—and I'll walk you to the cashier.' I mean, what do I need that for? If it's a big store, I make them walk around for miles. It's great fun. Then you, like, walk through a hallway. You know he's standing and watching you out of the corner of his eye. So you take something off the shelf and stick it somewhere else, on another rack or something. I always used to pull that sort of thing on them."

Ilse doesn't see anything funny about being followed around in this manner. That which is taken for granted in the case of a Dutch customer—to be able to move around freely in the store—does not apply to her. Therefore she feels forced to avoid stores where it has become too much. If necessary she'll walk a block farther, a "voluntarily" imposed inconvenience.

"When you go to Zeeman stores [a five-and-dime chain], they walk along right up behind your ass. That's also the only store where it really gets to me. That's why I don't go there so often. They really just walk right on your tail there. Now I go to a branch of Zeeman way out that way, a lot farther."

Why do they do this?

"They just want to see what you're up to. Or they stand gaping at you from a distance, so that when you look up for a moment you see one of them standing there staring at you. I don't like that one bit. But it's the only store it ever happens in. In other stores there's no problem."

Do they do this because you're Surinamese, or is it a routine procedure in that store?

"I don't know. Well, I've noticed they don't pay attention to the Dutch shoppers. And not all the salespeople there do it, just one girl and the manager. The rest of them don't. It makes me think you should just stay away from their store, so I don't go there often. Only when I have no time to go all the way to the other shop, then I do drop by here. I just get what I need and get out."

Repeated observation has given Ilse insight into the racism she experiences in the store. She knows how it occurs, who is involved, and how these people behave toward white customers in similar situations. In the examples above, the women are not suggesting that white customers never get checked and blacks always do. Rather they suggest that the checking that would otherwise be carried out on white customers is prejudicially transferred to the lone black customer.

Olga describes how she confirmed her suspicion that as a black she is watched closely. She carries out an experimental study of the behavior of a particular salesman. "When you go into the drugstore here, that man starts following right behind you. Once I wanted to buy some baby lotion. He's just standing there watching, pretending to write. I say, 'I can't enjoy my shopping. Look, if I had a store, I wouldn't want anyone to shoplift in it either. I'd also keep an eye out. But not the way you do. I'd stand in a corner and do it inconspicuously.' 'Sure, Ma'am, but so much gets stolen from here.' I say, 'You're paying attention to me while those Dutch people are shoplifting.' He says, 'That's not true, I'm not paying any extra attention to you.' I say, 'Well, sorry, but I can feel it.'"

Although the man denied having watched her especially rigorously, Olga saw it otherwise. She did not want to draw any hasty conclusions, however. And so she put the salesman to the test.

"The next day I go in there deliberately, to buy sandwich bags. I was thinking, I'm going to see if he's really watching me. And he does it again. I leave the box of sandwich bags there and go stand next to the perfumes. He comes up to me saying, 'Can you find what you need?' I say, 'If I can't, I'll ask. I'm just

looking.' Well, he *still* keeps following me around. I say, 'Listen.
I've been living in this neighborhood a long time. If I'm short
of cash when I'm paying, the cashier girls always say, "Oh,
Olga, we'll get it from you another time." I never steal anything. If someone trusts me, I don't steal. Why would I?' Can
you just imagine a person like me taking a few packs of
baggies and risking that a policeman will come to pick me up
for it? So I just said to him straight and honestly, 'You won't
see me in your store again.' He said, 'I'm sorry about it, but I
do have to keep an eye out, of course.' I said, 'But why especially
when *I* come in? So many other women came in at the same
time I did. But you weren't keeping an eye on them.' He says,
' Yeah, but those Surinamese.' I said, 'What *about* "those Surinamese"? You're watching me, and all the time other people are
shoplifting.'"

Olga knows that because she is black she will be suspected
of being a shoplifter right away. Therefore she expects that she
may actually be charged for it—unjustifiably—at some time. She
believes she can avoid this by taking all sorts of precautions to
ensure that they will have no grounds on which to humiliate her.

"I purposely bought a plastic shopping bag. It is *so* transparent that anyone would *have* to see whatever was being stolen
in it. Then, when I went to the drugstore, I even said to that man,
'I've got this see-through plastic shopping bag. You can sure as
hell see what I do or don't put into it.' By the way, it wasn't only
at the drugstore, it also happened at the supermarket. I know
they're watching us, so I always leave my bag at the cashier. I
only take my purse in with me."

Olga takes yet another precaution. "That's why I also never
go with three or four friends when I go shopping at the department store, for instance. I never do. On purpose. I say, 'You just
go ahead; I'll go to a different department.' Because I know they're
paying attention to us. And if someone blames me wrongly,
well, they're not going to get off with, 'I'm sorry!' But it
wouldn't occur to me to steal anything, either. I mean, if I don't
have the money for one thing or another, then I just do without
it."

Olga seems hardly willing to show how painful it is to be
continually treated with mistrust. From the precautionary measures she takes, it is apparent that this kind of prejudice can have
a drastic effect on the organization of a black woman's shopping

errands. Even these precautions are not enough to prevent store personnel from continuing to pay undue attention to her. This means extra stress: feeling uncomfortable because she constantly feels suspicious eyes piercing her back.

As we've seen, the experience of being unjustifiably mistrusted results in a certain degree of indifference when witnessing whites shoplifting. Olga: "I sometimes see them stealing things. But I don't say anything to the salespeople, because I'm thinking, you're busy watching me, so why should I say anything? Recently it was one of these old ladies, a real *old* lady in the supermarket. She was tucking away a roll of toilet paper. I watched her. She says, 'Yes, everything is so expensive, isn't it?' I just walked away. I'm thinking, why should I care, she's such an old person. It was a little pathetic to hear her say how everything is so expensive. But they aren't watching those old people. And *they* steal! I would have said something if it had been someone my own age, a Dutch girl. Then instead of saying to the manager, 'You only watch Surinamese customers, and meanwhile . . .' I'd say it directly to *her*. Then they really feel it. What could she say to that?"

Racist conversations

The anti-black (or anti-foreigner) atmosphere in stores is well illustrated by conversations between Dutch customers and salespeople, overheard by the Surinamese women when shopping.

Mavis gives an example. "At the market, you hear them talking about Surinamese. They think we're noisy, that we speak too loudly, and act like the city belongs to us. That kind of thing. Or when something happens at the market, they all start talking. That's when you notice how much happier they are to see us leaving than coming."

What do you do if you're there?

"I stay out of it. But it does get me angry. You could probably read it on my face, but you won't catch me saying anything. Only if a Surinamese child is involved—then I'll sure make noise."

Mavis goes on to describe an incident in a newsstand. As soon as she came into the store she could tell that her entrance came at an awkward moment for those present. "As I came in, there was a lady there who was very upset about something. She was telling a story to the man behind the counter. I heard something about foreigners. 'I put my umbrella down over there and all of a sudden it disappeared. So I say to myself, what's going on here? Maybe he stole it.'"

Mavis suspects that the blame is again being pinned on a foreigner. She recognized instantly the climate in which such things are said, as this kind of scene is familiar to her. With the sudden reaction of the agitated woman, her suspicion is confirmed.

"She says, 'Well, some of them are nice,' because I came into the store. The man was also getting sick of her. But you know, he probably has his own ideas about Surinamese."

This comment illustrates very clearly the difference between active and passive racism. The woman in the store expressed the prejudice actively. The storekeeper simply accepted it, passively. His own opinion remained unspoken, making his attitude unclear.

Being accused of theft

Carla: "Once I went into a cigarette shop somewhere on the east side. It was one of those little stores with candy racks at the counter. I had just withdrawn money, and I wanted to mail a letter. [Some Dutch cigarette shops and newsstands handle postal and bank transactions.] I only had to write the address on the envelope. The saleslady was watching me, so I bought stamps right away. It was cold, so I had my hands in my pockets. She counted up the stamps and then said, 'And that Nuts bar, too.' 'What do you mean?' I said. 'Yes, you took a Nuts bar, didn't you?'"

As Carla tells the story, she relives her old indignation. With an agitated voice, she continues, "I say, 'What gives you that idea? I didn't take any Nuts bar.' I emptied my pockets for her to see. I said, 'Sorry, but I'm not paying for it.' So she looked at me, she saw my hands in my pockets and thought, she must have stolen something. I say, 'I'd never pinch a bar of Nuts! You saw how much money I just changed here, didn't you?' And she says, 'Let's just forget it, Miss.' She tells me to just forget it, as if everything's fine if I haven't really taken anything. I was really pissed off! As it happened, there weren't a lot of people in the store, but I did say out loud what I felt. It was so insulting. For one reason or another she doesn't want to say, you stole something. But she's thinking, I'll charge her for it. And *I'm* thinking, lady, fuck you!"

A black woman's experience of everyday racism extends beyond the discrimination and prejudice directed at her personally. Witnessing racism directed at or expressed about others also affects the Surinamese woman who is present. Witnessing racism toward children, in particular, provokes the women's anger.

Olga tells the following in relation to this. "Once I was in the V&D with my younger sister. There was a little Surinamese boy there. He had bought some note pads and paid for them already. But he put them in another bag, a bag from another store. So the man in V&D thought, that boy pinched those. He grabs the boy like this, saying, 'You stole those things and I saw it. You stole them.' My sister had seen him paying for them, and the woman at the cash register too said, 'That boy paid.' 'Yes, but I still just want to check if he has any other things, even if he didn't steal them from *us*.'"

Apparently the prejudice, cost what it may, had to be confirmed.

Olga did not let it end here. "It was an eight-year-old boy. He just cried and cried. It was pathetic. I let them have it. I said, 'He isn't my little brother, but he might just as well be. That boy's mother gave him five guilders and he bought one guilder's worth of note pads. He even has a receipt for it!' But the man went on accusing the boy anyway."

Olga is personally affected by the unfair manner in which the boy is being treated. She is not talking about injustice in general, but ties it in closely, speaking as if it were her own little brother. She was so deeply hurt by the incident that she could not immediately express her outrage. "It was really upsetting. That day I really felt angry at every Dutch man I saw. Everyone. When I got on the tram, I thought, if any one of them tries making any wisecracks today, I'm going to lay right into him. It made me feel furious at everyone. I really felt bad for that boy. He went away crying. And that kind of man is just cold as ice. He couldn't give a shit whether it's a little kid or not. I mean, if he comes at *me*, I can give it right back to him. But a little kid like that can't. Oh, it was so pitiful to see. I have a little brother of 11, too. So sad, that boy didn't have anyone to help him out. I mean, the people they should be getting, they leave alone—because there are plenty of Dutch boys who rip things off, you know."

Public Situations II: Public Transportation

Laila: "I don't notice any discrimination in the tram. They just come and sit next to me, and I also just sit next to them." The empty seat next to the black passenger in an overcrowded tram has become an almost stereotypical symbol of racism in public transportation. Although none of the women interviewed mentioned that example, they did speak of other forms of racism with which they are confronted.

Less right to a seat

When asked if she has ever experienced discrimination in the tram, *Joan* answers immediately, "Oh yes. People often look disapprovingly when, as a brown person, you've got a seat."

Other women describe having been "cold-stared" right out of their seats. Typically what happens is that someone comes and stands where the black passenger is seated until the latter feels socially obliged to relinquish his or her seat.

Ilse: "When people are getting into the tram, older people, for example, they look around and then they always come and stand where Negroes are sitting. So I usually look at them and just keep sitting. If I see that someone really can't stand, I'll stand up of my own will. But no one's going to come to me and say, 'You have to get up.' I stand up most often for Surinamese people or Turks."

Carla, too, has experienced discrimination in the trams. "An old woman got onto the tram. She came and stood right next to my seat, even though there were Dutch women there too. She stood next to *me*, deliberately, hoping I would stand up for her. But I didn't. Then the whisperings began. 'They have young legs and they can't even stand up.' But I didn't react. I thought to myself, why do you have to stand right at my seat? They've played it that way often, you know. Especially these old people."

Whites will often pressure black children to give up their seats. The discrimination lies not only in the double standard—the fact that the black children, more than Dutch children, are expected to relinquish their seats—but also in the rough and rude way in which the request is made.

Ester experienced this personally when she was younger. "You'd be sitting in the tram, and a Dutch child of five would be sitting in front of you, for instance. They'd come right up to you and say, 'Hey, stand up.' They don't go to the [Dutch child], they walk up to you! And if you don't stand up, man, what you have to listen to! 'Filthy damn black! Whaddya come here for?' and God knows what else. Certain people curse at you all the time. But that's what got me to fight, in those days."

How old were you then?

"Twelve, thirteen. But I don't do it anymore. At school they didn't have the courage to say 'filthy black' to me. They would have learned a lesson they'd never forget if they had. But later I thought to myself, what am I doing? They're just stupid people. I didn't let it get me down anymore."

When Surinamese children are addressed rudely, the Surinamese women present feel offended and immediately come to their assistance. We recall that *Mavis*, when speaking of the racist comments in the market, said that she would only get involved when a black child was concerned.

"I was sitting in the tram. There was also a Surinamese boy with his little sister sitting there. Two cute little children, maybe seven or eight years old, sitting together in one seat. An older woman gets on. 'Hey you, get up!' I found it really disgusting. You just don't *say* it like that! She could have asked, 'May I sit here?' I said, 'You might ask that more politely, Madam. You wouldn't have dared say it like that to a Dutch child.' I've often seen how their own children talk right back to them. You can't start thinking, oh, it's just a Surinamese child; he can stand up. Of course he can stand up. But you can certainly ask it a little more politely. Those two children just sat there staring at me. They just stayed seated, you know."

Mavis immediately associates the incident with the fact that she also has a younger brother who might receive the same uncivil treatment. "I always say to my little brother, 'If someone asks you to stand up, they mustn't think they can say anything they want to you just because you're a foreign kid. They have to ask you politely.' Usually the really little ones will just get up without a word. Well, I think that's wrong."

Joan often rides the tram with her son. "Once we were sitting together, each with our own tram ticket. A woman comes along and first starts going on about how 'that child could certainly sit on his mother's lap.' That sort of talk. That really gets me angry. As I see it, if you want to sit down, ask me politely,

'May I sit here?' Normally I would move over. But if you start giving me dirty looks, then don't expect me to do anything at all. Anyway, she started carrying on. So I said, 'If you want to hold that child on your lap, then please have a seat.' She didn't do it. So I just sat and enjoyed the ride next to my child. Well, there we were. When we got out, she had two seats to choose from."

Have you experienced this kind of thing in the tram at other times?

"Yes. But my son stands right up when he sees elderly people standing. On the one hand, that's very courteous. As long as the people are a little bit civil, I don't mind that. But I do notice people discriminating against *him* more readily than against me. But he has a more Negro look, you know? People look at me so strangely for his being my child. But you know, I can't always jump to his defense. It's tough for him; it's nasty. I sometimes think to myself, you people start this yourselves. A child like that can't understand it yet.

"I have a friend, a woman from the Antilles, who teaches her eight-year-old son everything [about discrimination]. But I don't want to do that. I think they'll learn it through their own experience. I'm not going to drill him on what's what for every single case. You do tell them certain things, about how it used to be, for instance. But a child gets completely confused when you tell him too much."

As we see, Joan's reaction differs from Mavis's. Joan believes her child will learn from experience what it means to be black in Dutch society. Mavis, on the other hand, began drilling her little brother at an early age, to teach him that he cannot be treated as inferior and doesn't have to accept such treatment from anyone. It is also interesting that Mavis is the only woman who described having been warned by her mother, albeit implicitly, about the racism she might encounter as a black woman.

Ilse once appointed herself protector for a Surinamese boy in the tram. In this situation she went a step further than Olga, who had defended the boy unjustly accused of theft in the V&D by saying he could have been her little brother.

"There was a little boy sitting in front of me. It was just noon, so the tram was full of Dutch children. This bitch walks straight up to the boy and says, 'Stand up. Let me sit here.' I said, 'Get lost!' I said to the boy, 'You just stay seated, honey.' I said to her, 'He's my brother.' And you know I'd never seen that child's face before. But I said, 'Fuck off, lady. He won't stand up. He paid to sit in this tram, too, just like you.'"

Ilse has experienced so much unkindness and aggression in buses and trams that she seems to be at the end of her rope. One incident after another is remembered and related; two ended in fights.

"For my birthday I got a gift certificate for a houseplant. I had to go all the way to Osdorp [a suburb of Amsterdam] to pick it up. My nephew went with me. We get into the bus with this plant, and at the next stop a woman and her dog get on. Just at the moment the bus arrives, I see her picking up her dog. With that dog on her arm she gets into the bus and walks up to my nephew. 'Would you stand up? Let me sit. I have pain in my knee.' I said, 'Like hell! Put down that dirty dog. If you can't walk, how can you carry that dog? You have a knee problem, right?' 'Yes, but that's none of your business.' I said, 'He's not going to stand up.'"

Ilse then points to a Dutch boy sitting nearby. "Why can't he stand up?" She is unaware, however, that he is wearing a sling around his arm. Right away, an argument begins. "The whole bus began yelling at me. Everybody there."

Ilse attracted the aggression of the entire group of whites, who were almost all adults. When a little boy began cursing along with the rest, it was the last straw. "I didn't mind so much that all those adults were bawling me out. But that little squirt thinking he could be a part of it too! I stood up and gave him a whack. Wham!"

Ilse felt extremely threatened and reacted wrongly by picking on the boy. The bus stopped and the police were called in. Just at the moment the police were about to take her away, someone came to her defense.

"The police were ready to take me away. Then a woman came out of the bus, a young woman. She said, 'Sir, I was sitting in the bus the whole time. They all abused this woman, calling her names and provoking her deliberately. That's why she grabbed the one she could handle and hit him.' Well, the police drove me home. *With* my plant!"

Ilse tries to conceal how hurt she felt at the time. As she tells the story, she passes from Dutch to Sranan Tongo and makes it into a "cheerful" story. She is particularly angry at the driver, a Surinamese, who shut his eyes to the entire scene. In contrast, the white passengers acted in solidarity against her. She words this terrible story in such an amusing style that we both end up laughing about it.

Ilse then goes right into another story. The fact that the whites in a conflict situation have an extra trump to play—namely racism—makes her burn with rage. In a moment of extreme helplessness, she found a rather unfortunate double-edged solution: to turn a racist attitude against its user.

"I once fought with a Dutch woman in the tram. It was terribly crowded, so if someone pushed you, you didn't pay it any mind. But I felt a really sharp jab in my back. At first I thought, oh, forget about it. It's just because it's crowded. You have to expect that. But then she hit me again! I looked around without saying anything. She shoves me a third time, with, 'Now will you move over?' Since it was so crowded, I couldn't do a thing. When a seat became free, she sat down. I went up to her then and said, 'What you just did, you better never do again!' 'So what are you going to do about it?' she said. 'What are *you* gonna do about it?' Then I got furious. I grabbed her long hair and yanked it; we started fighting. They separated us. When the fight was over, the girl suddenly comes out with, 'Go back to your own country! Go back to your own country!'"

Ilse reacted swiftly to this racist cry. She thought, so you're a racist? Then I know the other prejudices you must have. "So I said, 'I should go back to my country, huh? Say one more thing and I'll stab you.' All of a sudden the whole tram went silent."

Of course she had no knife with her. But she was well aware of the dominant prejudice against Surinamese. It would probably be assumed that as a black she would indeed have a knife or some other weapon with her. "I didn't even have a knife. But I thought, I know what you people are afraid of."

The sad part of this experience is that Ilse felt so driven into a corner and so humiliated that she was forced to confirm, as it were, an existing prejudice in order to defend herself at that moment. She wanted to show that whites couldn't just push her around and shout whatever they wanted at her. What she wins on one front, however, she loses on another, for the people on the tram go home with yet another story of a black threatening a white with a knife.

Verbal Abuse

Shirley offers another example of a conflict situation that becomes a racial issue. "When the bus or tram arrives, I always want to get right in. But there are always these old people just standing there. They take their time coming, and then stand there talking. You are supposed to let them go first, right, but I never do. When the bus stops, I shoot right in. And then I hear, 'You haven't learned any manners,' and, 'Get on back to your own country.' Well, I'm not about to just let that go by. So I say, 'What do you mean?' I don't make jokes with them, man, I don't look for trouble, and I don't come down on them. But when that kind of thing happens, I give them hell."

Clearly, an argument like "go back to your country" can only be used when it is a Surinamese, and not a Dutch woman, who has too little patience to wait a moment.

The argument that the Surinamese "should get the hell out of here" is heard by the women so often that even innocent comments that imply something similar seem suspect to them. The following excerpt from *Ilse's* interview is an example. She describes a situation that other Surinamese are likely to recognize quite readily. She has just answered "yes" when asked whether Dutch people ever ask why she is in the Netherlands.

What do you think of when they ask that question?

"I think, go to hell! Because they always ask that. And in the winter, when you're standing at the tram stop, they stand like this [shivering and rigid] and say to you, 'Cold, isn't it? Where you live it's nice and warm, isn't it?' It's always the old ones. Always. 'Cold, isn't it?' Standing like this, brrrr. Even if they have a fur coat. Meanwhile you're just standing there, normally. And they come over to ask if you're cold. So I say, 'Why no, I'm not cold at all.'"

What do you feel when they ask this?

"It makes me so angry. I think to myself, mind your own business!"

The problem is that Ilse must guess at the motivation behind the remarks. Sympathetic interest? Or would she receive a very significant look if she admitted that she was indeed cold?

Do you get the idea that they are suggesting that you ought not to have come here at all?

"Yes, exactly. Especially since it is always the older generation, not the younger ones. Yes, they discriminate too, but not as badly as the older people, because to them [the older people] we are still intruders."

Prejudice is also articulated overtly in stories and comments the Surinamese women overhear while riding to work, home, or just downtown.

Ilse: "Recently I was sitting in the tram, coming home from work. Two old ladies were sitting and gabbing, 'Yeah, those Surinamese and other foreigners are so lazy. They don't work. They just collect welfare.' They were complaining that they get so little money. I responded right away. I said, 'I am one of the Surinamese who works. I'm coming from my work right now.' 'Yes, but we're not talking about you.' I said, 'But you're talking about my people. I don't like that.' That kind of thing happens often in the tram, and when it does I give them a piece of my mind right away, because I hate it."

Laila is affected when she hears people on the tram express prejudicial ideas. "If they say something like, 'We better keep an eye on those guys,' meaning three Surinamese boys standing together, I do feel like I'm involved."

Mavis explains why it is so unpleasant to overhear such comments about people from her country. "You sometimes hear remarks like, 'There's another one of them in the back of the tram.' And if some Surinamese boys are standing in the back, for example, and you get onto the tram and walk on in, then you hear all around you, 'There are a couple of 'em standing back there. Pickpockets, for sure.' Whether or not they're pickpockets, you feel awful, just because it's your own people they're talking about. So it really isn't nice to hear. I feel the same way when I see them do something cruel in the street, when they're rude to someone. It seems like it's meant for me, too, when they talk about a Surinamese standing in front of me or behind me. It affects me too. They know I'm standing there, so they should keep their mouths shut. They shouldn't talk about, 'Those Surinamese. Why do they come here? Let them go back to their own country.' You shouldn't say that. I mean, if it was only intended for that boy, then you would have kept your mouth shut. You just don't say that sort of thing when other Surinamese are standing right there, do you? I do think that's discriminatory. And you get that a lot in the tram. A *lot*."

Black Pete

When the interview with *Rita* touches on provocative incidents in the tram, she says, in a somewhat dejected voice, "I've never experienced anything bad myself. And I hope I won't, either, because I think you feel really awful when it happens. My brother, he's experienced it. It happened around Sinterklaas time [The feast of St. Nicholas—the children's Christmas holiday]. Black Pete and all that, you know. There was a little girl of about four. My brother was standing behind her. He wanted to give her his hand, and he smiled at her. Out of friendliness, you know. And the kid began to scream. "Look, Ma, it's Black Pete!" Thank goodness other people looked too. They saw that my brother didn't want to do that kid any harm, that he was just smiling at her. Well, when that happens you just feel like absolute shit. And then you've got to have an answer ready for that child. An answer that isn't aimed at the child, but at the mother. Because it's purely a matter of upbringing."

Ester has had a similar experience. "When you sat in the tram, you used to hear, 'Oh, Black Pete,' if one of those kids was riding." Ester is not so much offended by the child's exclamation as by the passive attitude of the adults accompanying him. "The mother will never say to her child, 'You mustn't say that.' No way. They're all having a good time in the tram. That's what makes those Surinamese guys get so aggressive at times. What do they do? They hit the kid while his mother is sitting right there. Then you get the whole tram against you."

Being denied a seat

One way in which racist feelings toward black women may be expressed is by refusing to offer them a seat in the bus or tram. This problem was raised especially by those women who had experienced a pregnancy while in the Netherlands. *Mavis* is the only one who has directly experienced that people would stand up for a Dutch woman sooner than for a Surinamese. "I find that they are more likely to stand up for an elderly Dutch woman than for an elderly Surinamese. That's right. I still remember it: A really old Surinamese granny comes in. Well, what a long time goes by before anyone stands up! If it had been a Dutch woman, they'd have stood up for her much sooner. They won't usually admit it, but they *do* do it, you know; very discriminatory. Some people are very courteous and offer their seats right away. But there are a whole lot who would stand up only when a Dutch woman is standing, if they have a choice."

Carla tells about a friend of hers being insulted while she was pregnant, though she does not place the incident in the context of racism. "I was once riding the tram with a Surinamese friend of mine who was pregnant, and all the seats were taken. Then a Dutch woman asked a little boy, 'Wouldn't you like to give your seat to this lady?' He said, 'How can I help it if she's pregnant? It isn't mine, is it?' A little boy! He didn't get up. 'I paid for my tram ticket too,' he says."

Various women indicated that when they were pregnant, older people would stand up for them more readily than young people.

Lita: "They would just get up for me when I stepped into the bus or tram. The younger people don't offer their seats so fast. Older people do. I noticed that when I was pregnant. Once a very old lady wanted to give me her seat. But I said to her, 'Please keep your seat.' And yes, men—actually the men give up their seats even before the older ladies."

Myra, however, found that "everyone" gave up their seat for her when she was pregnant. "Yes, they did. And when I got into the tram with the baby carriage, I was helped too. Since I've had such good experiences, I always give up my seat to other people too. So when I see a pregnant woman or an elderly person, I offer them my seat. If I hadn't had that experience, maybe I would have been hardened too. Sometimes I hear people saying at the top of their voice, 'I will *not* stand up.' Look, if they hadn't done it for me, I wouldn't do it for them either. But that's not the experience I had. Maybe it has yet to come. You never know. I hope not. But maybe it'll happen someday."

Public Situations III: Aggressive White Men

Do you ever have trouble with Dutch men on the street?

I asked most of the women a question similar to this. I intended to find out whether black women are confronted specifically with the sexism of white men.

Rita: "Well, sure, once in a while."

Do they say something? Touch you? Whistle at you?

"No, I've never had that. I was always approached in a very friendly way. I mean, they say hello, I like you, and that kind of thing, you know. But then I just say, 'Sorry, I have no time. Gotta go.'"

So they simply greet you in a friendly way?

"Yes. But I've heard from some people that they get certain things yelled at them, like 'blackie' and 'monkey' and that kind of crap."

"Well, it isn't exactly an assault," says *Linda*. "Okay, when I come home late sometimes. They just walk along with you and ask what you'd like to drink, and all that. I say, 'No thanks.' They walk me to my door. I say, 'Okay, 'bye now.' That's all. A few of them maybe want to shack up with a Surinamese girl. Or just to screw, I'm sure. So when they come up and talk to me, I get rid of them right away. Because I'm not into that. I'm just not into that."

The racist-sexist prejudice that black women are supposedly always available and willing is the source of unpleasant experiences for several of the women.

Shirley: "Some Dutch men, not all, but some, find brown women more attractive. Maybe because they're looking for some action. Or maybe they want an exciting half-breed. But not all of them like Negresses."

Have you ever been approached in the street?

"Yeah, sure. But then I know just what they've got in mind. They just want to have a little Negress, you know. Just for a night. That's all. They're curious about it. They say Dutch women are different from Surinamese women in bed. I don't know whether or not that's true. But they think there's more fire in us. So they want to try it out.

"Once it happened that I was going to the hospital with my child. There was one of these guys who was really out to get a Negress. And you get a line like, 'Don't I know you?' But I had never seen the man in my life. Then he says, 'Feel like a cup of coffee?' I say, 'I don't really like coffee. And in addition I don't have much time. I have to take my daughter to the ear doctor.' It must have taken 2½ hours—but he waited. When I came out of the hospital, I thought to myself, he's gone now. But he was standing patiently, waiting at the corner. Then he started asking if I had a boyfriend, if I lived alone, more of those questions.

He wanted to go out to eat with me, and all that. But I figured out pretty fast what that guy had in mind. He was really set on making it with a Surinamese girl. Well, the game ended for the moment. But he came around often, ringing my doorbell. I didn't answer it, and finally he stopped coming by. I've experienced that frequently, these Dutch men who are just greedy for a Surinamese girl. Well, that just doesn't work on me."

Shirley does not immediately reject all white men's advances. She says she differs from her Surinamese friends in this respect.

"My Surinamese women friends are different from me. If a Dutch man were to come up to them in the street, they would send him off right away with, 'Get lost!' But I don't think there necessarily has to be something behind it. Maybe the guy needs to talk to someone, or just wants to make a friend."

Ilse had a Dutch boyfriend for a while. "He had a really great family. When we were going over for dinner, they always called to tell us, 'We'll be cooking such-and-such, do you like it?' Always new things, and I always tried them. They were really nice people. But you know, they were used to it from their son. He never came home with a Dutch girl. He had been married to a Dominican girl. When I met him, they had a 2-month-old baby. He left her and came to live with me. So they were all used to his not having Dutch girls. He himself said that he couldn't stand the bitches."

Why?

"I never asked. He just didn't like having relationships with them."

When I ask Ilse if she thinks Dutch men find Surinamese women more fun, she says, "Sometimes, yes. Most of them just want a quick affair. They come with expensive cars and all that. It's always older guys who want young Surinamese girls. There are a lot of them, you know."

Did you ever experience that?

"Especially when I was pregnant. Some Dutch men are crazy about pregnant women. One guy kept pulling up behind me every time he saw me. Sometimes he happened to see me in the bus. He'd drive alongside the bus, right up to my stop. And now there's another one in a Mercedes. I seem to have a power of attraction for men with a Mercedes! It's only old guys."

How old? Fifty or so?

"Yeah, around there. They follow you around in their cars. Once I was standing at a bus stop, and a Dutch woman said to me, 'Miss, you're being followed.' I said, 'No I'm not.' She said, 'Yes, you really are.' She had been walking behind me for a long time and she saw a car following me. She said, 'It's that car.' The guy kept driving behind the bus the whole trip. When we'd stop at a bus stop or traffic light, he'd wink at me and motion to me to get out. When I arrived at the end of the line, I *ran!* Down the stairs, gone. I didn't see him again. Those guys are sick. That kind can really tear you apart. You never know what they're carrying. Leave me out. I wouldn't mind having the car! But that's the beginning and the end of it."

Was anything ever said to you?

"Often. But I don't mind. I like feeling that I attract attention on the street. But that's the beginning and end of it, too. I've already got somebody. Just out of the blue they want to give me money, they want to take me for a drive, or out for a drink, that kind of bull. I don't know what it is with me and the old guys, but one of them followed me from my door. He says, yeah, he's seen me walking here before, he's keeping an eye on me, I'm such a good-lookin' chick, and all that. Says he can give me anything I want. I said, 'I have a boyfriend.' But that didn't matter to him at all. I thought, see what happens. I said, 'If I tell you I want a thousand guilders, can I have it?' He says, 'Yes, but then I have to get you.' So I said, 'Piss off!' There are a lot of these old men who are after young girls, here in this neighborhood, you know. Some of them are just crazy about Surinamese women."

Why would that be?

"I don't know. They think Surinamese women have big asses and all that."

In the discussion of *Carla* and *Olga's* experiences with nursing home patients, we explored the racist idea that black women are always ready to prostitute themselves and that they may therefore be approached casually with an offer of money. A further illustration of the fact that the oppression of black women is defined by both sexism and racism is to be found in the women's experiences in city night life. *Rita* mentions that blacks are not permitted into certain discotheques. But, she adds, women have less trouble with this than men.

Linda describes how such a situation can actually occur. "Once I went to the disco with a Surinamese friend. There were just the two of us, and when we wanted to go in, the bouncer said, 'If you come here, you come without black boys.' "

Since Linda and her friend are women, their freedom is not impeded by the racism that black men would have encountered: refusal of admission. Linda immediately showed her solidarity with the men of "her" group.

"At that point I said, 'Let's get out of here.' My girlfriend said, 'No, we already paid, didn't we?' I said, 'I don't give a damn, I don't want anybody to say things like that to me.'"

But the friend was determined to stay. Because of the tradition, familiar in the Netherlands and Surinam, "out together, home together," Linda was persuaded to go in with her friend after all. Then they experienced what it means for unchaperoned black women to be permitted into the disco: to serve as prey for pawing white hands.

Linda: "At some point my friend and I start dancing. One of the white men started to dance too. Only him. Then he started touching me." The story comes out in fits and starts, as if she is feeling the rage rise in her again.

Can you describe just what happened?

"Well, he started dancing too. He comes over and touches me on my bum. I almost went crazy! I swore at him at the top of my lungs. I was terribly angry. I said that he shouldn't imagine that he can just grab any black chick in the house. And I was already feeling so pissed off about the one who'd said, 'You don't come here with black boys.' That meant you couldn't come with your boyfriend. Well, then I didn't feel like going there at all. They discriminate, pure and simple. And I don't take that shit from *any*one!"

Conclusion

One of the most important conclusions we can make from these interviews is that, initially, each of the women, in her own way, indicates she experiences little or no discrimination. After being questioned further, however, it becomes evident that all of them have experienced a wide range of injustice, unkindness, contempt, and hostility because they are black women.

The women share with the Dutch the taboo on the word "racism." Racism and discrimination are viewed as "loaded" concepts—terms that may only be discussed with reference to public, blatant, or violent acts against black people.

The women *do* experience the frequent humiliation, harassment, insults, sabotage, discouragement, imputations, accusations, and aggression as painful obstacles. They also state that these experiences inhibit them in their freedom and possibilities for development. Educations remain unfinished and work circles are left prematurely. They cry. In blind rage, they scream and curse, and sometimes even come to blows. Yet racism seems to be too big a word for them to use.

Rather than working from generalizations, we now have actual examples of black women's daily experience in contact with whites, and we can test specific assumptions and beliefs about racism. Such systematic analysis of firsthand accounts is especially important in revealing the many covert forms of discrimination with which the women are confronted.

These stories and analyses of everyday racism offer us a first impression of its meaning. Everyday racism refers not only to the prejudice and discriminatory treatment actually experienced, but also to the *stress* caused by the *threat* of racism. It is the fear of being hurt suddenly and unexpectedly. It is the precautions you must take in order to evade possible discrimination and the strategies you must develop in order to react adequately and be alert to whatever happens around you. It is the sense that your social environment is not safe.

We can see that the Surinamese women are treated as *inferior*, kept at a *social distance*, and confronted with *social aggression* if they give evidence of not accepting that distance and their inferior position. While the women do not immediately interpret all their negative experiences as a result of their being Surinamese, they do seem to learn to observe the experiences systematically, and they begin to outline a pattern of the various forms of racism they encounter in contact with whites.

In order to determine whether they are experiencing prejudice and discrimination—and if so, in which situations—the women make use of a number of what I will call *control strategies*. These can be summarized theoretically as follows:

a. The use of *their own knowledge, opinions, beliefs, or expectations* in such situations. For example: "I know they discriminate"; "There aren't many whites in the Bijlmer, so ... "; "The housing agency was located on Beethoven Street, so you can imagine ... "; or, "Foreign tenants may be rejected."

b. *Systematic observation* of the behavior of the white people involved, to test one's suspicion of racism. For example, "She always went to bed at 7:00, but when there were three Surinamese nurses there, she just stayed up." Or, "The next day I went back deliberately to see if he was really checking up on me."

c. *The opinions of others* about the person concerned. "Later I also heard from other people that he really discriminated." In other words: I was not the only one who thought that he discriminated.

d. *Comparing one's experiences with others.* For example, a comparison with a Dutch woman: "She was allowed to, and I was not." Or with one or more other Surinamese or "foreigners": "She couldn't stand that teasing either"; "All foreign girls had that experience."

e. *Comparing one experience to other similar experiences.* "It wasn't only at the drugstore, it also happened at the supermarket."

Although it remains a modest first impression, this theoretical structure can be a foundation for developing interpretation strategies that may help us understand more about covert racism.

I hope that further research will lead to a model with specific guidelines for the rapid and effective identification of more subtle forms of discrimination.

Chapter III

———————— ✳ ————————

African-American Women's Experiences of Racism

Handing Down the Knowledge of Racism from Generation to Generation

Almost all of the Surinamese women interviewed express a distrust of the Dutch. They feel that the Dutch are "two-faced" and that "they don't mean what they say." At the root of this distrust lies a reality with which they are continually confronted: The "we-Dutch-are-such-tolerant-people" smile can transform itself without warning into vicious racism.

Mavis, who has lived in the Netherlands most of her life, is the only woman who described having been prepared for the racism of Dutch whites. Her mother often warned her of the "nasty things" she would encounter in the Dutch, and she, in turn, tells of having tried to build up her little brother's defenses.

In contrast to this, a striking aspect of my interviews with African-American women in the U.S. is that almost *every one* of them mentions having been ingrained with a sense of her situation as a black girl and of the fact that whites could harm her.

In this chapter, 11 African-American women speak of the racism they face in their daily lives: Lorraine, Gloria, Bernice, Audrey, Sojourner, Gwendolyn, Margaret, Eleanor, Pamela, and from my follow-up interviews, Paule and Grace. They carefully observe what happens around them and interpret specific incidents with the aid of their sophisticated knowledge of racism and the behavior of whites.

Black Americans have long passed on this kind of information from one generation to the next. It is in fact a survival strategy, reflecting the necessity of anticipating as far in advance as possible what kind of racism can be expected. It is a strategy employed regardless of economic class. Some of the women grew up in poor or very poor working-class families, others in middle-class or lower middle-class families. The significance of the African-American women's experiences lies especially in this transfer of knowledge.

We discover that, on the level of everyday contact with whites, racism manifests itself similarly in the two countries, despite the structural differences between the North American and the Dutch societies. At times, in fact, the African-American women use almost exactly the same words to describe their experiences as the Surinamese. In addition, they offer perspectives that illuminate the Surinamese women's experiences, making them more understandable in terms of racism and ethnic/racial group relations.

The first group of interviews presented here took place in the Bay Area in California, in 1981. The experiences of these women should not be considered fully representative of the broader American situation. This area is traditionally considered "tolerant" and "mild" in terms of racism. In the 1960s, it was one of the most important centers of black resistance. In contrast to the Dutch situation, the word "racism" is anything *but* taboo.

Almost all of the African-American women told of ways in which they, as children, were made aware of the existence of racism:

> " 'Sticks and stones may break your bones but names will never hurt you.' That was the kind of toughness they [black parents] had to teach children . . . . " *(Bernice)*

Since African-Americans have had to deal with the racism of white Americans in their daily lives for many generations, they have integrated education about racism into the socialization of their children.

"Racism is here all the time in this country. We live with it on a daily basis." *(Lorraine)*

"I grew up in a black environment ... but I always knew that there were whites close by. I ... know how to switch roles." *(Bernice)*

"I grew up with a lot of discrimination. It's so much a part of the experience here in the U.S. that you almost take it for granted." *(Pamela)*

"I have experienced so much racism that some of it I've totally blocked out." *(Eleanor)*

Various women talked of the 1960s when segregated drinking fountains and other designated places for whites and "coloreds" made way for integration:

"I was 12 years old .... We were the first integrated class at X Junior High School. Oh, Lord!" *(Bernice)*

"In the sixth grade, I was bused to an all-white school. And I became an experiment, a statistic ... a black child taken to white school, where I experienced this extreme alienation." *(Eleanor)*

Despite integration and years of progress, the violence against blacks persists. Several women experience terrorism from white Americans as a real threat:

"I don't feel safe. I don't know if this is just my own upbringing, but my mother said there is nothing more frightening for her than a gang of white boys, that somehow they had it out for black women." *(Eleanor)*

"The Klan is working. I would never go too far out in my car, because I was always frightened of what they could do." *(Margaret)*

"There's a feeling that the Klan is back. And right near here, the KKK has been chasing kids, breaking windows." *(Eleanor)*

The few times that the Surinamese women raised the issue of racism explicitly during the interviews, they made little mention of its various dimensions. As a result, the meaning that the women attach to concepts such as discrimination and racism is ambiguous. The African-American women make a clear distinction between what they call "blatant" and "subtle" racism. In this way, they communicate a vivid and detailed image of what they understand racism to be.

Blatant racism

Much of California has the reputation of being progressive or liberal on issues such as racism. According to one woman, racism in California is different from that in Chicago, for instance. As a black in Chicago, you absolutely could not live in certain areas because white Americans would set your house on fire. Another woman contrasts California with Washington D.C., where white neighbors organized themselves to prevent her parents from moving to "their" street. In other words, there is less "blatant" racism in California, according to these women. Blatant can be defined as "completely obvious," "vulgar," or "offensive."

"Completely obvious" is related to the *identifiability* of racism. In this sense, "blatant racism" is described as:

"Overt kinds of acts against [you]." *(Lorraine)*

"Calling you names." *(Lorraine—and others)*

"Saying, 'I don't like you because you're black.'" *(Gloria)*

In addition to its relationship to the identifiability of racism, "blatancy" is also a significant indicator of *what racism looks like.* It can occur in a "vulgar and offensive way":

"Being gross, like saying black people are inferior, black people are not smart, that we cannot learn certain things." *(Eleanor)*

The term "blatant" can also refer to the *consequences* of racism. These may be dire; racism can destroy the future of a black child even before he or she has the chance to develop.

"School situations where teachers pass a [black] child even though they aren't learning." *(Pamela)*

"For an advisor to discourage you from seeking higher education is blatant discrimination." *(Gloria)*

Subtle racism

Several women feel that a change has come about in the nature of racism in the U.S. since the 1960s, particularly in California:

> "After the turmoil of the 1960s and since the 1970s, they wanted us to believe that racism doesn't exist anymore." *(Lorraine)*

> "I moved to California. And everything became real muddy, because it was so subtle, that racism .... Everything is so sunshiny and everybody is so groovy and so nice. California has this reputation all over the world ... but it's different." *(Eleanor)*

The women offer various definitions for the concept of "subtle racism." Some definitions touch on the *invisibility* and *intangibility* of certain forms of racism in social situations. "Subtle racism," then, corresponds to what I have called covert racism:

> "Not openly racist acts." *(Lorraine)*

> "A certain underlying attitude." *(Lorraine)*

> "There are all kinds of unwritten ways that people can practice discrimination." *(Bernice)*

> "Hard to pinpoint." *(Eleanor)*

> "I think it is hard to put your finger on it." *(Bernice)*

> "It's hard to say exactly how I experience it." *(Eleanor)*

Other ways in which the women phrase this indicate that subtle racism is sometimes a question of *seemingly "minor"* or "trivial" actions:

> "There are a thousand ways." *(Eleanor)*

> "It becomes smaller. The smaller, more refined things come out." *(Eleanor)*

> "Little insulting kinds of things." *(Lorraine)*

The term "subtle racism" can also denote for the women *the way in which the racism is communicated* and how they react to it:

> "It's confusing, it's very maddening." *(Eleanor)*

"It took me a while to really catch on." *(Audrey)*

"You really have to work out how you counter that kind of behavior." *(Bernice)*

"With whites being subtle, you also become much more sensitive to and aware of the kinds of things they do." *(Bernice)*

Finally, one of the women draws a connection between *class* and "subtle racism":

"Especially when you're dealing with whites who are highly educated, it is always going to be very subtle." *(Pamela)*

The interviews that follow have been edited. In general, I used the same interview format as I had in the Netherlands. I asked about all kinds of experiences in different situations: the workplace, neighborhood, school, and various public situations. The stories of the Surinamese women showed us that racism operates through many different agents and in many contexts. The same holds true in the U.S., where the problems raised have much in common with the patterns of everyday racism portrayed in the previous chapter.

To avoid repetition, the interviews with African-American women are organized by woman and not by issue. Each woman has a unique story to tell, and reading the complete story gives us a clear impression of the way racism pervades her life. The interviews are presented without much commentary until I reach the end of the first series. There, I discuss some of the major similarities between the U.S. and Dutch accounts. I have also provided some general background to elucidate or explain certain situations. For the rest, the African-American women speak for themselves.

Lorraine R.

Lorraine, a community project evaluator at a university, is 37. We talk together in a 9-by-12 room, a room originally intended for storage purposes. Surrounded by old typewriters and piles of dusty papers, we sit on chairs borrowed from one of the other college rooms. The cluttered environment gives the meeting a kind of congenial ambiance right from the start.

This is my first interview in the U.S. Not yet used to the situation, I fall back on the routine of the interviews in the Netherlands, asking Lorraine about the community in which she lives.

She is renting an apartment in a racially integrated building for the first time, having lived her whole life in all-black neighborhoods. Thus I immediately find myself face to face with one of the greatest differences between the history of black Americans and Surinamese: the reverberations of the apartheid system that legally separated black and white Americans from the turn of the century until 1964.

Have you ever experienced racism from neighbors or in your neighborhood?

"Racism is here all the time in this country. We live with it on a daily basis, but in a subtle form. The forces are always against us here.

"I was the first black to move into that apartment building. There was just a certain aloofness from the rest of the neighbors, no real blatant or overt kinds of acts against us. Since I didn't come into daily contact with them, even that was minimal. But it's an attitude you pick up from them."

In Lorraine's story I recognize *Mavis's* experiences with her rich neighbors in Amsterdam. No openly racist acts, but their faces showed that they did not want foreigners in their midst.

When I ask whether it was difficult to find housing, Lorraine says she was lucky. The owner of the building is a Filipino man.

"Had I gone to others, I think I would have been turned down, because I believe there was a concerted effort to minimize the number of blacks living in that area. I've lived there a long time. I was the first black to move in. Recently it has changed; there are more moving in. But there are still not as many blacks as Caucasians. I think I was just fortunate to go to that particular person, who was also from the Third World."

The university department where Lorraine works is a center for minority projects. This is reflected in the composition of its staff. The director is a black woman; a few other women of color work there as well, in addition to a Vietnamese man and a white woman. This situation is completely new to me: a university department in which both the highest positions and the administrative jobs are staffed by a black majority. Lorraine likes this kind of work situation.

Was it difficult for you as a black woman to get this job?

"No, I think because so many of the projects involve Third World students. They are so conscious here, the director being a black woman. I didn't meet with any difficulties in getting the job. Had it been reversed, with more Caucasians in charge in this particular office, it would have been more difficult."

In her more than ten years of work experience, Lorraine has had many white colleagues. We discuss her job at a welfare agency, where she worked until coming to the university several months ago.

Did you have good contact with your white colleagues?

"Not in that last position. I encountered a certain arrogance in the office. Several women with more authority, at a higher, management level, were black women. I found among the white women a certain underlying attitude; they did not respect the authority of the black women in charge. They could not accept a black woman in a position of authority over them. It meant you had to deal with a certain amount of arrogance. So it was not a good relationship."

The situation sounds familiar. Wasn't it *Olga* who told of not being accepted in a management position? I ask Lorraine how exactly the arrogance of the white women was manifested.

"I'll give you a specific example. I worked with a white woman at the same level. There is a certain hierarchy in the welfare department system. You have levels and channels that you have to go through to get things accomplished. But when this particular white woman had a proposal for a project, a change she wanted to suggest, she wouldn't follow the normal procedure, which involved approaching your direct supervisor. Both her supervisor and the woman at the next higher level were black women. I maintain that she had no respect for these women. She felt that *she* should be in their position, that the roles should be reversed. She couldn't accept it as it was. So she bypassed these two people and went to the *next* higher level to present her proposal."

And the next higher level was occupied by white males?

"That's the thing. White and male. I would have been involved in the project to some degree, but I had no knowledge of it. It was something she wanted to promote for herself. When she was asked about the input she'd received from her coworkers —myself and another black woman—she had no answer, because she had not even mentioned the existence of this proposal to us. She hadn't told those of us who would initially be involved in it anything about the existence of a proposal at all. She simply did not want us to have any part in it. So she admitted that she was really caught. It was just a product of her sheer arrogance that she could not deal with black women in positions of authority."

This is reminiscent of *Olga's* head nurse D., who preferred having an unqualified white student-nurse distribute medicines rather than leaving it to Olga, the qualified woman who was black.

"And there were other instances when she would do the same kinds of things, you know, just naturally. Say you are going to be out of the office for the day for some reason. It is common office courtesy to notify the others. 'I'm leaving for the day, I won't be returning,' that kind of thing. She refused to do it! She'd just leave, rather than telling her coworker. It was more or less that she didn't want to put herself in a position in which she would feel subordinate to the other people."

Could you talk to her about it?

"Well, I think she understood me very well. And knew that I understood her position and what she really thought and felt. She knew I was a very strong person and she approached me very rarely. She was very, very leery of me.

"She was one of those people who tend to smile a lot, not actually challenging anyone, but doing little insulting kinds of things. It begins with that sheer arrogance that I think is inherent to the majority of Caucasian Americans. They want to see blacks in a subordinate, inferior position."

Do you experience this kind of arrogance also on the street or in shops?

"On the street, yes. Once when I was walking, a Caucasian woman walked by with some cups of coffee or something in her hand. The point was, she was just about to walk right into me. It disturbed me. It happens a lot. To me that expresses a certain attitude: 'I don't respect your space, so I'll just walk right into you.' They do it a lot here on campus. Or they may just be rude, for example, reaching right across you when you're standing in line for something, instead of saying, 'Excuse me.' Just the common courtesies you could expect. But if someone doesn't respect the person you are, they ignore personal customs. These daily racist things are very subtle. They're not always overt; no one's calling you names. But I think the racism *is* there because it is inherent and very institutionalized in this country."

I am particularly interested in just such daily, subtle forms of racism. We never read much about it.

"I think most people just accept it. You encounter it daily. In the newspaper, on television . . . .

"Once I was standing in a long line to collect some notes. A white woman was in front of me and it was her turn to go to the window. I said, 'Well, go to the window.' She turned around and spoke very sharply to me. Although I didn't respond verbally to her, my expression let her know I didn't like it. After she'd collected her things and I mine, she did apologize.

"I think people are used to seeing people accommodate to and accept such things. When you challenge it, you're outside the norm and they're very taken aback. They're so used to the masses accepting it. I teach my child about it."

You mentioned on several occasions white women having been arrogant in their attitude toward you. Have you experienced the same with white men?

"I just don't come into contact with white men, except possibly in the classroom. But yes, they're equally so. This is a white male-dominated society, and their arrogance trickles down to the white women and children."

I bring the conversation back to the subject of campus life, asking how the situation is for black women.

"It is difficult for black students to be here at this university to begin with. They have a deliberate policy here that keeps black students out. There is a lot of pressure on the black students here, and a lot of them don't make it through. Because no one's really responsive to their needs. I mean, if you aren't strong enough to handle everything yourself, nobody's going to take you by the hand here. You are definitely on your own, one among the thousands."

It makes me think of the university course catalogue I'd just bought that morning. I was surprised to read the clause stating that the university did not discriminate on the basis of race, color, national origin, sex, or handicap. While I understand the positive intent behind "equal opportunity" statements, such a declaration gives me a cramped feeling. It is disappointing to realize that such a fundamental right as equal treatment of ethnic students needs to be protected and explicitly stated in this way. But look once again at the Dutch educational system. Didn't *Mavis* and

Carla drop out of school because they could not handle the discrimination? *Ester*, too, quit her training as a nurse's aide because she could not bear the criticism and harassment. *Carmila* only managed through great effort and perseverance.

So Lorraine's next remark about universities has a familiar ring. "They are quite willing to see you take a passive role. I think the universities here try to weed out black students. You know, to make you fall by the wayside."

How does it feel to be in classes with so few blacks?

"The black students here are relatively young. I find that they don't speak up, that they are not very aware of a lot of the things I've experienced. I find them so apolitical. That's very disillusioning to me in this society, in this world. And I see them identifying so readily with what's American. They haven't extended their minds a step beyond. They don't see themselves as part of a larger Third World community.

"In class discussions, I have found the other black students to be very unaware and very reticent. They just sit there passively. And I find that I'm always the one to challenge the whites in the discussions."

Do you have any white friends?

"I do interact with white coworkers, but I never consciously cultivate friendships with whites. There is a certain insensitivity about them that precludes my choosing them as friends. I know just one black person who has friendships with whites. But then, they're European whites. They're different from American whites. I can't quite put my finger on it, but they're different. They tend to be in academia, too. That also makes a difference."

Can you explain the difference you experience between American and European whites?

"I think it's basically the attitude. Americans tend to be very narrow and rigid in their thinking. And they're so caught up in being American and in the patriotism. That's not to say that Europeans are free of prejudice. It's just different. For example, I was in West Berlin for one year. I could feel a certain amount of racism from some of the German nationals. But others were very open, very responsive."

Do you talk about racism with whites? Is it something you can talk about?

"I don't. I tend to find that on the few occasions that I have tried, they were uncomfortable or tended to be defensive.

"I do talk about it with my black friends. We have discussions frequently about the forms it takes. Just generally, we talk about how it affects our children, how we want to deal with it in terms of our children, that kind of thing."

Have you ever had a white boyfriend?

"Never, never."

Would that be unthinkable?

"I think so. White males are the dominant figures in this society. Because of that, I think, racism is inherent in them. This is the oppressor, and I could not relate to an oppressor. So I can't ever see myself having a relationship with a white man, if just for those reasons.

"I really think it has something to do with the psychology of the black woman, that she is not able to be in that situation. But for some reason—I can't put my finger on it, I don't know what it is—this is starting to change. It used to be extremely rare to see a black woman and a white male, other than in the entertainment industry—you know, celebrity types, movie stars. There it was common, but not among average people. But lately I've seen more black women with white males. I think it's because they feel there's a shortage of black males for many reasons. For one, a lot of black males are in prison."

In discussing the question of beauty, skin color, and sunbathing, I ask Lorraine if she thinks it is true that black women are jealous of the white woman's complexion.

"If you have a poor self-image, maybe you take on such ideas. But I certainly do not, and my child does not. I always taught her that we people of color are beautiful people. Most American white females only imitate black women anyway. When we wore our hair in the natural style, they eventually tried to make theirs look like ours. Then this white movie star Bo Derek comes along wearing her hair in braids. As soon as she does, it's suddenly popular among white women, whereas African women have been wearing it that way for centuries. So you see they only imitate. And what do they do in the summer? Roast themselves brown!

"I even think white women are probably jealous of black women. We are very sensual, beautiful people. Our movements are very graceful. They try to take this on. If you watch carefully, you'll see that white women who associate closely with blacks tend to take on their characteristics. I think they feel more or less threatened by a black female in those situations. I do believe that. I found that when I lived in Germany, a lot of the young [white] women dated black service men. I think they felt very threatened seeing these men always return to black women, so in their speech and so on they tried to take on the characteristics of a black woman to remain attractive to that black male."

Do you think white men find black women attractive?

"I think they do. Black women *are* extremely attractive in their movements and their looks. And I think even the most racist white male secretly admires black women. The most racist bigot you could find. I talked with a friend about it, that European males found black women very desirable, you know. But this friend was a black male who had worked quite a bit in Europe. He said the black woman was really sought after by European males. I myself experienced a certain amount of stares and such things there. I was very uncomfortable when I first went to Berlin. They were not at all rude—they wouldn't touch you or anything like that—but they were definitely kind of interested. The European male admired you openly. Not doing anything offensive. Just admiration."

Do you think whites are correct in their belief that blacks are hypersensitive to racism?

"I don't believe that. I think they say that because they think racism doesn't exist.

"After the turmoil of the 1960s and since the 1970s, they've wanted us to believe that racism doesn't exist anymore. If you believe it doesn't exist, you can't fight it! I mean, it is very purposeful to push that idea, right? You can't beat racism if racism doesn't exist! If they can promote that idea and sell it to the black masses, we won't fight. But we know it does exist. In a different form, a more vicious form."

Gloria G.

Gloria works in the same department as Lorraine, as an executive secretary. At 23, she has already had several jobs. She has a warm smile and receives me in the office as if I were a cousin who has come to visit her.

She is greatly amused when, late in the interview, I ask why none of the black Americans I talk to speak with the accent you always hear on television. She tells me that that kind of "black talk" sells well in Hollywood. (Another explanation may be that most of the women I interviewed had a high level of education.)

Although Gloria works at this university, she is studying at another. When she enrolled several years ago, she was the first black student.

What was it like to be the first black and female?

"It was hard. I had a lot of hidden agendas to fight. I was fighting changes that were endorsed by the chancellor's office. It was always a question of watching what you said and how you said it, in order to get what you wanted. I didn't like having to do that. But it was a very valuable experience for me, because it prepared me for the challenges of work. I was constantly being challenged on what I said or wrote. I enjoyed the challenge, but it was hard to deal with at first, knowing that someone was rejecting my ideas simply because I was black."

Can you describe one such instance?

"I was trying to arrange for a guest speaker to come. They had promised us we could have a whole month with black speakers. Suddenly it was cut down from a month to a week. That hurt. And this was two weeks prior to the event. I was told they didn't have the money, so they were going to cut it down to a week. What can you say to that? You know they're always lying about the budget. So you try to find out why. One of the white ladies, who said she really liked me, said, 'Gloria, you know why it was cut? Because you were grouping [black] people together, you were organizing black people. It showed force, and that can't be tolerated!' I said I appreciated her honesty—and then I resigned. It was just too much for me. It was a blow. That was the type of barrier I was fighting. It wasn't as blatant as saying, 'I don't like you because you're black.' But you can't dispute budgetary reasons. That was the case that touched me the most."

What did you do at that point?

"The university is situated in a beautiful place. I just sat down and watched the sun go down for a while, and I cried. In all honesty, I just sat there and cried. I was crushed. So that was all I could do. And I went home and talked to my mother. She described a similar experience to me. And she told me it was just one of the tests of my faith and of myself. She said it was a good lesson for me to learn.

"I resigned and went back to being a full-time student. It made me fight even harder. I went as far as refusing to attend a class in which I'd have to listen to someone say things about the black race that I knew were not true. It was hard, and it made me more alert—or aware, let me put it that way. A lot of people would see it as negative, but it made me more aware of how society takes advantage of me, and of the fact that I have to do more scheming in advance, because I don't feel I should have to kiss anybody's ass to get what I want. I really feel this. It made me a lot harder."

Could you talk a bit more about everyday racism at the university?

"An example I have of racism is of the time I petitioned to enter my master's program. It's not the only one, but it was the first serious one."

As Gloria recounts this experience, I feel as though I am hearing *Carmila* speak again. Identical experiences. The dean in the Netherlands and the academic advisor in the United States discourage the black woman student from continuing her studies, when it should be their job to stimulate her to develop her abilities as much as possible.

"I wrote my application for the master's program and sent it in, and they rejected me. I asked my advisor why. I said, 'I have been in this program six months; I have successfully passed six classes. Why am I not admitted?' He said, 'We on the committee felt it was better for you to go out and get some practical work experience. Don't *think* about getting a master's degree right now. Come back in about five years.' And I just sat there and said, 'Sure.'

"To me, for an advisor to discourage you from seeking higher education is blatant discrimination. My advisor was white. All the lecturers and professors are white. I came across another lecturer who realized he couldn't keep me down, so he gave me an incomplete for the course, saying my paper wasn't good enough. I took the paper to a different professor. He graded it, and it was a B, which was sufficiently high. It cost me a year's hassling going back and forth to that first professor on a weekly basis to get this paper the way he wanted.

"When you give an oral presentation and you're talking in class, that's another thing.... Last quarter, we had our presentations and this brother from Nigeria was giving his presentation. It was excellent. To me, the format of a presentation is for that person to present all of his materials and then there is a section open for questions. But the professor started critiquing him after, oh, the first 15 minutes, and I stopped him. I said, 'Don't.' I said, 'I think I understand what he is saying. But every time you interrupt I lose my train of thought. Please stop all the interruptions, I'm begging all of you, my classmates, let him finish his presentation.' During the break, the instructor called me to the side and said, 'Gloria, why don't you quit saving him?' I said, 'What do you mean by saving him?' He said, 'When I have a question, you don't let me ask the question.' I said, 'But your question might be answered further along in the presentation if you take time to listen!' You know, I fight battles like this with professors and that pisses me off. You know, it is not blatant discrimination: It's bias, it's ignorance."

Giving unjustifiably low grades, not listening to the black student's contribution, always ready with negative criticism—these are all examples of the same minutiae of racism experienced by the Surinamese women in the Netherlands. The consequences of these kinds of "micro-inequities" can be far-reaching.

"I would like to see true integration, true mix, a true 'melting pot,' which America is supposed to stand for. And it is not there. Because most of the brothers and sisters get fazed out. They have several fazing-out processes and you have to be there and stand for what you believe in; you have to show them who is the strongest."

What do you mean by 'fazing-out processes'?

"Eliminating, putting you down, not providing you with the support that you need to make it. Like the application process, when you apply to go to school and petition the department. If they don't like your style of writing. That's one way. Your GPA is another way. There are several fazing-out processes that brothers and sisters aren't even aware of. And you have to be sure that you're writing a paper that is acceptable, fits a mold, maybe typical American or international, so they will not think that you're radical or militant. There are a lot of fazing-out processes.

"In an institute run by white folks, our needs are not taken care of. I remember one time I was reading budget allocations for black studies and I noticed that every year their funds tended to decrease. And the scientists, their budgets were increasing. Why limit the knowledge that the university can offer the students? You see, budgets, that's how they control you."

I ask Gloria about her work history. She lists a long series of jobs, varying from office work to sales.

Were you faced with racism or arrogance from white customers or colleagues?

"Well, when I was a salesgirl, always. It was, 'Hey, girl, I'm on my lunch, come here . . . . ' Don't call me 'girl,' when I have a nametag here! It's either, 'Please excuse me,' or, 'May I have some assistance?' I know your mother taught you better; I know your mother taught you how to be courteous. It was very hard for me to interact publicly as a salesgirl. That was real hard.

"Besides that, there was this supervisor. My last supervisor was an Italian girl. We were the same age. She had finished her degree about six months prior to me. She would stand there at my desk to see what time I came in. I felt that was pure harassment. And even if I wasn't late, she documented me as being late. I couldn't understand why she didn't like me. I could not understand. And I would appeal to her. I said, 'Let's go for a coffee, let's talk. Tell me what your feelings are.' And I could never get that feedback from her. So, I just chalked it up to maybe it is a racial thing. Or maybe she did not know how to communicate with blacks. Or I just didn't know. Still, to this day, I can't place it. So it had an impact on me that was a little too much for me. I see it as a conflict that cannot really be resolved. I couldn't even transfer to another unit without her signature. So I quit there. I don't know if it was racism or it was just too much responsibility for her."

Some people say that black women are jealous of white women's appearance. What do you think?

"Really?! As you can tell, I can't trip on that. To be perfectly honest with you, I think a white woman is ugly [whispers and then laughs]. It is not that they can't make themselves appear to be glamorous. But I feel that black women have more to offer naturally. I think *they* have something to be jealous of. Because if they didn't, why would they lay in the sun all summer long to get brown? So wherever that came from, you can tell that person I said to sit on it. Because I think it is the other way around. When it comes to hair texture, you know, we hear white people say they have 'naps.' And I say, 'Darling, you do not have naps, you have knots and refined curls.' I think I am just as good and maybe even better. No, I *am* better! So I haven't experienced that and, to be honest with you, I don't think any woman in my family has experienced that. We really believe in supporting each other.

"The black woman, I feel, is more supportive to her man

than a white woman. Because, if you look at it, the black man was freed out of slavery, he was freed without anything but his family. The unity comes from the woman and the man, and without that, you can't have unity. So I feel black women are stronger and better. The white man has always had it handed to him. His woman has not had to give him any support. So I really think it's the other way around. I have serious concerns for the black person who said that [they are jealous of white women]. That one I never heard."

Do you think white men find black women attractive?

"I think they find her attractive. It could be out of heritage, you know, from what they were taught a long time ago.

"You know, when you look in history, white women have always been jealous of women of color, because women of color have been able to steal their men without even trying. So one never knows. That's a point I will have to think upon. White women are constantly trying to put you down verbally and I don't appreciate that. As to a white man, he may not do it, unless he sees he can do it and get away with it. That has been my personal experience."

Can you give examples of white women who try to put you down?

"Everyone in the department knows that Sojourner is the director of the department. My white coworker over here told someone that Sojourner was a coordinator. Now to me, that is a mild form of putting her down.

"Here is a more recent one. This was an experience I had at the bank. You know, it wasn't just what the lady said, it was how she said it. I was going to cash my check, and she said, [harsh voice] 'Give me your driver's license.' I said, 'What? *Give* me? I think you'd better backtrack and *ask* me, "May I please see some identification." ' To me the way she addressed me was a put-down. You don't say, 'Give me your driver's license.' You ask for identification. And to me that was a mild put-down.

"I try to pick up on my own levels. It may be very subtle. You have to listen to them all the time. They always try to pass on misinformation and then we have to be there to correct them tactfully, which is hard. It is very hard to do."

One of the most marked differences between the Surinamese and African-American women interviewed is the manner in which they deal with racist experiences. In the Netherlands, it seems as if nobody talks about it to anyone else.

Do you ever talk to friends about the racism you experience?

"Yes. Especially with my female friends. And my male friends—I hate to say this—but the ones who feel it the hardest are my lighter brothers and sisters. Because they are always asked, 'What are you?' Which I feel is a form of disgrace and disrespect. You know, can't you accept people for what they are? They feel it in a different manner than I do. They get it more than I do because you can look at me a mile away and tell that I'm black and [know] you should watch what you say, because I'm not going to take it. We talk about it a lot, especially the females, how we get double discrimination as opposed to the black male. When I say double, I mean the chance of being sexually harassed."

Did you ever experience sexual harassment?

"No. I have my own strange way of telling a man off. If he thinks he can be dirty, I bet you I can be dirtier. And so with a smile . . . . "

Bernice L.

Bernice is 30. She is currently working on her thesis in Ethnic Studies. Just before noon I find myself circling the campus, searching for a parking place. I finally find one, but the parking meter only allows half an hour. Just crossing the huge university green will take at least a quarter of an hour! With map in hand, I walk along the lush green lawns, down one tree-lined lane after another alternating with romantic little bridges and sun-drenched squares. Quite a difference from the university in downtown Amsterdam, where the university buildings are dispersed throughout the city, and no "campus" exists at all.

Unfortunately, Bernice is unable to begin right away. Time presses. We make a virtue of necessity; she walks back to the parking place with me, and it turns out to be my first interview in a car—a solution that works out so well that I repeat it several times thereafter.

Can you remember the first time you experienced racism?

"I was 12 years old. It was right after integration, so we were the first integrated class at X Junior High School. Oh, Lord! I was in the exceptional, or the bright—the gifted, we called them —gifted classes, when you're ahead of your grade level. Here I was, 1 of maybe 3 blacks in a class of 20. In one class, I remember this child told the woman that she was 'not gonna sit next to a nigger, 'cause her ma was head of the PTA.' And I was the only black in the class. It was the first time I had ever been referred to as a nigger. And I walked out and went home. My mother politely turned me back around, marched me up to the school, apologized for my behavior, which angered me no end, and told me in no uncertain terms that if I ever came home for something so insignificant again, she'd kill me.

"'Sticks and stones may break your bones but names will never hurt you.' That was the kind of toughness they had to teach children at 12 and 13. Right. It was just killing. But that was the kind of thing, because you couldn't fight. Whites didn't know how to fight. If you fought them, you just beat them up and you would get in trouble. So it wasn't like you could counter the argument if someone called you a bad name. I was only dragged to that school. So they got the chance to call us niggers and a whole lot of other things, and we had no recourse."

What is the effect of racism on the socialization of black girls?

"It is a lot. For instance, it was three years that I was at that particular school. Each year we were the first ever to get to that section, in the sense that we were the first blacks that white teachers had to encounter. We were the pioneers. There was no preparation in terms of people having had to deal with blacks.

"Part of it was the quota. Although they said, okay, we are going to have all you blacks here, they didn't mean *all*. They were only going to let in one or two."

Bernice goes on to describe a situation that has much in common with the experiences of the Surinamese women, who were often likewise the first black students in a Dutch school. Bernice kept coming up against the prejudice that blacks were not bright and the refusal to recognize their intelligence.

"The other part was the frustration of going against brick walls, basically. Knowing that no matter what you did, because you were black, you were not going to get any better than what you had ... and it really made a significant difference. I pretty much made straight As. I had, for instance, the *Encyclopedia Brittanica*. We had those books at home, and I would use them for writing my reports. And teachers a lot of times did not believe I knew how to use that. My father and mother had gone to college, so I knew how to use a reference and things like that."

Wasn't *Carmila* also accused of not having written her paper herself? Many Surinamese women found their abilities doubted.

"We were tested, and I got awards, and they would argue and bicker about a black receiving the top such-and-such award. It was all right for us to receive the physical education award, it was all right for us to receive the music award, but when it came to math, social science, English, language, arts—how could we possibly achieve above whites? So what I found was that as blacks in that integration model, which was in the late 1950s, early 1960s period, although you were qualified, you had to be twice as qualified because you were always challenged for making the equivalent achievement that a white made.

"Also, I taught for a number of years at this school that was very close to the campus, so I was teaching my professors' children. I also got children from the flatland community. It was a small school. We tested the children to see who was highest, and this little black kid in my class got the highest! Do you know, every parent in that school wanted their kid re-tested. They could not believe that he achieved past them, with all their material things and all the things they were able to provide. So I think, for a lot of whites, what they could not handle was the fact that it was not necessary to have all this money to be gifted or intelligent. So, to counter that, the public school district came up with another classification, called 'potentially gifted.' Which meant you met every intellectual requirement but you did not meet the social requirements. So you could be a smartass, but you did not have the economic background.

"They gave me the math award for my junior high school. Later, I was selected for Harvard with some other black students. We were printed up in the paper. I mean, the comments that came out were just so ridiculous. For instance, when we graduated, they're supposed to mention that commendation. But it was, you know, 'Maybe we can overlook this.'

"Another thing is that you are being told, 'You're exceptional, you're the one and only.' Then you begin to feel you're exceptional and the one and only, where really, I feel, this is a matter of circumstances. You were in the right place at the right time. Because there are many smart blacks, and you see them and you have gone to school with them, and you know the only reason they didn't get the same opportunity you got was they only wanted one more black."

Luxury and wealth bring us to the subject of consumer power and shopping.

Do you experience racism in stores or on the street?

"Mainly in the stores. They'd rather—you know I've seen them—they'd rather not serve you. They'll walk around and serve two or three people. And sometimes—it may depend on how I feel, I mean, I've gotten a real bad attitude—I've complained and they've been reprimanded sometimes. And other times I just don't; I walk out of the store. It depends on how I feel, what I do."

What does that racism look like? What happens?

"Basically they won't serve you. They won't. They'll ask every other customer in that store if they want service, except for you. Particularly here, where the stores are like one big store and you'll have the shoe department and various departments. They'll walk all around you rather than serve you. That's the basic one they'll use; they just ignore you altogether. A lot of times they'll make the assumption that because you're black, you can't afford whatever you think you want. And they'll automatically go to the cheaper item or something like that. You may very well know what you want, but their assumption is that this is what you can afford, you're black. I mean, this is their sizing up. Suppose you want to see some jewelry or something; they'll immediately go to the counter, as opposed to something under glass. Small things like that, which are very annoying at times. I've gone in and asked for a watchband. They directed me, 'Here,' and I said, 'Look, I want a silver Seiko, etc.' As long as I know what I want and I'm asking for it, then they'll do that. But they'll immediately, sometimes, direct you to a smaller, cheaper brand of the same product."

I mention that in the interviews in the Netherlands, the point is the reverse. They run up to you right away to prevent you from stealing anything.

"You can have the reverse, too. Here, a lot of the stores have many more security devices and then they have the roving security people. I'm not going to say it is impossible to steal, but the fact that you may or may not steal is another thing. What they are basically concerned about is maybe you'll go away and they won't have to help you. What I used to feel in a lot of stores [was that] they didn't want you to be seen in their store because you were black and they might be accused of servicing the black population, or something like that. I get more of the other, when you get so discouraged you go away.

"I think it is hard to put your finger on it. You really have to work out how you counter that kind of behavior. The other thing that's really hard sometimes is house hunting. I've gone to areas where they know what you can't afford. I went to a man one time, looking around, and you know he told me that a two-bedroom was $600, which was totally outrageous. But that was just to discourage me from coming to look at all."

I remember *Mavis* in Amsterdam, who also faced covert discrimination from the woman in the housing agency, who acted as if she had never spoken to her on the phone. Mavis says that she would have preferred that the woman react differently: "If only she had exaggerated the costs, because she knew what I wanted; then I could have at least said no. Instead of saying to me that she never spoke to me. That really upset me." The point here is that Mavis, in that case, would not have known that she was, in fact, being discriminated against. As Bernice reveals, however, sooner or later you see through even the most subtle tricks.

"And there are other ways. Where I'm staying now, they actually maintain a racial balance. How many blacks, how many Chicanos, how many whites they want to have. When you come in, I don't care who you are, they will tell you there are no vacancies, but you can fill out an application. At that point, they size you up and they can call you back the next day or they can just leave your application there. There are all kinds of unwritten ways that people can practice discrimination. And there is nothing you can do, because they've posted 'No Vacancy' and they've told you, 'No vacancy,' but if something comes up, they'll get in touch with you. Because of the nature of California laws against discrimination—they've had several cases—they had to be more subtle about it. But with whites being subtle, you become much more sensitive to and aware of the kinds of things they do. Like I said, that's one of them, that I know that they do at the place where I'm staying.

"It gets into little things like appearances. Your natural looks too big or you have on a black leather coat. So I find as a black you really have to be much more careful about your appearance when you have to make a public impression or want service. It cuts through a lot of red tape if you just go in fairly conservative as opposed to, say, being somewhat ethnically dressed.

"I remember going to one place and they asked my husband if he paid his bills. Well, of course he's going to say yes, but what

was the point of even asking, when they do a credit check? Of
course, we didn't want to stay there, just because of the way she
was handling that. The point of it is, you get a different treatment
automatically. I'm sure she didn't ask that to whites who came in.
Take away our black faces, there was nothing that would distinguish us from anybody, I mean anybody white over there.

"I think this is one of the problems that blacks find. They
have to not only be conservative but then have additional pluses.
I mean, you have to drive a decent car or you have to wear ... I
mean things like wearing an expensive watch or having a big
diamond on your finger. These are small things, but when someone is sizing you up, they really add a plus in their estimation or
evaluation of you."

Bernice's husband comes from Kenya. This leads us to an
important subject, as Bernice shows movingly what it means to
be raised from a young age in a predominantly white society. She
contrasts her experience with that of her husband who was—just
as the Surinamese—born and bred in a society where whites are,
in terms of numbers, no more than a small minority.

*Is there a difference between your experience with racism and your
husband's?*

"First of all, he is a foreigner, so I think he finds it a terrible
shock to be treated like that. I think the difference is that I grew
up in a black environment. We both grew up in a black environment, but I always knew that there were whites close by. He never
had that encounter. So he finds it even more difficult to deal with.
I at least know how to switch roles. He doesn't. But I do know
that he gets deferential treatment, in the sense that once he opens
his mouth and they hear that accent, they're willing to make more
allowances for him, because he is *not* a black American, than for
me, because I *am* a black American."

*What exactly do you mean by switching roles? Can you give an
example?*

"When I go in and have to talk to these professors on
campus, okay, they are all white. I have to extend certain kinds
of courtesies; I have to give them a certain kind of discourse.
There is a certain thing I have to learn which makes me equivalent to my white counterpart in terms of how I go in and ask for
information. I can't just say, 'Look, I need such-and-such.' I have
to know about their kids, or I have to know about the last book
they read, what they're doing now. And I have to have some

formal chit-chat to do with them. Whereas you and me, we can sit up here and we can start talking. You know there are a lot of commonalities that we can immediately talk about that we don't have to necessarily totally verbalize.

"I find when I deal with my white counterparts in terms of professors, I have to constantly start over from square one and repeat everything over and over. And it's not that they don't have a memory, but it is part of this little ritual procedure I have to get into every time I want to talk to them."

Is that because you're black, or would it be the same for a white student?

"I think part of it is being black, in the sense that I never feel comfortable enough to move to square two or three because I feel like they don't remember. I'm not making that kind of impact. So part of it is my own feeling of inadequacy in the situation. I find that they really do not understand. It is very hard for me to remember the last thing we talked about. The relationship, in terms of rapport, who you are, where you're coming from, I have to re-establish that a lot of times with them. I think it is different with black professors; I think it is different with other black people. The signaling process of what you do to say —'Hey, remember me? I'm Bernice. I'm such and such and I'm doing this'—is different than when you talk to whites. With whites, I have to be very careful about how I say what I want to say. Everything I think is important has to be verbalized.

"I have two black professors I work with, so I can contrast. You know, we do have a different kind of discourse. It's important for you to verbalize with the [white] professor. He doesn't have to reciprocate. I find with the black professors, they do reciprocate. They will ask, how is my daughter, how is my husband. So you really get a sort of dialogue or exchange. I never get that with my white professors, unless there is a catastrophe or crisis. To me, they're just—I mean, I'm not going to say it's lack of concern, but it is! It's a real lack of concern for you, outside of you being that student at that particular time.

"I've seen men come in with their wives: 'This is So-and-so, this is my wife, and you know So-and-so. Jim is doing really good work and we're so glad to work with him.' My husband came in with me and he [the professor] couldn't think of a damn thing to say! I was really pissed off about that. Those, to me, are common courtesies. They don't even have to go any further than that, you know. They couldn't handle it. And that has happened repeatedly."

Is there also a difference for you, as a woman?

"I couldn't really differentiate that well, how that is compounded. But I know, for instance, a black woman can get a lot further ahead in this system than a black male. In terms of the discrimination and in terms of barriers being set up, whether it's moving ahead in the job, whether it's just trying to get information, service, or whatever, a black woman can get it a lot quicker than a black man.

"Of the two, the black male has threatened the white infrastructure, white society, more than the black woman. Plus, as black women, we've been domestics, we've had certain kinds of positions in this society where we were closer or more in touch with whites. The men were cooks, porters, and valets. You had many more women who worked in the home, taking care of the children, taking care of—you know, cooking, and those kinds of things. So you have a lot more women who've had more of those kinds of opportunities. And I think because of that, the whites have had more exchanges with black women. For instance, within our department, there are very few men, I mean almost no black men. And the few we do have—let me put it like this: They're not the macho black. We do not get the macho black man in [the department]. I think a lot of this has to do with how they [the whites] feel about it. I know a lot of them appear definitely threatened by just the masculinity, the sexual problems, I mean, for a variety of reasons. They are very much threatened by black men."

How does it feel for you now to study at and graduate from the university?

"It was really trying in the sense that I had several things to overcome. One, being a woman, and then being an ethnic minority in addition to that. In the department, they encourage you, they admitted you. I think a lot of them really didn't expect people to finish. Women get married, have children, or whatever the problem is, and they didn't expect you to persevere. I only had maybe one or two real, say, racist or ethnic encounters in the department with people. Most people managed to hold their tongue or not really come across purely on a racist level. But I know that as women, there were limits that we found ourselves facing.

"The few women professors here came during the era when women in the profession were not allowed to marry. So a lot of times women give women harder times than the men do. Oh, let me see, what did they do? There was no leniency or leeway of any kind. Say you didn't have an assignment ready. You could say, 'Look, I only read half the book but this is the part I wanted to be confident in.' You could easily negotiate that out with most male professors. I found with the women it was totally inexcusable to ever have that kind of thing. It was like, if you can't do it the way I did it, then you don't need to be here.

"And a lot of it is the socializing aspect of it. I think that was the other part. For instance, as a woman I might want to date or do something outside. It was very hard to have a private life. It was all right for a man to date an undergraduate or someone beneath him. It was not the same for a woman.

"And then, too, being a black woman, you had to constantly deal with the sexual stereotypes. We have had sexual harassment in the sociology department here. I had one case. It was sort of an overtone, I couldn't really put my finger on it . . . whether the professor was coming on to me or not. But I know that they find black women have a mystique. And a lot of it is just real curiosity. I found that a lot of them are 'anthropologizing,' acting as if they knew how—supposedly knew how—to interact with people of different cultures. They seem to have a very poor rapport with the majority of black students."

I ask whether she can remember incidents when she had the impression of being sexually harassed.

"You look at any of the books, you look at any of the movies, the stereotype of the black woman is either she's a mammy, which means she is fat and an overprotective kind of person, or she's this sexual hotpack. And they always try to figure out which one you are. To me, it's always a big trip. And then for women, I mean black women in particular, we have a history. For instance, if a black woman is raped, it is never the same as if a white woman is raped. 'She must have asked for it,' that kind of thing. So you always have this double standard that's already put on you and then you have these people looking at you, expecting you to somehow or another match up to this standard. You know, fitting to one or the other, and there is no middle ground.

"A lot of the time it's just the whole interaction. In a lot of cases, I would go in expecting someone who was, say, a Caribbean expert, to be able to give me certain kinds of information. And rather than say he didn't have any expertise in the area, he got into this whole bantering kind of thing, where he would never really come out and say he didn't want to work with me. What I found out later as a result of the encounter was that he didn't *have* the expertise in the area, hadn't been in the field for over 20 years. So my knowledge was much more current than his. When I went in and asked for certain kinds of information, and said, 'This is what I want to do in a reading course,' he agreed to the course. But then he was constantly fighting me over the areas I wanted to get into, because these were not his areas of expertise. On one hand, it was a miscommunication, I feel, but on another level, I can also say I felt that, as a woman, it was, 'You don't know what you want—I can tell you what you need.'"

I ask her to explain what little gestures or sentences make her feel that the other person is trying to find out which "kind" of black woman she is.

"One of the things is, when you go in to the professor's office, it's bantering, but it's more than bantering. You are linguistically or communicatively trying to size each other up. And as if they know anything about blacks, they'll tell the latest black joke. For a lot of them, they see no difference between telling a dirty joke in male or female company. I mean, up to a certain point, yes, I'll sit through any kind of joke, but once you become an adult you save that for the locker room, with the other men. I want the same respect, but for me to demand that respect is an affront. You should be used to it; it shouldn't be any kind of problem.

"I ran into a professor who thought he could engage in playing the dozens [a black bantering game] and he thought he could get as vivid, because he had read enough. I said, [contemptuous voice] 'You don't want to do this, not with me. Do you understand there are no limitations if you begin to banter like that? I can talk about you, your mama, the dirt under your toenails. I mean, it gets to that. You don't want to do that.' I tried to make him understand that, and he just thought, now its your turn to give me an ethnic pun. So he could write it down and collect it and put it in his data!

"I think they have a very WASP sense of what it means to be black. And so this professor, this white professor, wanted to do this with me. Other students told me that this is what they had to do to get anything out of him. I told him I really didn't think he wanted to do this with me because, first of all, the majority of the black students who've had to, they have been middle class. I am not middle class, so I can get filthier than filthy. I told him, I will really hurt your feelings.

"All the way through the conversation, he kept trying to get it going. It was like someone who just got a new recipe for cake and they really want you to taste it, even though you know it's not any good. I wouldn't do it, and he insisted, and it just really got down to, not what I wanted to do and why I came to see him, but was I going to do that? That was clearly an ethnic thing. He didn't even understand that there are different barriers for men and women in terms of that [banter], and that when women do it, it's a different kind of thing.

"So that was a very pointed case, as far as I was concerned. It was just really crazy. That's probably one of the worst cases. But you run into little things. They get to a point and they leave something open or withdraw and they expect you to fill it in with something ethnic. A lot of them expect you to tell ethnic jokes or ethnic stories that they would not be privy to. And they'll turn around and use it in a little, you know, wine session, or share it around with other friends to impress them.

"I had been working in a black community where I did my research on African religion, and one of the professors asked me, 'What about the voodoo ceremony?' I said, 'What about what?' 'You know, the voodoo.' And I said, 'What do you mean? I mean, it's there. So what? What about it?' He wanted me to tell him about blood, about people taking off their clothes. First of all, when I go to a black community, there are certain things I will report and certain things I will not report. And I just don't think it's worth anybody's while to get into these exotic scenes where they break chicken heads and they spill the blood. I mean, so what? Everybody knows about that; why do I have to retell that, when there's something else that's perhaps even more important? He really wanted to hear about the blood and the dancing and this whole sexual thing that was going on."

Bernice tells another story about a professor's program on cross-cultural notions of what the body parts are all about.

"The professor, it turns out, was only interested in the genitals. We all wrote these papers. Now, every part of my paper was detailed, except when I got to the genitals. Because first of all, I had a male informant and I didn't want to embarrass him, nor embarrass myself. And it was the only part of the paper that had to be rewritten. I felt very manipulated."

Do you think he would have tried it if you had been a black male?

"No, I don't think so. I think the other thing of it is, like I said, the class was predominantly female. And the professor was male. So you tend to find a lot of things that they do or they tend to get away with because we are women."

Do you think that black women are jealous of white women because of their looks?

"I don't know if they are jealous. I think there's an anger in the sense that beauty is defined through what white women are all about. I mean, to be beautiful in this society you need to have straight hair. To be beautiful in this society you need to have the nose, the mouth. I mean, when you look at models, when you look at what is 'the image of beauty,' nowhere does it begin to address what a black woman is all about. And I think that you have anger about that. You have anger in the sense that as you have children and you begin to teach your children self-esteem and things like that, you have to define it through those models, whether you want to or not, because you constantly have magazines, you have TV, this kind of thing, where you see so few blacks.

"I think part of it is the media, and part of it is stuff we've done to ourselves. And for that reason I can see women getting very spiteful about it, because it is a goal they'll never achieve. You can only get white-light. You will never *be* white, you know, and even if you go and get . . . I mean, we go into skin bleachers, pressing, processing your hair, plucking this, doing that. I mean, it's just really abomination, what black women do to look nice [laughs].

"Well, one thing, 'black is beautiful' changed a lot of that. There is a wider range now of what is acceptable. But for those who grew up in the 1950s, who were becoming women in the 1950s, it was a lot more difficult because if you had short hair you had to press it, no matter how much hair you had. People bought wigs. It angered me in a lot of ways. It angers me when I see women who press their hair. Pressing their hair, that kind of preparation—to feel they have to negate what they are about, that's the biggest problem. We've lived in a society that says in order for you to be a plus, you have to negate everything that you are about."

Like almost all of the other women interviewed, Bernice, after discovering the effect of racism in subtle forms of contact, touches on the history of oppression that African-American women have faced for centuries. She describes proudly the black women's support groups that have been operating for years, which started even before the white women's movement began doing such things.

"One thing I wanted to mention, too, one of the things we did have here—and I hope you get the chance to really look into—is that we had black women's support groups to help us deal with the racism and that kind of thing. We got together and we shared these stories, so that you didn't feel so alienated, isolated. And we helped each other strategize: How do you cope, how do you deal with that? So I can say that although we ran into a lot of these things, as women, we came together much better than men did. Men have just recently started to have black men's support groups.

"We got together very quickly. We first started talking about where do you go shopping, where do you get the best quality of this, where do you go to get your kids' clothing, sharing kids' clothing. 'My kids have outgrown this, you can have it.' We started off from that kind of thing and very quickly moved to academics and the kinds of things that we needed as tools for survival. We [exchanged] phone numbers. We aligned ourselves with other black women as they were coming into the schools and we aligned ourselves with each other for crisis-like things that happened.

"I had a professor one time, he just didn't want to approve this paper I had written. And I had done everything he said. I began to feel it was racism, so we strategized about what to do next. Another woman who was a law student said, 'Look, you take this paper to one or two other professors, get their comments, and then go back and say this.' And that helped. After that, he approved it. It was that kind of thing; she had had two or three years' experience beyond me.

"So we had that kind of sharing network, and it was really important, because we did run into the sexism and did run into the racism and it helped to be able to verbalize and talk about it. It also helped to have people say, 'okay, yes, I remember this, and this is what I did.' We really had solutions to everything."

Audrey T.

To my surprise, when I ring Audrey's bell, the door is opened by a young woman with pink cheeks and dark blonde hair.

"How nice that you've come to interview me. You come from Amsterdam, don't you? I've never been to Europe. Jeff, come say hello. This is Philomena—did I pronounce your name correctly? This is Jeff, my husband. Jeff, could you bring something for us to drink?" Audrey makes me feel instantly at home. It turns out to be a very intense conversation, about which I later write in my notebook: "Just saying the word racism was like opening a faucet from which a constant stream of information flowed. I was sometimes so overwhelmed and absorbed by it that I forgot I was there as an interviewer."

Audrey is 25. She received her master's degree in sociology less than a year ago. Now she is teaching in a high school.

"It's funny, I noticed today that, during lunchtime—we have one big lounge that everybody sits in—and it just dawned on me today, maybe because I was thinking about this interview, that there was one table where all the black teachers sat and at the remaining tables were all the white teachers. Now, I'll interact with the other teachers. But most of the black teachers that are on campus socialize and interact with their own ethnic group. So there is not a lot of extending. One of the problems is that a lot of the white teachers there don't extend themselves. If there's a social event or a social function, a lot of the white teachers are inclined to invite maybe *some* of the black faculty. Now some might go, but for the most part, they don't. If I would give a party, probably less than half of them [the white teachers] would show up, whereas probably all the blacks would show up.

"I think that there is probably a lot of anger among some of the black faculty members because of the problems that you get in the school system. A black teacher might have been in the school ten years. And say a white teacher has been in the school five years. If there is a job [opening] for a principal or vice principal, that white teacher is more likely to get it. It's very difficult for a teacher from a minority, especially a black, to move up. She has to not only have experience but also have a lot of degrees in order to get a position that a white teacher who has fewer degrees and fewer years of experience might get. So I think that there's a lot of animosity among the ethnic groups in terms of discrimination they have experienced in the job market."

Have you experienced any discrimination in the job market?

"Yes, I have. I think I have had a lot of discrimination. But I only began to realize it as I got older. The first time, I think, that I was really discriminated [against] in a job was when I was working as a teller for a big bank. A lot of people there seemed to be threatened by me because of the type of person I was. I came in ready to work, you know, having a very good attitude about my job. I established very good relationships with my coworkers, and I got along with the people. And my customers, they came into the bank and they would wait for me to wait on them rather than go to another teller. I think there was a lot of jealousy and envy around."

Audrey was still in her trial period. The story she begins to tell is very reminiscent of *Joan's* experience, since Joan, too, was immediately discriminated against in her trial period and left the position because she was so miserable about constantly being watched. It would all sound very familar to Joan if she could hear Audrey speak.

"I was on probation and my supervisor was real hard on me. Any mistake I would make, any little mistake, and she would make a real big issue out of it. Also, if I was maybe 30 seconds late coming back from lunch, she'd give me a big lecture about it. Whereas a lot of the other employees would be late 15 or 20 minutes and she'd make a joke out of it. So I had a lot of discrimination from this supervisor. I eventually ended up quitting. One, because I went back to school, and two, it was just like I was constantly fighting and fighting . . . just not getting along with the other workers. It got to a point where I was very unhappy with my job. It was very stressful for me. I just quit. I went back to school and I found a better job that paid more, [where] I felt they really valued what I had to offer. Whereas the other people just totally tried to destroy me, get rid of me."

Did you encounter discrimination in other jobs?

"Not yet. I just graduated from college in June and so this is really my first professional job. I've been on the job since October and I'm starting to move up slowly. But, you know, it seems like the problems begin when I start to move up. As long as I'm down there below them, it's cool. They are real nice, you know, and they are really interested in me. But as soon as I come up with some idea, they want to know right away, 'Is she going to take over my job?' or, 'Is she she going to become head of the program?' So that's where I usually have trouble. But I haven't had any yet. All the discrimination has been during my academic experiences in school. At the university, that's where I experienced more discrimination."

It is as if I hear *Carmila* talking, constantly coming up against a wall of obstinacy and aggression because she, a black woman, wanted to have a higher education.

"I've grown up among blacks all my life. When I came to the university, it was the first time that I had ever experienced interacting with people in such a large institution, with so many whites. The university was 1% black in 1965. I think there is less than 1% now. So, for the first time in my life, I experienced being in classrooms where I was the only black. I experienced interacting with teachers who, right away, thought that I was inferior. So [the] discrimination basically was that a lot of my instructors doubted my ability to perform and to compete with the white students.

"I'll give you a perfect example of where I felt discrimination. I did my thesis on child abuse. It was all new to me, so of course I had a difficult time. I used to have a lot of problems with my writing skills. When I was in high school, I don't think I was prepared adequately for the type of writing skills that I needed in graduate school. But I worked on it and I improved. So, I had done a research project, and I wrote my proposal. I think I got an A on the paper, and at the bottom, he says—this is an exact quote—'This is an excellent research proposal. I'm very interested to see how this will turn out.' And then he says, 'Did you do this alone or did you get help?' In other words, he was saying, 'There's no way that you did this by yourself. You had to have had help.' I read the comment, but I didn't realize what it meant until a year later, when I did the final project. The first two graded periods, I got an A and an A+. When I did my final proposal, what happened is that he didn't want me to bring in ethnic issues. Basically, my study was that child abuse is related to cultural attitudes toward discipline. Well, he didn't want me to look at this at all.

"All my life, throughout my education, I have been doing what the teachers wanted me to do. Never what I wanted to do for my own benefit. Well, I went and I studied [what I wanted] anyway. And I was punished for it, because he gave me a C on my final project. He just cut it down. He said it was the worst paper I'd ever written. He said, 'How could you do A+ work the first two quarters and then hand in such a horrible thesis?' The only reason he passed me was because I was graduating. That's what he told me. Basically, he was just angry that I was looking at cultural attitudes. He didn't want me to bring in anything that had to do with ethnicity."

Audrey was punished for her motivation to study a subject out of a political involvement, as a black student. *Carmila*, you will recall, was also threatened with punishment (an unfairly low grade) when she defended ethnic groups in the Netherlands during an exam.

"And no one has ever done any research on that topic. That's what prompted me to do the research. I thought that it would be great for me to introduce that issue, that concept. The teachers ended up keeping a copy of it. They hated it so much, but yet they kept a copy. Maybe they wanted to use it for their own benefit, but I don't know. I never found out. Anyway, that was one of the worst things I ever experienced. It really hurt me, because for once in my life I was doing something that I believed in, that was related to blacks—that would teach me something and teach other people something—and he just cut it down."

How was your contact with the white students?

"They never wanted you involved in any political activities. We have what is called a Black Student Association, BSA. And whenever we tried to obtain funding to have a speaker, have a workshop, we had to go through so much political hierarchy to get what we wanted. You had to go to the president and to the vice president. Whereas any white organizations on that campus could get money like that [snaps her fingers]. I mean, if they wanted to have a speaker, they always had money, but whenever we wanted something, they never had the money. I offered to help plan the graduation ceremony, which meant guest speakers, the reception, etc. I said, please let me know when you start organizing. No one ever let me know. I had to go on my own and find out. And then, any advice I had to offer, they wrote it down but never followed up on it.

"Last year when I graduated, I had to ask that a black faculty member be on stage to represent us—5 or 6 black students among 180 white. There has never been a black faculty. And I felt, well, hell, I'm graduating, my family is going to be here, and I've had this black counselor who helped me during my whole six years of the university. I said, I want someone on stage to represent my ethnic group. And I had to request that, because they would not ask her to come on stage. She is in charge of admitting blacks and minorities and they never even had her on stage.

"And the students don't open themselves to you. The only time you might interact with them is if *you* ask them something, or you need something from them. Take study groups, for example. They form their study group before you [black students] get a chance to even ask. So you end up studying on your own."

It is as if *Carla* is speaking about her experiences with Dutch students in social work school, the friends who stuck together. No one asked her to join their group. There was no one with whom she could have contact.

Have you ever experienced very subtle forms of racism?

"I had a scholarship to go to school. And if you got below a B, it was possible that you might lose that scholarship. I was one point below, because I had had one C. They sent me a letter saying that my scholarship was going to be taken away from me. I didn't have a job at that time. I went to them and I told them that I knew I was capable of doing the work. And the dean, who was white, says, 'Well, I know you're a hard worker, but there are a lot of students who can perform in graduate school; they can use this money.' So, in other words what he was saying was, 'Really, even if you try, you can't do it, so why should we continue to give you the money?' And that was probably one of the things that was very subtle. But see, I didn't know all that. It took me a while to really catch on."

Why didn't you realize it at once?

"You see, because I had never been in an institution like that. My mother is Russian. She grew up in Russia. My father is black and Indian. When I got older and left that environment that was predominantly black and went into an institution that was predominantly white, I had never interacted before in my life with people of that caliber. And so I didn't know anything about discrimination. I wouldn't even think about discrimination existing because we didn't talk about it in our home."

Audrey is the only American black woman who was not taught about racism during her upbringing. This is probably because her mother is white and, moreover, did not grow up in the United States.

"Even though I know my parents went through it, they tried to hide it from us because it was something that was bad. I wished they would have taught me. Because then I probably would have known. I would have attempted to deal with it better. Now that I am on the job, if I experience discrimination I can identify what it is right away. I think I know how to deal with it better. Whereas in college, I just didn't know how to deal with it. I didn't even know when I was being discriminated against."

Do you experience any racism in shops or on the street or in restaurants?

"Yes. For example, this is a fairly wealthy city. Most of the kids who attend the university are extremely wealthy. So most of the services here on the campus cater to wealthy students. And it is very obvious that black students who are going to college right now are basically on financial aid. They don't even have money to pay their way to school. Whereas a lot of white kids, their parents pay for their education, plus they give them an allowance. And they can buy very expensive clothes.

"I happen to like fashion; I love clothes. There's one store up on the avenue where I shop. One time I went into the store. First of all, if you're black, it's very difficult to get a charge account there. To get a charge account, you have to be making $2000 a month. If a black person goes to a bank for a loan, they will investigate everything. They'll see how long you've been on your job, how well you've been able to pay your bills. Whereas if a white person comes in, it is much easier for them to get a loan. As long as they have credit. But they are much harder on black people, because they don't feel that we are good at being able to pay back.

"Anyway, I went to that store one day and I was buying a pair of pants. It was my first time shopping there. I think the pants were over $70, something like that, and they were marked half off, so that was $35. So right away, the lady said, 'I can't sell these pants to you because someone has changed the price. These pants are not $35, they are $70. And I don't know who could have tagged it. It looks like it was just changed.' I said, 'Are you insinuating that I changed the price?' She said, 'Well, I don't know who could have changed it; I'm not saying you changed it, but someone did.' And then I said, 'Look, I can afford to buy anything in this store that I want. If I couldn't, I wouldn't shop here.' And then I said, 'I don't care if the pants are $100. If I want them and I can afford them, I buy them.' She really thought that I had changed the price tag. And she said, 'Do you still want them? They are $70.' I said, 'No, thank you, I'll go next door and get them.' And I went next door and paid the same, I think it was two dollars less. They can't believe you can afford expensive clothes.

"And in restaurants, especially if it is a very expensive restaurant, they always ask you for your ID, always. The reason they ask you is because they won't believe you. Even if I look like I'm 25 years of age. I've been in places where they won't believe that I'm 21, at least 21, and they'll ask me for my ID. Whereas a [white] couple come in that look just as young as I do, and they won't ask for their ID. So they try to discourage you from coming in, but I still go, you know, because I feel what makes them angry is that you don't get mad. And I'm very calm. If they ask for my ID, I say, 'Sure.' I don't get mad or anything. But I will not let you accuse me of changing the price tag on those pants. I didn't get mad or curse or anything, I said, 'No, thank you.' You see, they expect you to get mad or get violent because they think black people can't control their anger and that we're very violent. And so it shocks them when we're not violent."

Are you always alert when you go to shops? Is racism always on your mind?

"I never used to think about it as much as I do now, now that I know that it exists. I wonder sometimes if I'm paranoid about it. Because I'll go, for instance, for a job and they are so intimidated by a black woman who comes in in a three-piece suit with a briefcase and can sit up and articulate. And they're so intimidated by that that they try to find things to discourage you. Basically, they want a person who has credentials, who has experience. First of all, they don't think that there are many black women who will apply for those jobs, or blacks in general, because they don't think that you have the qualifications.

"I'll give you a perfect example. I went for an interview right before I got this job, for a finance company. I wore a very nice suit, I had my briefcase, I had my resumé, I was all prepared. I came, I was very relaxed, and I was on time, in fact I was about ten minutes early. I sat down and the guy said, 'How is it that you feel that you can combine business and social work?' That's what I have a degree in, I told him. He was just taken aback. I mean, he just couldn't believe that I could sit back and explain to him how it is that I planned to integrate my credentials with that particular job. And so I had an interview for about an hour and a half. They wanted my transcripts from school. Now, any time that someone interviews you for that long and then requests your transcripts, it looks positive, right? They asked me to get my transcripts from the university and I did that. They even wanted my transcripts from high school. They did a whole credit check on me.

"The whole week passed and they didn't call. So of course I called and said I was wondering if they had made a decision on the job, and he said, 'Well, I'm still doing some investigating. I'll call you back in a couple of days.' Another whole week went by; he didn't call back. So I finally called him back and he said the office was going to be transferred to another city. 'Would you be interested in working over there?' I said, 'Sure, that's fine.' He said, 'Okay, call me back tomorrow and I'll have a decision for you.' So I called him back the next day. He was out of his office the whole day. He never returned my call. I finally got in touch with him the next day. He told me that he'd changed his mind, that he wasn't going to be hiring any people at all.

"I made a mistake, because I should have followed up on him. I should have called and . . . Hell, I went through all this running around for three weeks, getting all my documents, taking time off for an interview, calling him like I was licking his feet, you know, chasing after him, and then he tells me this! Well, my mother and all my girlfriends and my boyfriend said, 'You should have asked to speak with his manager. You should have filed a complaint.' I was so angry and so hurt that I just got depressed for a couple of days. I was so pissed off with this man that I never called him back, but I should have followed up. I should have embarrassed their corporation. I should have called and asked to speak with his manager and I should have told him how unprofessional they were. I mean, they never sent a letter. Nothing. No 'thank you,' nothing.

"I think I was just really shocked, because it was my first time on the job market. I had never experienced anything like it. It gave me a taste of what I would be experiencing through all my life. He never even told me why. But I never did anything, I just dropped it. That was a mistake on my part. Now if this happened again, I would follow up. I think it is because I just couldn't believe the world was like that. I was so naïve in that sense.

"I think what it taught me is that whenever I go for an interview now, I kind of expect it. And the thing about being discriminated against, what I'm learning, is that it's not so much that they're discriminating against the color of my skin or my sex, it's that they are so afraid of what you can do. They are so afraid of the knowledge that I have to offer or any black person will have to offer. They are afraid that I can think, that if I get in there, I might learn too much, and I might take over. That's always the fear of the white man. The main fear in this country, of the white man, is that you will learn his mentality. In other words, that you will learn how he thinks. Once you learn how he thinks, you can conquer.

"I don't know exactly how they think, but I've learned a lot about how to get a job. If you want to get a job, all you have to do is kiss ass. Just be a slave, do what they want you to do. But, you see, I'm not going to lower myself. I know that in the job I have now sometimes I will have to do things that I won't always agree with, because that's part of this system. But I'm not going to lick anybody's feet to get a job. I'll clean floors before I'll do that. And I think what they fear more is how much knowledge you have, that I can sit up and organize an activity. They're very afraid, 'Is she going to be president of this company? Is she going to make more money than me?'

"I stand up for what I have learned about my ethnic group. I'm not saying that black people are perfect, that we don't have any problems. Hell, we discriminate against each other. You know a lot of the discrimination I experienced was from black people also. But as far as my job experiences and my academic education, most of the discrimination has been with whites, through whites."

I ask whether there's a difference in the discrimination coming from men and women.

"A black woman has a better chance of getting a job if a white man interviews her, as opposed to a white woman, simply because of the myths about what black women represent, that we're just a sexual object in this country. A lot of white men would love to have a black woman. That's what I feel. And a lot of times a white man feels, I can hire this black woman and if she wants to move up in this position, I can get her to go to bed with me. Or I can have an affair with her. So they feel it is an opportunity for them to sexually abuse you. A lot of black women fall for that. A lot of black women have gone to bed with a white man to get a job. And a lot of black women have gone to bed with a black man to get a job.

"Whereas what the white woman is afraid of is that we're going to take her job. The white man doesn't worry about that because society does not allow a black woman to take over a white man's job. But society will allow a black woman to take over a white woman's job. So the discrimination is different in the sense that I think that the white woman is more intimidated and afraid that I might move her out of the way. Or I might become more successful. The white man doesn't worry about the black woman becoming more successful in the end, because he feels that he can manipulate her."

Have you ever experienced that a white thinks he can manipulate you?

"Oh yes. With teachers at school. I have had teachers who have made passes at me, who have propositioned me to go to bed with them in order to get an A. Not directly, but very subtly made passes at me, like, 'How would you like to get an A in this course? You know I can help you. If you want to, we can set up some time when I can work with you on an individual basis. You can come over to my house.' And right away, you know, when I see that happening, I just transfer out of the class, or I just tell him, 'Look. I'll turn you in. I don't play that shit.' On a job, I have never had a white man for a supervisor. I've always had either a black man or a white woman or a black woman."

Do you think that black women are jealous of white women because of the way they look?

"Yes, I do. Because this country idealizes the blonde-hair-blue-eyed woman. There are so many black women who have never appreciated the beauty of black skin or curly—what we call kinky—hair. They perm their hair to keep it straight, they perm their hair to curl it so that it looks white. In the 1960s a lot of black women used very light bleaching creams to bleach their skin. Women would wear wigs, trying to look white. A perfect example of that is cornrows or French braids. On a job you cannot wear French braids or cornrows. If you do, you risk getting fired. There was a woman who was on Channel 7 News and she used to wear French braids. Very, very stylish, a beautiful black woman. And they told her that until she got rid of her French braids, she could not come back to work; this happened in 1980. She took it to court and she won the case. She sued them for discrimination, but it took her months and months before the court would even hear her case. If I would go for a job and wear French braids, I guarantee you I would not get the job. Not if it was for a white corporation or company—there's no way!

"See, in this country, white people see blacks in two ways. They see us as as 'niggers' and they see us as 'blacks.'"

What is the difference between "niggers" and "blacks"?

"There is no difference, but to the white man there is. To the white man, the difference is that a 'nigger' is someone who is uneducated, who is inferior, who is dogmatic, who has very, very dark skin, has very kinky or nappy hair. Maybe what they would call 'black' would be someone like you or me. 'Black' is a more sophisticated person, more sophisticated than a 'nigger.' You have more flash because you're light-skinned and you have straight hair and to them you are more beautiful. All they look at is the physical attributes. They don't look at what's inside the mind or heart."

Audrey explains that because she is fair-skinned, she is sometimes seen as Puerto Rican.

"I've had some people even think that I was white, when I know I don't look white. I know I'm very fair-skinned, but you can put a white person next to me and you know that I'm not white. I know that I have gotten jobs because of my physical attributes, which makes me angry sometimes. Because I can go to a job and because I look close to white, they might give me the job before they would give it to someone like my friend, whose skin is dark and whose hair is a different texture than mine. And if you ask that question to any black person, especially someone who is dark complexioned, she would tell you the same thing."

Have you ever had any white boyfriends?

"No, I have not. Two of my sisters do. My oldest sister's boyfriend is white, Jewish, which is the same."

Her younger sister also has a white boyfriend. Both sisters have never had a black boyfriend. Audrey thinks it has to do with the fact that both are extremely bright, so they were put in high-potential classes that were predominantly white.

"They never were in classes with blacks. They only interacted with whites, because of their ability to excel academically.

Most of their girlfriends were white and the guys that they met at class were white and they never made an effort or attempt to see what it was like to be with a black person. And I also think, because of a lot of myths that they have heard about black men, that they have a lot of fears. I have a real good attitude about black men. And my older brothers, they have always dated black women. They have very good attitudes toward black women.

"If I would have married a white man, I would probably be ostracized like hell by the black men and the black women. Black women hate with a passion the fact that a black man would pass them up and go to a white woman. And I can understand that, even though I feel that if you love that person .... A lot of black women are so tired of being with men who misuse them physically, abuse them, give them babies and leave them, that they'd rather be alone. And so they are very choosy about who they want to be with. Black men feel that a white woman will give up the money easier, give up sex easier, and take care of them. Which is true. There are a lot of white women in this country who will do anything for a black man. The black man feels he'd rather be with the woman who's not going to fuss at him, who's not going to give him a hard time, who will let him do what he wants to do."

Do you experience different kinds of racism than your husband?

"Yes, I do. I have a better chance in this world as a black woman, simply because a white woman will hire me for a job before hiring Jeff. Jeff is extremely bright. He is an extremely talented person. And anybody who talks to him sees that. So the white man is, from the beginning, extremely intimidated by him. Whereas with me, the white man doesn't worry about me taking his job, not because I'm black, but because I'm female.

"White women try to use Jeff also. Because the white women out here feel that the black man would love to have them. White women feel like black men see white women as a fantasy, something to experience or to investigate. He teaches mathematics at the university. White women in his class will come on to him sexually. They will proposition him and feel that if they give him their bodies, that will get them through a class. But he is not that type of person. He hates any woman who will do that to him. He just lets them know right away that they cannot be in his class. See, if Jeff were ever to be accused of having anything with a white woman, he would be fired. And he could go to jail.

So that's why his relationship with white women has to be totally professional. He is never seen alone with any white student. He has an office. If a white student comes to see him, a female, the door is always open. And he never lets anyone call the house, never gives any student his phone number. He will not see you after office hours.

"When a white person sees a black man with a white woman, he hates it. And especially older people. They hate it! They'll give you a very dirty look or sometimes they won't serve you. Jeff and I have a lot of white friends and we've been the only black couple sometimes to go to social events. Some people treat us very nice, they love us, they're glad to have us. And other people are very stoic toward us. They're just very cold, you know; no one will take your coat, no one will offer you a drink. And then the only thing they'll talk about is sports, because they think that's all black men are able to talk about, football and basketball."

Audrey comes back to the subject of her own position: too white for the blacks and too black for the whites. An outcast in a system of rigid beliefs.

"When I was growing up, I received a lot of ostracism from both blacks and whites. Blacks were envious of me because I had light skin and blonde hair. That's what they wanted. A lot of my black girl friends were very envious of me. I used to get beaten up a lot by black people. And with white people, I was ostracized because here is this nigger who has white blood in her, and they hated that. So I received it from both sides. I did a paper on that one time in school."

Sojourner U.

Sojourner began working in a center for community projects 14 years ago in an administrative job and has since become the center's director. She is an awe-inspiring woman. She is tall and of large build, a 37-year-old who speaks in a calm, controlled way. Her department occupies two rooms: the secretarial office, where Lorraine, Gloria, and others work, and the small room (work room, coffee room, storage room) where our interview takes place.

It is early in the morning. As I wait for Sojourner to arrive, I make use of one of the typewriters to type my report from the previous day. I am constantly impressed by how helpful and kind everyone is. Outside, on the street, it is the same: I am always greeted by other black pedestrians.

Sojourner arrives. She paints the last of her perfectly polished nails, so that they can dry during the interview. With a wink, as if to say, "I'm ready," she leans back into the couch.

Is it difficult to be a black woman in such a high position?

"Extremely. In fact I'm sure that if I were not black, I would not have as many problems as I have had. It is extremely difficult and hard every year to continue to work in the way that I like to work. This wall, which separates the department from other rooms in the building, is a political thing. If you go outside this door, you see the staff out there is white. Our staff represents several minority groups, so that it predominantly consists of people of color."

When I ask Sojourner what kinds of problems she encounters, she is brief and to the point. Her description is so vivid that the words stay printed in my memory a long time.

"The difficulties that I run into .... Well, I am a black woman, and I am very outspoken. And I am for what is right and what is fair. I respect when respect is given. The problem that I have is I don't receive the proper respect for [my] knowledge or experience, or just for me. As a person, I am always tested and challenged in some way. And there is a lot of jealousy about things that I have accomplished as a full-time employee and things that I have done to better myself. Also, the whole thing of me always pushing affirmative action... 'Oh, here comes [Sojourner] again with this affirmative action shit.' Or I'm black or African and they don't like to hear you talk about your culture."

I ask for examples of discrimination.

"There are several instances I can relate back to. When I first came to work here, how others checked on a regular basis, you know, my personnel director coming by the office to see if I and another lady were there at a certain time of the day. And then this white woman telling her that I had not come in one time when I had been in. Other cases involved jobs. One particular job I had applied for, I was told that they couldn't afford to have me away from this office. I applied for the position of director of student affairs, which is open right now. They still beat around the bush, although I was told I had a very impressive resumé.

"Another case: I had a friend who had been a student here, and he got into fundraising full time. He wrote a proposal free of charge and I submitted it to the senate. They tabled it, indefinitely! Didn't even look at it! Now if a white person had submitted that—it would have been different. They didn't say it was bad, they didn't say it was good, they just tabled it. And now they have to scrounge for money. Whereas if they had accepted that proposal and implemented it, they would have had money. But because I was instrumental in bringing it to the senate, it was tabled.

"[There have been] several instances where I have made a suggestion or brought something up and it was either shelved or put to one side because I was the one who had said it. The thing is that my creativity and ability to think for the future is more advanced than theirs. And of course they don't want to give me the credit for having ability. But I know that the university people don't really understand what's going on in the community.

"I don't get support from the university. I know that I'm the only so-called director that does not have his own office. You can see the circumstances that I have to work in, and it has been this way for years. This whole room here [the back room] was supposed to be my office and the rest of the staff was going to be housed up in front. Now I don't know any other director running a program who has to go through this.

"The department gets support from all over the country and [there are] so many schools that want to adopt our way of working. Every year [the university] picks up on how much money we have left, looking at us like a watchdog. Watching over us, waiting to see if we're going to make some mistake so they can throw us out. I'm the controversial person here. They don't want me to come to the budget hearings, because they consider me to be a troublemaker. And the little things that they say. Well, I just either defend it or address it."

I ask her for examples of those "little things" they say.

"Negative things: 'Well, we understand that the money is not being spent.' Taking anything that they can from letters or whatever. Financial things: I'm not paid a salary commensurate with other people in my position. Also, I am supposed to have a well-informed supervisor, but the person who is in charge isn't any help. He hardly knows what's going on here."

This is the only interview that retains a formal tone throughout. I suspect that this is partly because we are sitting at Sojourner's workplace, literally. Something keeps me from asking more personal questions. After she has spoken at still greater length on the organization of her work, I ask:

Have you ever heard people say that black women are supposedly jealous of white women because of their looks?

"I don't know where this idea comes from. I've never known anyone in all my years here on this earth being jealous of white women. It's just the opposite. White women are jealous of black women, because of the way they look and the way they dress. And I say that because if they weren't, they wouldn't try to get a tan. I have never felt jealous of any white woman or ever wanted to be any color other than what I am. Simply because I'm a proud person; our people are proud. And actually I know that African people as a race have more to offer. And white people want that. You know white women want our men, because they see them as studs or whatever it is. And of course the white race is afraid of the African race. Because we have so many hidden powers that they still have yet to discover and to grasp.

"There are so many things that I have to be proud of, being a black individual and looking back in history at what blacks have contributed to this world; I cannot ever feel that I'm jealous of the white woman. Because I know that white people have never contributed anything to the world other than to steal from others. This country was built from thieves and robbers kicked out of other countries. They all migrated right here and then started to steal slaves from Africa. I mean, they have robbed from every culture.

"So I feel that white women are extremely jealous, because they know that their white men would love to be with a black woman or to get her. And that's all there is to it: knowing the black woman has certain powers that they would like to be close to. We are a race of people that they still do not understand, and they wonder how we could have been [hurt] so much and still survive. We'll continue to survive. You know, the thing is, they try to kill us off, kill off some of us. Through wars and prisons. And also too now the worry is the way they want to have another draft. And most of the people 18 to 21 are people of color."

Do you have any white friends?

"I have some white relatives. We grew up around no white people. High school was my first experience going to school with white people. I don't have any close white friends. I choose to have it that way. There are some good white people, don't get me wrong. I had white people to my house for dinner, once. And that was the only white couple I did have. There was another white guy that used to work here. They were all Jewish. I never thought of dating a white man, I never have. I guess because I've always thought black. I don't feel comfortable around white people because I always feel like there's something they try to get from me. And I have to always stay two or three steps ahead of them. You have to deal with it, not let them think that you are vulnerable. I hope I never fall in love with a white man [laughs]. I'll not even give that opportunity a chance."

On the last day of my stay, I happen to notice Sojourner standing in a large store. I walk up to her to say hello again. Then we each go our own way. I suddenly feel very alone. Apparently it has affected me more deeply than I realized: the struggle of that strong woman at such lonely heights.

Gwendolyn I.

Arrol is a black student who received me at the university and introduced me to several of the women I interviewed. I am planning on interviewing Arrol's girlfriend, Olivia, who lives at a bit of a distance, so Arrol drives along with me.

When we arrive, it is already dark. The neighborhood is poorly lit. We turn into a narrow alley. When Arrol rings the bell, Gwendolyn, Olivia's sister, opens the door. She is wearing a robe. Olivia is not there yet, and Gwendolyn does not know when she will be back. She invites us to wait inside, and apologizes because she is ill. She then turns to me, saying, "I would also like to talk with you, but I really can't." Then she leaves the room as Arrol is putting water on for tea.

A little later, to my surprise, Gwendolyn suddenly appears from the bedroom, freshened up and dressed. She draws a chair up to the table and asks what all these interviews are about. I tell her they are about the daily lives of black women and their experiences with whites. Gwendolyn looks at me and suggests, "Why don't we try it, one of these interviews?"

My talk with Gwendolyn is something of an exception among the interviews. She clearly has less education than the other African-American women I talk to. Her language, work situation, and social experiences reflect this. Yet, in many ways, I am grateful for the different perspective she provides.

Gwendolyn does domestic work at three different addresses. She tells of having tried to find other work and of the humiliation of having to live on welfare and food stamps. One cigarette after another goes through her fingers. Sometimes she sits staring out into the space before her.

"Before my job cleaning houses, I wasn't doing anything. I was trying to collect general assistance. And instead of giving me money, they sent me up in the mountains to work."

What kind of work is that?

"Well, it's to get you off the general assistance. They find you work and they tell you what to do. And if they hire you up there, then you have to work there for a long time. 'Cause if you refuse work . . . . "

She speaks very softly, and in a low voice, which makes me miss a lot of what she has to say. Sometimes she even murmurs as if speaking to herself.

I ask whether she likes the work she is doing now.

"No, I don't, but this is all I can do now. I can't go to school because I don't have the money to catch the bus.

"See, I don't come in contact with that many people. Mostly I'm by myself. I don't even go out that much. I don't go to discos."

Gwendolyn talks about her daily activities, the kind of books she reads, and how she has not been able to make friends since she came to California.

"Like I said, I was working up there in the mountains for a while. And they had made it important for me to go down for my food stamps and my Medi-Cal [health insurance]. The woman down there was asking me all kind of questions. I haven't been working, so I didn't have no income. I kept trying to tell her this, you know. How can I tell you how much I've been making when I haven't been making anything! And she kept telling me that she had to know what my sister was making and my mother making and all that kind of bull. I didn't like what she was doing. She was asking me all these questions that didn't have nothing to do with me. So I got pissed and just walked out of the office.

"I know that that broke my chances right there of getting food stamps and Medi-Cal. They make you mad. And maybe that's what they want to do. They make me mad. So just forget it. I only did it anyway because my sister told me. You know we needed it, we sure did. But hell, I didn't know it would be as hard as all that, you know. I didn't know that they send you up here in these mountains to lift logs. They were having all kinds of women doing that work."

What kind of work do you do there?

"We lift logs! We'd lift them, we'd lift logs. We bring logs off from the mountain, then put them down on the bottom. We saw, we . . . . "

That's hard work!

"Sure it is! But they don't care. They don't care. And like I say, they hire you. If they come up to you and they see that you're doing a good job, they will say, 'Here, you're hired.' And if you refuse and say you don't want to work there, then you don't get general assistance. See, that just knocks off your money. You'll still be eligible for food stamps and Medi-Cal, but you won't get no money. So they pointed me out and hired me. I was mad. But I couldn't refuse it."

Are they harder on black women than on white women?

"Well, I guess you could say that, because I didn't hardly see any white women up there. I know there are a lot of white people applying for general assistance, but you don't see them up there in the mountains. I saw not more than five up there. But you couldn't count how many blacks were up there. Yes, I guess you have to say that they was pretty rough on us. I'm not a prejudiced person. But I guess with that kind of attitude, I won't go nowhere. Because I know white people are prejudiced out there. It came to me twice, you know, discrimination on jobs. And I was hurt, I was really hurt. I cried. Because I never had a door slammed in my face before."

Can you tell me what happened?

"I applied for this receptionist's job. It was in the paper. There was this white woman in the background and this lady was at the reception desk. And I asked her, were they still hiring for the receptionist's job? So she went in the back and she told the boss that there was some girl here for the job. And he said, 'Well, what color is she?' And she told him black. And then he said, 'Well, what does she look like?' Those were the words, 'What does she look like?' And he came out and he looked at me and he said, 'No. It's been filled.'

"So this white friend that I knew, her name was Nancy, well, she wasn't really a friend. She was living in the building that my sister was living in. She knew us. She was all right, you know,

Nancy was okay. Nancy went down there to apply for the job. Well, they were ready to hire her on the spot. So she came out and she told me. I was hurt!"

Gwendolyn saw through the boss's racism immediately. To obtain evidence, she set up an experiment with the white friend. She could have gone to court with this evidence. It is characteristic of the American situation that she was very conscious of the fact that she could file charges. In contrast to the Netherlands, special provisions have been made for this in the U.S., such as anti-discrimination organizations where charges can be filed immediately. I should also emphasize, however, that factors such as money, education, and class status make the courts more accessible to Americans of the middle and upper classes than Americans from the working class. Most African-Americans are of the working class. And at the moment of the crisis, the immediate pain and anger felt can make the bureaucratic route through the courts seem unappealing and far away.

"And instead of me thinking about the things that I could have done, I went in and I just blew up. You know I called him all kinds of names and all that kind of stuff. And then I called the NAACP. They told me there was nothing they could do about it; they gave me another number to call. So I just said forget it, I'm not even gonna bother with going to this discrimination court. My sister Olivia was mad at me, because she thought I should have went through it. But you know, I get to the point where I just won't go through all that red tape. That was the first time.

"And the second time was ... there's a restaurant that just opened. They had a sign in the window. I went up there and filled in the application, so maybe they saw that I was black and didn't want to hire me. I called and they told me they were not hiring anybody, but they left the sign in the window. That makes somebody think that they were still hiring.

"And the shops around here, I didn't apply for; they won't hire us because we're black. There are no blacks working in any of these shops around here. In none of them.

"So that was discrimination. Olivia had told me, 'Well, you know, that happens.' But it never happened to me. I thought people were people, that they were all nice. I wasn't that naïve, I mean, but it never happened to me, until then. I was hurt, I didn't know what to do. I just don't want to go through that red tape and go to court, because they still wouldn't have hired me. So that's about it. The only time that I really hated white folks. But then I get over it and it doesn't bother me anymore."

Have they ever been unfriendly to you in the shops?

"One time. One time it sure was. I went in this expensive shop. I was just looking, you know. And if I wanted to buy anything in there, it wasn't like I couldn't. Because I did have the money on me to get something. I could afford something in there. But I didn't want to buy nothing in there, 'cause it was an expensive store. This lady came over to me and asked could she help me. And I told her no—this was a sister too, this was a black woman—I said, 'No, I'm just looking.' And she went over there to this white woman and started talking, 'Oh, she's just looking, 'cause she knows she can't afford nothing in here.' I just couldn't believe what I heard. And I just walked on out of the store. Of course I told Olivia about it. Olivia wanted to go there to the store. I said, 'No, just forget it, just forget it.' "

Do you think white people are arrogant?

"I think there is a bad side and a good side to everybody. If there is anything I hate about white folks it is when they try to act black. You know, you can be my friend, but don't try to act what you're not. They really make me mad. I'm not prejudiced, but once they get up here, they find their black friends and they just think they can do what these black folks do. But they can't. You know, then their voices start changing, trying to sound like they are black. That tees me off. I don't like to see that. I think they should stay in their own territory."

Why do they do that?

"'Cause they try to belong. They want to be one of us. Just like when I was little, I used to want to be white. Because, you know, they had all these nice dresses and stuff and the money and the long hair."

Gwendolyn used to work in an office. The racism she experienced there had much in common with *Olga's* experience with night nurse D.: keeping control surreptitiously; trying to find something against the black employees; making them out to be arrogant if they actively opposed this treatment; and, especially, trying to keep black employees from giving each other support. In Gwendolyn's situation, they ultimately went a step further, finding a pretext on which to fire her.

"It was an office job. And I thought I was doing good work too. But I guess to them I wasn't, 'cause they surely did fire me.

I was working for white folks. Our supervisor, she was a court
jurist, something like that. She was going to be gone for a couple
of days. And she wanted everybody to come in when they were
supposed to. Well, while she was there, we could come early and
leave early. So I thought I would come in early one day, 'cause I
had something to do. So I came in early and I left early. They must
have told her what I did. She came to me about a week later and
told me I was fired. And I said, 'Why?' She said, 'I don't owe you
an explanation.' And I blew up. I wanted to strangle her, you
know, 'cause it was so hard for me to get that job.

"I knew the reason why they did it. It wasn't because I was
late, 'cause I never came in late, I was doing my work. It wasn't
like I was late from my lunch break, 'cause I wasn't, you know.
They wanted me and this other sister out of there. They fired both
of us at the same time. And it was because me and her were
friendly, going to lunch and talking just like everybody else in the
office. But I guess they didn't want us to become friends or
something, I don't know what it was.

"So sometimes they treat you good and sometimes they treat
you bad. I had got that job through an agency. And that was the
last one I got through that agency too. Every time I called in for
another job, they would tell me they would not have another job
for me to go on, you know. So I didn't have nothing to do but to
turn to housecleaning. I couldn't even get a job with these
agencies."

Do these people where you clean like the work you are doing?

"Oh sure, 'cause we're good! We know how to clean! And if
I don't feel like working, I don't have to go to work. But they're
not going to fire me, you know. Because it'll be hard for them to
break in somebody new. Usually when I go to their houses and
clean, I hang my coat up and then I just start doing what I usually
do. They don't have to tell me what to do. And the convent where
I work, they don't tell me what to do either. There isn't a black
nun in there. The other day they took me to this restaurant. It was
a Sunday brunch that we went to. I saw a couple of black nuns
in there; it shook me up. I said, 'Right on!' I never saw a black
nun! I mean, even when we were going to Catholic schools, I
never saw a black nun.

"I just stopped going to school. I just didn't sign up for the
next quarter and decided that I had to work. I didn't have enough
money to stay on campus. I don't like school anyway. I'd rather

work, you see, I would rather work. So this is what I end up doing. No, I'm not proud of it. I'm really sick of it, but this is all I can do right now. I have no other choice but to clean up folks' houses, until I can save enough money to go to places to look for other jobs."

A young woman of 27. Black, uneducated, no opportunities for a job. Her rights are pulled out from under her time after time. When she said she was "ill" when I arrived, did she perhaps mean that she is simply sick of the whole system, and that it's just not worth the effort anymore?

"You'll find that I don't care about a lot of things, 'cause I don't. It doesn't, it don't bother me. I really don't have time for it. I have my own changes that I have to go through. The only time I really worry about something is when it happens in the family, then I worry. I have enough personal problems dealing with myself than dealing with outside people.

"I ain't jealous of nobody. I can't afford to be jealous. I'd rather have time to struggle; I ain't got no time for no jealousy. I'm not jealous of no white person. I'm not jealous of no black person. And I have nothing for nobody to be jealous of either, you know. I'm just living—a comfortable life, you know.

"My man isn't black. He is Mexican. We get a lot of stares when we go out, 'cause he's a much older man than I am. He's 15 years older than me. They probably do envy me because I have a nice-looking man. Plus we're a mixed couple, and that probably blows people's minds. But we don't care. 'Cause we just enjoy each other and that's it. We don't care what nobody says."

Gwendolyn's stories show that she leans heavily on her older sister Olivia. When I thank her for letting me talk with her, she says: "I thank you for coming over and interviewing me. Too bad Olivia wasn't here."

Margaret G.

I am standing in a women's bookstore, wondering what to do. There is a note for me with the cashier: The appointment with Eleanor, who works there, has been canceled. My gaze falls on a young black woman standing in front of the same rack where I had been browsing a few days before. There is no question but that the book in her hand is one from that long row of black women authors. Should I . . . ? Before I have the chance to consider the possibility of a disappointing "No, I'd rather not," I am standing beside her. "Oh, sure. I'd like to talk with you," she says.

A moment later we are sitting in the car around the corner. The time flies by. We have learned to block out the many curious glances in our direction. Why does it attract attention, two black women absorbed in conversation? A white man goes so far as to park his car a hair's breadth from us. With a lot of sighing and loud mumbling, because he "really wonders" if he'll ever be able to get out again, he squeezes a heavy belly between the cars. Exchanging a knowing look, Margaret and I confirm that there is plenty of space on the other side of his car. Fine, we've seen you. The interview continues.

"I went to an all-girls' private school [in Los Angeles], predominantly black and Hispanic background. If you didn't look a certain way, if you didn't have the hair like everybody else, you were like the ugly duckling and you were cast out. I didn't like it. The farther you go west into Los Angeles, the worse it gets. Because upper middle-class blacks moved there. And at one time I'd say I was middle class, but then things just fell in my family and I wasn't middle class anymore.

"I lived in Utah [as a child]. It's not racist, but it's predominantly white, predominantly Mormons. They kind of own Utah. Not too many blacks get far there. They just keep them where they want them. I went to school there with all white children. I was young and there was never a problem of color or anything. The closest thing that I got to, you know, color, was with one of my best friends. Her little sister, who was about 4 years old, asked me, 'Why is your skin color different than ours?' And you know, we all laughed and I told her, 'Well, I just stayed out in the sun a little longer than everybody else.'"

I ask whether it was difficult for her to travel from Los Angeles on her own as a woman.

"There is a lot of stigmatization in southern California that I don't particularly like. It frightens me because everybody has a place, you have a clan. So moving here I felt free, and then somebody told me that there is a lot of racism here too.

"I used to live in Richmond [California], just for a little while. And on the other side of Richmond the Klan is working. I would never go too far out in my car, because I was always frightened of what they could do. Not afraid of death, but afraid of them. I just felt there's something wrong with them."

Many of the women I met talked about the everpresent threat of physical violence. Most of their fears centered around the Ku Klux Klan (KKK), whose continuing terrorism and racist ideals they see as a real danger to them. Later in the interview, she will talk more about the KKK. She is very disturbed by the fact that "normal" people can do such horrifying things.

Margaret is still quite young, at 21. After she graduated from junior college, she moved from southern California. It was hard for her to find a job, because a lot of employers told her, "You have good experience, but you are not stable."

"I feel there is racism at my job, from my manager. I think I'm highly intelligent in some ways. And if you're intelligent and black, she has nothing to do with you. She wants to make you feel small. You know, make you feel stupid. And I didn't particularly like that. She figures that all black folk are alike. There's a lot of Uncle Tommy in there, and I don't believe in that. There is so much of us kissing up to that; you have to do it to succeed. Well, I think she is a bigot. You know, she smiles in your face one day and the next day she's . . . . "

The rest we know. Margaret's experience lends emphasis to the experiences of the Surinamese and of the other African-American women: subtle harassment, prompted by racist feelings.

"She'll explain something to you, okay? And it's a really fast explanation. You pick it up, but maybe you miss a few points. That doesn't make you dumb. She says, 'I told you that once, don't you understand?' And often she looks at me, and I feel, is there something wrong with my hair? And she says, 'You have the prettiest white teeth.' That's a stereotype for black people, teeth, or, 'How do you make your hair go like that?' It was meant as a compliment, and because I was looking for a job, I grinned and said thank you."

This kind of experience has made Margaret cautious. She is always on the alert.

"A lot of people say I appear to be a snob. That I don't talk much to strangers. I don't. I mean, *this* is surprising [I think the surprise refers to her talking to me, a stranger]. I've been making this outward effort to meet other people. Because I don't know anybody but my roommate, her sister, and her sister's husband. Other people, they know me, but they really don't know me. Do you understand what I'm saying? Other people intimidate me with what they could do to me. Like, I need a job right now. So

I'm very close-minded at work. You have to be careful because there are so many people [who] can do you harm."

At the beginning of the interview, Margaret had told me she is lesbian. I ask if that also plays a part.

"They can do harm to you because you are gay, because you're a woman. You have to be careful with the men you talk to. I don't turn off to men, I enjoy them, I look at them. But some of them can be dangerous mentally, physically. And so they may think, well, she's a real snob! But I'm not. I'm protecting myself. Females have this homophobia, they're always afraid, 'Oh, she's gonna touch me!' You have to protect yourself."

Is it more difficult for you to cope with situations or with life as a black gay woman?

"My blackness has nothing to do with it. The only way it affects me is . . . they [whites] have this stigmatization that black women are freaky. Maybe they *are* freaky. Everything that white people taught us is not within ourselves. So that's the only way it bothers me. I figure all black women's minds are like this big . . . they don't want to open it. And it has nothing to do with the church, it has nothing to do with their upbringing. They just don't want to see it. I open my mind, why can't they open theirs?"

It bothers Margaret that she can never talk freely about her weekends, her dates, because she doesn't go out with men.

Would you rather deal with white men or with white women?

"Now, because of my lifestyle, I'd rather deal with the women. Men have a tendency of being bigots more than women do. They also have the tendency to think all black women are promiscuous. If I wear a low cut blouse, I get more looks from white men than I do from black men. It goes back to slavery. They felt we could do more for them. And all they want to do is have intercourse. I'd rather deal with a woman, 'cause she isn't going to look at me that way unless she is gay."

Do you find whites arrogant?

"Some, not all of them. You'd be surprised, the ones that have been around black people the most are the ones that are the most arrogant. The ones that have never been around a black person, they are just wonderful people. They wonder about you as much as you wonder about them.

"What used to amaze me was stuff that white people could sit around and think about. On a talk show I heard somebody say some things that aggravated me: 'How does your hair go like that? How do you get your hair to stand up? How do you braid your hair to show the scalp?' They don't say very much. 'All black people look alike. All black people are lazy; they don't have any motivation. All black people have white teeth.' That's just ignorance, you know. And there was another: 'Blacks *want* to be the minority. We segregate ourselves.'

"In a way, that may not be ignorance, because I used to know that when I was going to school and caught the bus, for some strange reason all the black people went to the back of the bus. While for so many years people were fighting to get to the front of the bus! And I, even myself, just naturally went to the back. I finally stopped. Now when I get on a bus, I sit wherever I want to sit. They also say, 'All black people talk loud.' I've made my own conclusions about that. Department stores, that's a prime example. White people are around, but you hear the black people's conversations. I couldn't understand. It's true, they do talk louder than anybody else. And I think that the reason is that because for so long nobody heard. You know, there is an expression: I want to be noticed, I'm going to be noticed, so look at me.

I recall how many of the Surinamese women also mentioned being stereotyped as "loud." However, they had no framework for analyzing it, as Margaret does here.

"I never wished I was white. But there are some qualities that I like, like their ability to invent things. I wouldn't want to be anything else than black. I only want to get into people's heads that I don't understand. Somebody like a KKK member, I'd like to see: Why does he hate minorities and ethnic groups so bad? What is it about us? I like people, but people don't always like me."

I ask for the reason.

"I don't think this is a reason, but at school I never walked with my head down. It wasn't instilled in me by my mother. I never was a person who looked at my feet when I walked. So I walked straight up, you know, with my head up. When I first got to Los Angeles, I'd just finished eight years of going to school in Utah with nothing but whites. My grandmothers didn't let me go out in the black community all that much. I didn't pick up their slang. It was hard for me to say their slang. So when I first got to my high school, they looked at me really funny and for a long time, without saying anything. And finally one day, one said to me, 'You talk like a white person.' It shocked me. I'd never even thought about it. And then somebody else said, 'Oh, she thinks she's stuck-up 'cause she holds her head up.' I never knew what I was supposed to look on the ground for!

"They didn't like me in high school because I didn't have long straight hair. In my school, there were a lot of creoles. They had, let's say, more than one-fourth white in them. So they thought they were better than you. I had three close friends. One was just intolerable and the other was like me—she wasn't Miss Goody-Two-Shoes, and she wasn't the woman of the street—so we always stuck together. The rest of them didn't like me. They always found something wrong with me.

"I got to the point where I thought, I don't care if they don't like me. If I like myself, I'm fine. So I like myself. There are a few things I'd like to change, but not much.

"Right now I have very few friends, because I've only been here a year and a half. Most of the people I know are black. I want to have white friends, I do. Not because then I can say I have white friends, but because they can show me something and maybe I can show them something. You know, have some exchange."

Are black women jealous of white women?

"Heavens no! I'm not jealous of white people. My mother said one day, 'I don't mind being black.' If I had to die and come back as somebody, I would come back being black. The one thing I wish I had was their hair! I think that's the only thing black women want from white women, their hair. The fact that you can cut it off in the springtime and by fall it's grown back out. You can wash it, go swimming, it doesn't frizz up. Otherwise, heavens no. There's nothing in the white person I want. I have seen beautiful black women. To me, black women are more beautiful than white women because we come in so many shades, as you know. We can do so much to our looks with make-up or without make-up. A lot of [black] women can go without make-up.

"I think white women might be jealous of my color. The ones that sunbathe for days and days, you know. I won't go so far as to say they're extremely jealous. They're probably no more jealous of us than some black women are jealous of them. I'm not jealous. I can only speak for myself, you understand."

Can you remember the first time you felt racism?

"The first time, I didn't feel it directly. And I probably, hopefully, won't ever have to deal with it directly. I was watching a television news program and there was an exclusive interview with a KKK member and his wife. He was saying how he was jumped on by three black men in central L.A. and that's what made him go and join the KKK. Now I may not be answering your question, but this is what I felt: How did that force you to join the KKK? You know, how did that *force* you? Because the same thing could have happened to you in a poor white neighborhood. If you got beaten up there by three young white boys, what would you do then? Join the Black Liberation Army, or what?

"White people don't know what it's like to be black. They've never been singled out. I felt it when I heard somebody say that black people should go back to Africa. That enraged me. I said, 'Black people should go back to Africa! Nobody asked to come over here!' And after you get to digging in my genes, in my roots, I'm not full black anymore anyway. The black people of Africa won't even have me. Because we're not full black.

"So it's like we're lost. Because you're not white and you're not African. You're just American. And that's how I think it should be. That anybody who lives here on this continent, that is born here, is American. That's the nationality. You're not black, you're not white. That's how I'd like to see it. But I know that it can never be."

Eleanor E.

My first appointment with Eleanor had to be canceled, but we were able to meet a few days later. Right from the beginning I am very impressed by her. I have finally come into a feminist bookstore with not only the most extensive selection of literature about women of color, but also a black saleswoman. It is a relief to be able to talk to her about studies on women of color. Usually white saleswomen can do no more than point to the newest acquisitions in the field. But one can see that the staff in this bookstore is aware of problems of racism. While browsing, I come across the following note attached to one of the books: "This book has been seriously criticized for its racism. Buyers are advised to read the article by C. as well."

Eleanor walks to the car with me. We ride around the block and park on a quiet street. It turns out to be a very exciting conversation, and I often find it difficult to choose between discussing racism in the white feminist movement, or in general. The former gains the upper hand.

Tell me about what you're doing for a living.

"I work at a woman's bookstore that is run by a collective of six women. In the collective there are four lesbians and two heterosexual women, and two of these are women of color.

"I've worked in collectives before. Usually, these collectives are places where they try to reach out to women of color to work there. But I find that what they want is a woman of color who can talk like they talk and be culturally assimilated, at least while at work. Especially while at work. And if I want to show any other things culturally, problems arise. Right now is a very tense time at work, because some racist things have been said. And it is very hard to fight on that battleground. I feel like they want to have a black woman work at our bookstore, but they want a certain kind of black woman who can be with them in a certain way that I'm not, that I can't be. I'm not able to be nice and, you know, play by their rules in a certain way that doesn't take care of me."

What did they do that makes you feel that way?

"Well, for example, we are having a big struggle right now. It's on the level of struggle, not just fighting. We're trying to have some political unity. We're all feminists, but some of us are Marxists, some are anarchists. Some people don't call themselves anything except feminist. But our bottom line is that we're all feminists. Well, in working with people, these political differences come up. Some of the people are separatist feminists. That means that they don't want to deal with men at all. I brought it up; there's a black woman in this area who is a very famous authority on children's books. Non-sexist and non-racist children's books. I thought that it would be wonderful for this woman to come and do an event for parents on non-sexist and non-racist children's books. That's one of our specialties in our bookstore.

"Well, people thought that it was great that she was going to do an event, but when they found out that I said 'for parents,' they said, 'Fine, it will be really great if all the *mothers* come.' And I said, 'Not just for mothers, but for fathers too.' It was a very big thing. 'No, no, no, no; we can't have men. The bookstore has existed for ten years; all that time we've had "women-only" events.' I said, 'That's fine, that's really good, but I don't think that we should have *every* event for women only. I think that it is very important that a father come and learn about non-sexist and non-racist children's books. How marvelous that there are men who are interested in contributing more than just the financial part to their children's upbringing.' It was very important for me, because this woman is a black woman, and she would be bringing more and different kinds of black people into the store. For business reasons and for political reasons, it was good that this would happen."

The problem is a deep one. Eleanor was accepted as a woman, but not as a black. Since white women are not confronted with racism, Eleanor is expected to leave that kind of problem at home. It doesn't occur to them that sexism is not the only form of oppression that black women experience; they are also fighting a battle in solidarity with black men.

"As a black woman, I feel that my struggle about racism and living in this country is linked up with black men. I am a lesbian; I do not have boyfriends, although there is a man who lives in my house. I cannot help but feel that as a black person my survival is linked up with black men. It's not just going to be black women surviving. It's got to be both. And I know there's a lot of sexism everywhere. There is a lot of sexism from white men; there is a lot of sexism from black men. But on some basic, bottom line level, which is survival, I think that we have to have some kind of struggle *with* them.

"So it turned into a huge fight. I thought this fight was being fought in an unfair way, because this was a black woman, who was an authority on this, and she's talking about doing an event for parents and also talking about bringing a certain kind of black man, and black people, into the bookstore. People said no. We vote by consensus; that is, everybody must agree. So for me it was a real blow, because I thought racism played a part in it, you know. We are willing to have all kinds of different struggles for women, but not for other people who are also struggling against racism and imperialism within this country and outside this country.

"The women's movement doesn't just stand alone. It is time to reach out from the women's movement and say, we can have a coalition. And I don't see some of my coworkers willing to have those coalitions. It's very frustrating for me, because I am a black woman and I cannot just be a feminist. I'm not just a feminist. I don't have that luxury, that I don't have to deal with anything else. They're not willing to deal with my blackness. They're willing to deal with me as a feminist or as a lesbian. And that's just *one* thing that I am. That's not the overall picture.

"I find one thing about being a feminist for over ten years . . . I initially found that the women's movement was very white and very middle class. I come from a working-class background, so there was a lot of adaptation, not only racially, but class-wise. And I kept thinking that people would deal with their racism and not say things like, 'Oh, you're such an intelligent black woman.' And, 'Oh, you're the first black person I've ever been able to talk to.' People treat me like I'm exotic.

"Recently, I guess in the last three or four years, a black women's community has surfaced inside the women's community, which has been really marvelous for me. Because there was a place to go to talk to other black women. You know, we felt so close to each other because people say such racist, typical things."

What do they say?

"I was recently called an 'uppity' woman by a white woman. I don't know if you know about that. It means you're stepping out of your place. It was something that white people in the South said to black people. If you were an uppity slave, you were punished. And this white woman called me that because I was arguing. I was being uppity; how dare I have a disagreement with her!

"I've had political arguments with women about black men and about their fear of black men, that all black men are rapists and are dangerous. And furthermore, [they argue that] the black liberation struggle cannot be as important as the struggle for women's liberation because, after all, sexism was the first oppression and so this is not a big thing. All black women should be libbers. They make judgments about black people and about black liberation movements. And they not only make judgments about it, they make them equal. They're equal kinds of oppression [they say], so why do I make so much noise? Why am I always trying to separate myself from them? Why can't I be *with* them, why can't I *believe* with them? Why isn't the struggle against sexism the same as the struggle against racism? 'After all, we're not racist, we're feminist. Feminists are not racist.' That was an incredible lie that I had to learn about the hard way."

When I ask how she recognizes racism in her contact with white feminists, Eleanor says that the racism of white women is very similar to the sexism of men.

"Most of them don't have any fear. I realize they don't have any shame. I find that women come on to me in a certain kind of way, they treat me in a sexist way. Women can treat each other in a sexist way, I think they can. I have experienced that in their attitude. I've experienced very interesting things in the bookstore. Sometimes two people stand at the counter and work. And if I'm standing next to one of my white coworkers, customers will say to me, 'Where is such and such a book? Where are the books on childbearing?' And they say to my white coworker, 'Well, have you read this book, and what do you think, and what are the central ideas of this book?' Do you know what I'm saying? To *me*, it's, where is something, and will you show me, and will you look up for me—service kind of things. To talk about the intellectual aspect of the books, the information—it's like I'm illiterate. I'm just a service worker.

"That's how I experience racism in the bookstore. Or they don't even see me at all. They come in, and I'm standing at the front desk and somebody else is in the back. They'll walk all the way around and they'll ask them a question and they don't even see me. I'm invisible. I have experienced that many times at work.

"It's very frustrating that people who have had some experience with black men come to me and feel like they can say things to me about it. People do a lot of dumping. They talk about their feelings, how they feel about black people and black men. They feel like they can say anything they want to me. And especially because I work here, they expect 'service with a smile' listening from me. That's part of my job. I have to give everybody a tit, you know, like, 'You want some milk? Here, I'm here to listen to you.' And that's really difficult.

"Or people accept me because they think I am a lesbian and in fact they don't know. Because I don't often tell people about it. But because they think that I am, they're willing to relate to me on that basis. But not because I'm black, and I may be coming from somewhere completely different.

"You know, it's convenient to not deal with me [as a black]. Especially if I don't talk to them in dialect. I find that if I have a lot of black friends who come in at one time, and we start talking, people get very threatened. Because they are not included. I get certain looks, certain kinds of smiles: Can I be included? I have several friends who are very nationalist, you know. They don't talk to white people. They don't socialize with them at all. So it's this way: [White] people come over, they smile, they try to participate, and they're shut out because the language is above them—the slang.

"Sometimes my coworkers say, 'What was going on over there?' And I say, 'Oh, we were just having a discussion.' They do feel left out.'

Several of the Surinamese women also mentioned these issues: Whites who are critical of blacks speaking in a language they can't understand, and whites feeling threatened when black women get together in their own group.

"And they want so much to prove they're non-racist. It's a really big trend in the women's movement, which is not anywhere else that I can see. There's a big trend for people to prove they're not racist. On the other hand, in the country right now, there's a feeling that the Klan is back. And right near here, the KKK has been chasing kids, breaking windows. Our government is very repressive, especially against poor people and black people. And in the climate of the country there is a real upsurge in racism. You can feel this tension in the women's movement.

"But on the other hand, there are all these people who are trying to prove that they're not racist, they're *good*, and would we please take them into our confidences, and please won't we listen to them.... I don't know, sometimes it is so much like they're trying to save us—'Please let me try to make you understand that there are good white people and we're on your side.' [Eleanor sighs.] Sometimes the way it is presented is so totally patronizing that I'm unable to hear. But I also think that it's time to try to have coalitions with people."

What I want to know is just how racism works, so other women can recognize it.

"It is so hard to describe what happens, because it's so subtle. There's this expression that my father uses about things: 'Don't piss in my face and tell me that it's raining!' In California you experience these constant, more subtle forms of racism. Everything is so sunshiny and everybody is so groovy and so nice. California has this reputation all over the world of being this great groovy place, but it's different.

"It's not like you experience racism as I experienced in Chicago, where there are some places where they tell you, you absolutely can't live here or we'll burn down your house and we'll shoot at you. Or Boston, places where if you're black, you can't go to school there, you're going to get killed, they overturn your buses. They had this big thing, I don't know if you know about it, that happened in Boston: riots in schools because they bused black kids to all-white schools. Even here in California, you can't live everywhere! There are places in this town black people can't live. Black people are being moved out of here. The houses are unaffordable. We used to have a large black population. Not anymore; it's a pretty white city now. Black people are being moved into the southeast part of town and farther. It's the same in other cities, where I used to live. Black people and poor people are being moved out, and that's a form of racism.

"I've experienced where I wanted to rent a house, and I had money, I had a job, references. And there was another man who was there, a white man, and he didn't have all this money, he didn't have his credentials together. But he got the house.

"I wanted to live in a place, subletting. The woman found out that I was black. She said, 'Well, no, I don't know what the neighbors will think and we all have this agreement to not do it. I'm sorry.'

"There are a thousand ways, but everybody is so groovy about it. It's confusing, it's very maddening here. Racism is taking on this more subtle form. It's hard to say exactly how I experience it, except people are so eager on one hand, and then they're not really doing it. People are eager to meet me, not because they know anything about me, but just because I'm black, and they're trying to have a clean slate, to say, see, I'm not racist. And there are other people who totally treat me like shit. It's very confusing. The women's movement is one of the more confusing places to deal with racism."

Do you also experience racism in stores or on the street, for example?

"Sometimes I find that I go into stores with my hands always visible. I'm always afraid they are going to think that I'm stealing. And people have accused me of stealing. So I always try to have my hands spread. Because I'm always afraid they're going to say something to me about it."

Had she experienced the same thing *Carla* did in Amsterdam, who had been accused of stealing a bar of chocolate when she was standing with her hands in her pockets in a cigarette shop?

"Yes, oh yes. There are places that I go to, like P, which is an upper-class lady's clothing store. People don't follow me around and watch me with suspicion, but they totally ignore me and won't help me at all. I have experienced that a lot of times, all of my life, in California, too. I experience this intense kind of racism from upper-class as well as working-class white people, that they feel perfectly free to work out in front of me. I think they look at me and think, 'This woman doesn't have money, she's just bothering me.' They don't know what kind of money I have. It's very bad to make assumptions. People don't know us. So that always feels bad to me and always hurts my feelings when people treat me like that, that I can't get a certain kind of service.

"I have experienced problems in shops, also. In upper-class shops they will not serve you. And there are some places I don't go. There are some bars where I don't feel I can go, because I don't feel welcome. Not that people won't serve me, but I don't feel welcome."

Why don't you feel welcome?

"Because of how the people look at me, or how they don't look at me. I see that they look at me in a really hard way, or they don't see me and take a long time serving me. And if a place is all white, it's maddening to me. I get kind of freaked out. I don't feel safe."

Eleanor was informed about racism from early childhood.

"I don't know if this is just my own upbringing, but my mother said there is nothing more frightening for her than a gang of white boys, that somehow they had it out for black women. You know, like that 'slave girl' book.[128] That was how I was raised. I shouldn't be afraid of black men, but I should be afraid of white men. I'm usually with other women; unless I go out with my roommate, who is a man, I'm always afraid. There is a place that I went to with a white woman friend, and I felt totally unwelcome. Just the looks, like, 'What are you doing here? How dare you.' These looks of disdain, you know. I try not to go to those places where I'm going to be the only black person. I've experienced that so many times. I'm the only lesbian, I'm the only black person. It's very alienating. It makes you feel very separate and very cut off."

Eleanor is one of the few women who has lived in Europe. This leads her to draw several comparisons.

"I lived in Austria for a year, about three years ago. As I say that, I realize all these things, these feelings come up for me. I lived in a small village for six months. I had never experienced anything like that. There were allegedly seven black people that lived in the village. I never saw seven. I saw one; she worked in the grocery store. I would stop traffic. I walked outside and people would stop and point at me. I went to a school once, a model school, and the children all burst out laughing at me. Or sometimes little children would burst into tears when they saw me, because it was such a weird thing. It was the most painful year I'd ever had. People treated me totally like I was exotic.

"I'd say, 'I am from America,' and they'd say, 'What are you doing here from Africa? How did you get here?' I experienced resentment, like, 'You're from a heathen country. We can't go anywhere; how did you get to come here?' I tried to be nice. I'd say, 'Well, I'm from America.' And they'd say, 'Oh, South America.' And I'd say, 'No, I'm from the U.S.A.' I think their resentment was toward the U.S., but also toward me as a black person. 'We hear how you're treated over there as black people. How dare you come over here. You're inferior to us. How dare you be able to get out.'

"The first time I experienced it, I thought, oh no, this is not happening, it's not true. But I experienced this whole rap about Africa too many times. It was just confusing to explain that I *am* African, yes, I am an African woman, but I'm from America.

"In England, I experienced an intense kind of racism. I went on a flight with 300 Austrians to England. I was the only black person on this flight full of white people. Everybody goes through customs . . . and they hold me aside and make me wait for an hour. They question me, they look through their book of terrorists. They want to know how long I'm going to be in England, how much money I have, what I'm going to do, where I'm staying. They put me through this incredible third degree, like I've never experienced before or since.

"My feeling in Europe was that racism was at the place [the U.S. was] in the 1950s; they weren't even sophisticated enough to talk about racism. I still think racism exists in a big, big way here, but there, it seems like people just treat black people any way they please.

"In France, it was really curious—it is a really chic thing to be black. It's chic if you are a certain *kind* of black person. But if you're just a worker and you just live there, they treat you in a contemptuous way.

"I think the English are incredibly racist. Because I wear my hair in dreadlocks, there was this other kind of hatred toward me from English people, because they saw me as a Rastafarian. I felt in danger from the police all the time. But I went to London a lot because people spoke English and I had felt so alienated by the white people in Austria. I went to London and people embraced me. All different people. African people said, 'Oh, you must be Nigerian, you must be Ghanaian.' And the West Indians said, 'Oh, you're from Barbados, you're from Jamaica.' You know, everybody was willing to claim me. I was so desperate and so needy to have that kind of claiming. That was family for me. People, I would hug them in the street. I didn't know them, but they would claim me and they would say these really loving things to me, and I needed that. So I spent a lot of time there. I met a group of Marxist women, black women there. We hung out together and that was really lovely.

"I found that black people in Europe don't seem to be in a place where they're talking about civil rights. A little bit in England, but people aren't even dealing with those things yet. The government seemed very oppressive toward black people. The black people were so loving. That was the thing that stood out the most to me, how people loved me. I was always struck by that. They were willing to love me without knowing me.

"Life is very brutal here [in the U.S.], systematically cruel, I think, for black people. Unemployment, for example. I'm not even talking about police brutality. The reality is that the position of black people hasn't really changed in the country since we've been here. There is now a black middle class and there are some black millionaires even. But it hasn't changed. Somehow that's cruel, to live in this country where there's so much to *not* have, for so many people to not have anything. I don't think it is bad having so much. Everybody should have so much. But it is cruel to me in this wealthy country, seeing it all around and not having it.

"I stopped going to [graduate] school at the time when it was very popular in the U.S. to drop out of college. And you know, it has never been popular for black people to drop out of college, because we can never get into schools, can never afford schools. So I think it was a particular middle-class attitude that I adopted. But I felt my work with battered women to be more important than school. I organized a conference for black women. That was much more important, organizing work.... I'm still too busy to go to school, but I'm feeling a little unsafe. Right now the climate of the country is too reactionary. I really think that a college education is becoming more important, especially if I leave my job. And I think I might leave my job some time, some day. It's not my life, the work."

A notable aspect of the upbringing of many African-American women is that they are stimulated from the start to educate and develop themselves as much as possible. This is evident in Eleanor's experience.

"I love books, but I [also] sing and I dance. My mother would say, 'Black people have always been singing and dancing; why don't you become president, or something?' Well, I'm not interested in becoming president, but I do like to sing. I like to dance and I do like theater. And I love to write . . . . It's an impossible field to get into now, in this country. Especially since the programs I like to work with are small theaters, Third World theaters.

"As a child, I went to an all-black school. I was one of the best students in the class, because I could read. A lot of the students couldn't. I served as the teacher's helper for a lot of years. Yes, I think my initial introduction to school was filled with racism, because I went to this all-black school and the students didn't come out knowing how to read. They weren't expected to learn how to read. I'm from a very affluent suburb of Chicago. This suburb had a lot of money, big millionaire kind of money. They could afford [to] teach [the] black working class, the servant-class population, how to read and write. And they didn't. I think that was very racist. There are people in my family who do not know how to read and write.

"In the sixth grade, I was bused to an all-white school. And I became an experiment, a statistic . . . a black child taken to white school, where I experienced this extreme alienation. I experienced alienation because in my old school I could read and write and I was the teacher's helper. Well, I went to this new school and I realized that even being the best of my class in the black school put me at the bottom of the class in this white school, because the quality of the education was so different. It was a very painful experience. I was a quick learner, but I had this total culture shock of going to school with these upper-class white people. It was horrible. I experienced days when people didn't talk to me, wouldn't know how to just talk to me like a person. I asked ten people where the bus stop was for me to go home; nobody would even talk to me and tell me that.

"I found out that they had these things called dance classes, where they learned how to do the jerk and they learned how to do the hitchhike, these dances that black people had invented. And I was told, 'Show me how to do these dances.' They would do some versions of these dances that were totally out. So somehow I didn't feel bad about not going to these dance classes. They also learned ballroom dancing. And it wasn't so much later that I realized that they didn't ask me because I was black. It wasn't something that was for me, it was for them.

"That was my initial experience of dealing with white people. It was something that changed my life. I realized that it made some separation between me and my family, because I had access to some information that they didn't have.

Eleanor's description of her schooling reminds me of the Surinamese discussions. *Lita* was put in a track below her abilities, and *Carmila* was set back two years by being pressured into a lower level. In Eleanor's case, she was tossed back and forth and began to feel confused about where she fit in.

"They tried to track me at that point into certain kinds of classes. They just tracked all the black students into low-achiever groups. So I was back with all my friends, but I'd had this experience of having this other kind of education by going to this white school. My mother found out about this tracking system. She went to the Board of Education and she said, 'My daughter is not going to be tracked into below-level math, below-level English. She is a brilliant student, look at her grades. I want her tracked into this upper bracket.' And then that made this *other* separation for me, that I was the only black student in this high-level class. It was hard. The teachers resented me, because they knew that my mother had come in. I was their only black student; they didn't want to deal with that. I learned to eliminate all my cultural—all these black 'Negroisms'—because it wasn't acceptable.

"And it wasn't acceptable to my friends and the neighborhood that I'd grown up with that I was not in their classes. They tracked all the black girls into home economics: sewing, cooking, you know. My mother said, 'You want to learn how to wash dishes, how to cook? You cook at home with me! I'll show you; you're not taking that!' And it meant this separation for me. I would be in class with these middle-class and upper-class white students, and always I was this exotic, weird one.

"I have experienced so much racism that some of it I've totally blocked out. Mostly I remember that tracking. This principal resented it a great deal that any black students would come to her school. But they wouldn't treat me like I was just a person. They wouldn't take into consideration that I had left this [other] environment. There was no adjustment done based on that. It was sink or swim. They were not helping you in any way. That's how it was.

"When it was time for me to go to college, I moved to California. And everything became real muddy, because it was so subtle, that racism. I had a wonderful English teacher, however, who encouraged me. She thought I was a wonderful person, that I was a wonderful student. And it's interesting, that's the person that I later went to Europe with and lived with for a year. We taught classes together. You know, she was this great person who helped me recognize things about myself that I didn't know.

"It is hard for me to really remember all these experiences of racism. I'm sure when I go back to school that I will experience it again. Then all those things will light up for me again. It seems so pervasive. It's so exhausting. It's so exhausting to talk about it. [In a very soft voice] It's this patronizing attitude that I don't like in the least."

Have you ever been jealous of white women?

"They tell us that being as light-skinned as you can be is beautiful. Having long, straight hair is beautiful. All things associated with beauty are white, and black people are not beautiful. All black children in America are given this message. When you grow up you want to look like . . . Jacqueline Onassis.

"I'm not sure that black women are in fact jealous of white women. But you're certainly told that you're not beautiful. I think what's happening now is that white women are jealous of how black women look. White people try to look like us as much as they can. I think the truth to me is that they're jealous of how we look.

"But there is a partial truth to that, that black people, and women of color, all women of color, are considered not beautiful. They're Asianist, because we don't have round eyes. If you're a Chicano, you're too brown. If you're black, you're too black, or your hair is too kinky. Beauty is always presented to us in this way. And I can't believe that it's not a phenomenon that all people of color experience in the world.

"A lot of the time, in America especially, it was really forbidden to have any interracial relationships, where people were trying to work out racism. I feel in a funny position saying it, but sometimes I feel that those relationships are unhealthy and sometimes I think they're healthy. It's hard to tell. In this country where things are so sick, sometimes I see these relationships, and I see the two people just rebelling. And sometimes I see two people that love each other. But I'm sure it's hard. It's hard from all quarters. It's more all right if you're a black man and you have a white lover, than it is if you're a black woman and you have a white man lover.

Why do you think it's harder?

"From experience I think it's harder. Because we're supposed to stand up for our black men, no matter what. Even if the men do whatever it is that they want to do, we still have a duty to produce children and have relationships with black men. It's sexism, that's what it is. It's a form of sexism that it's all right for black men [to do as they please], but not all right for black women. I mean it's not all right for anybody, but it's really hard [on black women].

"You could ask me about sexism and racism in relationships; I think I could tell you about that. I've had some white lovers, men and women. And for me it was very hard relating to white men, because if I look at it on a really gross level, they control the world, about 12 of them. But also in middle management and business, all these things are controlled by white men. And for me there was always this constant guilt: How can I relate to this man and what does this mean? I practically decided at one point I could never go home with a white man. The worst thing my family said that I could ever do would be to relate to a white man."

Eleanor is one of the few women who has had close relationships with whites. Her description recalls the comments by Dutch whites who used the argument, "Oh, I don't mean you," to justify making racist statements in the presence of the Surinamese women.

"I have experienced racism in my relationships. I remember feeling like my lovers were holding some attitudes about black people. But I was the 'exceptional' black person. It was a way to not make me be black at all. All these things they felt they could say about black people, but they didn't mean me. It became an intolerable situation.

"I have a white lover now, a woman lover, after I said I would never do that again. I didn't want to struggle with racism in my relationship. And I really feel like you have to struggle with racism whenever you have a relationship with a white person. But maybe when you have a relationship with a black person, you have to struggle over internalized racism. And you have to struggle over self-hatred and all those things that they've told you about black people and how we sometimes treat each other. No matter what relationship you're in, you have to struggle. If it's not racism, it's another struggle. I feel a little bit more whole if I look at it in that way.

"You know, my expectation is that all white people are racist. How could they not be, living in this world, living in this country especially? How could they not grow up with these things? Most black people are prejudiced, but because you're on the bottom in this country, it is a matter of power. You don't have a certain kind of power. So it's not acted out in a certain way.

"If somebody is your lover and your friend, it's much more personal, it's much more painful. Because everybody grows up with these feelings of racism. Internalized racism as well as external attitudes about black people. I think that it's absolutely true that white people are racist, because of what they're told about black people; I do. And I think that you can learn about it, you can let go of some of those attitudes, but I think that it's a hard, long struggle to get rid of all those things. What happens is that it gets more and more subtle. It stops being gross, like saying black people are inferior, black people are not smart, that we cannot learn certain things. It stops being that, but it becomes smaller. The smaller, more refined things come out more.

"I had one woman lover who became lovers with another person. The person was younger and white. I told her that she should break up with this other person, that I wanted to be monogamous. And she said, 'Okay.' She went to her and the woman cried and said, 'Please don't leave me.' So she came back to me and said, 'I'm not going to leave her. It's her first relationship and she needs to have a chance. It hurt her too much and she couldn't take it.' What was implied was that I *could* take it, because I was black and because I had had other relationships. Because I was black, somehow my feelings weren't as important as this younger white woman's feelings. And I thought that was racist! She didn't say, 'because she is white,' but that her feelings would be crushed. Not that *my* feelings—and I'd had a relationship with her at that point for three years—might be crushed. I couldn't work it out. I had to end the relationship. But because I didn't cry, and because I was black, I was strong or appeared stronger.

"This is something else that we're always supposed to be— the strong black woman. That's another way that I experience racism. That people can say and do things to me because I'm black, and because black people have experienced a certain kind of brutality in America, I can take it. It wasn't like she said, 'You're not smart, you're not pretty, you're not clean,' all these different things they say about black people. But what she said was the straw that broke my back, after knowing her.

"In our relationship, different racist things would come up and we would struggle about them and she would come around a lot of times to what I said. But in the end, she held on to those racist ideas. Now when I talk to her—she's still my good friend —I find that she says things to me that I still think are racist, and we have to fight about it.

"Sometimes I feel that when [whites] are with each other they feel more free. People start saying racist stuff to her and they expect her to comply and she has to say, 'Don't say this around me.' Or they say, 'You'll have another black lover.' She's had other black lovers, and they feel free to talk about her black lovers. 'Oh, you sure like them blacks, you like them that way. Are they good in bed?' When they're with each other, I'm afraid that they say all kinds of racist things. And I know that sometimes if I'm with a group of black people, we say things that are very prejudiced against white people. I know that we do.

"I don't know, it's very confusing for me to have a white lover. I've experienced too much pain with it. I hate it. I have this friend who said to me, 'So why do you want to have a race war in bed?' And at the time I laughed. Now it doesn't seem so funny.

"I feel like I'm getting it from all sides. White women feel like they can presume a kind of intimacy; because I love a white woman, that means that I love them and they can try to be chummy with me, say these intimate things to me. They assume this intimacy with me because they feel like, here is a black person they can finally work out all their stuff with.

"And with men you have to deal with sexism. You have to deal with sexism no matter what man. It can be your father, your brother, your lover, your best friend—you have to deal with sexism. And then if it's a white man, you have to deal with racism. It's too overwhelming for me to have to deal with that.

Eleanor also confirms all that I had heard in the Netherlands —from *Carla, Olga, Shirley, Ilse,* and others—about sexual stereotypes of black women.

"I think they have too many attitudes about black women, like black women as sex objects. That's how I feel white men treat black women in this country, as sex objects. In the street often, in the restaurants. Not so much the people working there, but patrons in the restaurant—men feeling like they can come up and buy me drinks or butt in on our conversation.

"I had several experiences with white men who always wanted, and they *told* me, they always wanted to make love with a black woman, that it's this big myth, how black women are in bed. And I think consequently we've gotten really uptight sexually, being portrayed as these lascivious, loose, sexual maniacs. Mick Jagger doesn't help us at all with that song, you know, 'Brown Sugar.' I think a lot of people are under this myth about black people's sexuality."

Pamela N.

Pamela is a social worker who mediates between battered children's parents and the court. She is 28, and her manner of speaking is quick and to the point.

Was it hard to get this job?

"It's difficult for me to say, because this is my first job in this career, but I think it is hard for any black person to find a job. For instance, there were only about six or seven black students in my program and only three of us are employed. I don't think that's an accident. I don't think that's coincidence.

"It was very difficult to get this job. I had been looking for four months. The position actually is a B.A. position. I have a master's. They were hiring five social workers with a master's and five social workers with a B.A. And what they ended up doing was hiring two master's level social workers who would be taking the B.A. positions."

How is that possible?

"I had been interviewed for the master's level position. The interviewer told me he had seen a lot of people who had a lot more experience than me, and he asked me if I'd be interested in a B.A. position. I said I would consider it. I said that because I had been looking for four months. I just felt at that point that I would take a position lower than what I was qualified for to get into the field and to be doing social work. And also it was a position where I thought there was a lot of upward mobility. It was a difficult decision to make, because I know that I'm qualified. I think of this job as temporary, just to open up the way to higher positions within social work. The agency I work for is very well known and I'm part of a unit that's going to become very well known. And so I will have exposure to things that I would not have had exposure to. I'll be learning a lot.

"But there's no way I'm going to be content with this B.A. position. A white person might say, 'What's wrong with the position? After all, you're getting paid.' They sort of expect that mentality from a black person, that we take what we can get from day to day. They're very suspicious and they do not reinforce a mentality which achieves.

"In this job that I have now, I'm the only female black worker. I'm sure they needed a black woman, and I'm it. I think in a sense there's discrimination, because they're given master's level quality work, but they're only paying at a B.A. level. Also I'm bilingual; I speak Spanish fluently. So they're getting quite a lot and they're paying at a bachelor's level. I don't think that's coincidental either.

"I think it's very difficult for an aggressive black woman to find employment. At least in my field anyway, [it] appears that's not something that is encouraged. I think it's held against me, being an aggressive woman and being black. But it's hard to say, because I haven't been working a lot in my field. So I haven't experienced it a lot personally yet. Although I know that I will.

"I know I experienced discrimination when I was looking for jobs. I was applying for a position with a Hispanic agency and I definitely felt I was discriminated against, for being female and black. They wanted a male, and they were very suspicious of someone who was black who would work in a Hispanic agency. Which I could understand. An agency that is geared to certain clientele or a certain ethnic group would want that ethnic representation on its staff. I think that makes sense. But what I objected to was that the employer was saying that because I wasn't Hispanic, I could not work with a Hispanic, which I think is totally false.

"I think it was my toughest interview. He asked how I could relate to the clients. And I told him very bluntly, as a female and as a black. I told him that I value my own ethnicity. I told him that I'm a black woman and I'm proud of that; I would never present myself as any other ethnic group in order to fit in. In other words, I'm not going to come into this agency and deny my ethnicity as a black person and try to assimilate into the Hispanic culture. I don't have to be Hispanic to work with Hispanics. I don't have to deny my blackness in order to be accepted. I'm an international person; I speak Spanish fluently. I spoke it better than him, you know. I speak it better than many Chicanos. I am very familiar with Hispanic culture. And I said that I felt that that was enough. If there was ever a situation where I felt my ethnicity prevented me from doing what I needed to do, I would consult another worker. So that was, I thought, discrimination.

"And also it was discrimination because I was a woman. You know, the assumption that a woman can't work with a male child, that male children learn about being male from men. That's not true. My father learned the male role from women. There were no men in his house; his father deserted them. He's one of the most masculine, steady, responsible men that I know, and he learned his role from his grandmother.

"There was another position that I applied for. The interviewer was a Hispanic man again, but he was working in a predominantly black agency. And he also asked me about ethnic issues. He was the only male non-black person on the staff. And he was very concerned about me coming in as a black person, black woman; would I side with the blacks? Basically, that's what he was asking. I gave him practically the same answer. He said that racial issues tend to get blown up out of proportion. Again, I was proud of my ethnicity, which is something you're not supposed to say. I feel that to come right out and talk about racial issues or to acknowledge my ethnicity is held against me.

"He was concerned about me coming onto the staff and turning clinical issues into a racial issue. I told him that basically I do not feel that you can divorce racial issues from human beings. That when I looked at him I knew right away that he was a Chicano male. And when he looked at me, he saw a black woman. I acknowledged that openly. I did not get the job. I think there's a lot of discrimination against being aggressive. It's really against held you, if you're being aggressive, as a black woman."

That is not the first time that a comparison with the career-oriented white man is forced to my attention. A black woman, it is commonly said, has to be three times as good if she is ever to get ahead—better than white men, white women, *and* black men.

"It's all very, very subtle. You know, here in the U.S., in this part of the U.S., it's all very subtle. You see a lot, you know. When you're a social worker, you see people who are working with black children. You know, a white teacher who says a black male child is too slow and can't learn has already predicted that he's going to fail. And that's the discrimination that I deal with every day. It's so pervasive that I almost think I take it for granted.

"I think last year, my internship, that was the most subtle form of discrimination that I had ever experienced. I was the only black social worker intern at this agency. I felt that they were very ignorant of cultural issues, and I was very blatant about it. I felt I was treated differently than the white intern. She was there a month before I started, from another program. But I noticed that she knew more things about the agency than I did. I noticed that they made an effort to go to her and say, 'Let me show you this.' Whereas with me, I had to ask. She got a whole different orientation. They would go to her and ask her to participate in things. Or give her information about the agency. And I noticed that they would not give that to me. I would have to get that information on my own. For instance, I am very interested in program planning. I remember once going to the director of the agency saying, 'I'm interested in program planning, so if you need any help in that area, I'll be glad to work on that.' I took the initiative. She sort of nodded, but she didn't do anything. But six weeks later, I noticed they were writing a grant and they had turned to the white worker for help, when I had said that I was interested."

Pamela's presence was only tolerated. The racism she experienced was the *neglect* of certain acts. The stimulation and attention that she could have had during her internship were denied her. As we have seen, several of the Surinamese women were similarly neglected by supervisors and advisors who were supposed to be their mentors.

Another aspect of Pamela's story corresponds to the Surinamese women's experiences—whites expressing surprise at a black woman's stylish or professional appearance. *Ilse* described vague harassment from her white colleagues in Amsterdam about her dress. She had said to me that she simply didn't know what to make of it. She couldn't figure out why they did such things.

Now notice the explanation that Pamela offers for such comments, which she encounters in her situation in the U.S.

"It's little things, like, I'd go to work dressed in what I thought were very casual clothes, I mean, not anything special. And I'd walk in the door and people would make a big deal about how I looked, how well I was dressed."

How would they say that?

"For instance, they'll say, 'Girl, you look nice today! None of our interns has ever dressed as nice as you do. You have more clothes than anybody I know. We're not used to our students dressing like that!' And see, that's very subtle. If I told people this, what I'm saying to you, they would say that I'm being sensitive. That is what white people always say about these things, that you are too sensitive. So, what they were saying to me was that they don't expect a black woman to have these things. And they certainly don't expect you to dress better than they do. That's what I hear.

"Why wouldn't I look nice? I'm in a professional program. I'm functioning as a professional, I'm working with professionals, so I'm going to dress professionally. I think white people don't like this. They expect black people to behave in an unprofessional manner. I think that was very subtle prejudice on their part. They didn't expect me to be able to conduct myself on that level.

"People always comment about me being bilingual: 'Girl, you speak Spanish.' I feel that part of the reason it's blown out of proportion is because black people are not expected to be bilingual. I'll really be very frank—I know white people very, very well. I was raised mostly in an all-white environment. My parents taught me about the white mentality very well. So I feel I know how they think. And I was trained to expect certain things from them as a group. One of the things that my parents told me, which I very much agree with, is to be aware of what they expect. They don't expect black people to have this or that. They'll expect you to fail. They'll expect you to be the worst in the group. And that's the kind of subtle prejudice that I find: They're expecting you to fail. Or they don't expect you to behave. Or if there's anybody in the group that is supposed to be the best, they certainly don't expect it to be a black person.

"Also, at this agency where I worked last year, the expectations that they had of me were different than what they had of the white worker. It was very similar to school situations where teachers pass a [black] child even though they aren't learning. I thought it was very subtle racism. Because they sort of let me go, they just sort of passed me by. I think that was racism. Oh, I see it so much.

"I was asked to participate in a research project on infant mortality in the black community. We had all these people who were white to do research on that. There was this white social worker who was doing a research project on teenage pregnant mothers and infant mortality and she needed some help. So I talked to her. I wanted to know what I was getting myself into, so I interviewed her. I didn't like the way she was handling ethnic issues and ended up telling her that I didn't want to participate and why. I felt that being a black person I could not participate in that kind of a research study.

"There's a lot of discrimination by professionals, especially in my field. Social workers make assessments every day about people. And that's a very powerful position to be in. You see a lot of it when you have professionals who are making assessments or decisions about black people. I'm used to discrimination in housing. I'm used to discrimination in employment. But, it's really interesting, since I've been in graduate school and now that I'm out in the field, I'm learning that there's another kind of discrimination in the professional field, as it relates to social work. In the mental health profession, there is a tremendous amount of discrimination against black people, in terms of people making assessments about black people that are racially biased. Black people in the mental health profession have had a horrible experience. They are the ones who get the worst diagnoses, they get the least amount of treatment, by the most poorly trained workers. That's historically what is known.

"What's on my mind most of all now is this kind of racism in my field, which is new to me. I'll give you an example. Last year we had a black man who committed incest. Every offender was supposed to be involved in individual therapy. So we have this 50-plus-year-old man who went to see a psychologist to be assessed. After the psychologist, who was white, had interviewed him, he made an assessment that he was not psychologically motivated, and he told the client, until you know what you want to work on, I'm not recommending you for therapy.

"Well, I was in a group and they were discussing that. I had to say something, because right there, that was an instance of discrimination. This black man was being assessed by a white psychologist and he was being refused treatment. I thought that that was racist. I told the psychologist—I didn't tell him in those words, of course—that I felt that as a black person, and particularly as a black social worker, I had to say something. I objected to the term 'psychologically unmotivated,' because that's a label that's been given historically to black clients. And I said that I felt that there is no way that anybody could interview a client in one session and make an assessment about his motivation. I also objected to the way it had been handled. He had said that the man was sweating and nervous—he had used that in his assessment. I said, the man is 50. He has never been to a psychologist before. It's a very frightening experience for many people, it's natural that he will be sweating. You really need to reassess that. And he did. But if I hadn't spoken up, that's another black person [who] would have been denied treatment because a white worker had assessed him as psychologically unmotivated. So there's a lot of discrimination in mental health. Believe me, there are a lot of decisions being made about black people by whites.

"I'm very much used to discrimination in housing and in schools. I grew up with a lot of discrimination. My parents, in the house that they live in right now, in Washington state—there was a meeting held by the neighbors to keep them out. And my parents fought that. So I'm used to the blatant and also not-so-blatant forms of discrimination. It's so much a part of the experience here in the U.S. that you almost take it for granted. I'm sure I'll experience more once I've been working longer in the field."

Tell me as much as you can about the kind of racism you experience and what it looks like here. Also, I am especially interested in how to recognize subtle forms of racism.

"It's very subtle. Especially when you're dealing with whites who are highly educated, it is always going to be very subtle. I think Audrey might have told you something about this; we went through graduate school together. Audrey and I helped out in the graduation of the second-year students. They have a ceremony, and they have faculty members on stage, you know. There wasn't a single minority faculty member on that stage, not a single one. I mean, you looked at that stage, and it was all white. I felt that was a shame. I thought that was subtle, or not so subtle really, and I thought, I can't believe it. And I said to myself, this is not going to be this way when I graduate. I want some of my people, some of my representation on that stage."

It is extremely difficult for Pamela to talk about this form of institutional racism.

"So we went through this thing where we said we wanted minority representation. If we hadn't asked, I'm sure that there would not have been minority representation up on the stage. I think that's racism, you know. I as a black person had to bring it up. No other white person in that group was aware of or sensitive to that, and they would have just let it go. These are people who are young; they're supposed to be sensitive. But that was racism right there. It's really hard. When you're a black person, you get used to it. And then again, you never get used to it. Somebody, something happens, and you are reminded, oh yes, that's right, I'm black and they're white, and that's how it is."

Pamela shows clearly how racism is rooted in the "in group, out group" principle, whereby the dominant white group has the means and position of power to ignore or exclude blacks. The patterns overlap each other. The white faculty's lack of interest in her progress as a intern is an extension of the nonchalant attitude toward black students who graduate. They can look on, but they don't really count. Everything is fine as long as the white students —the white hope of the white community—are well taken care of and have an unforgettable graduation party.

As an exception, Pamela sometimes takes part:

"In my home, I live in a group situation. And I seldom talk about racism and racial issues with white people, because I don't know if they can handle what I have to say. So I don't usually talk politics or racial issues. But I got into a conversation with some people where I live, some white kids. And they told me that they respected me because I had overcome obstacles, and that their respect for me gives me an advantage in terms of my relationship with them. In other words, what they were saying is that when they look at me, they see in me a black woman who has achieved in spite of obstacles. So therefore they have respect for me and their having respect for me is an advantage, more than if I was white, say. I said, well, tell me since when is having respect an advantage? That's not an advantage, that's a right! An advantage is something that somebody has, you know, that nobody else does. Respect is something that every person should get. They couldn't understand that. And I felt myself getting really angry because they thought that I should feel so honored. I felt, you're not giving me anything that I don't deserve by virtue of being a human being. In my mind I was saying, why did you even bring it up with them? They're white; how [will] they ever understand? They're white, they'll always think white, you know what I mean?

"You can never get too close to a white person here in the U.S. What I mean is, you must always, always, always, always remember that you are black and he is white. It's a defense mechanism. Because that way you will always be prepared for that white mentality. That is not to say that you should be unfair or hate, or that you can't associate with whites; I'm not advocating that. I don't consider myself a racist. I don't advocate just associating with one group of people. But I have to always remind myself of the white mentality. And what I mean by that is that I never expect a white person to understand the black experience. That way you never put yourself in a position of depending on someone you really can't depend on. Because you don't give them that much trust.

I would like to know more about your family. I understand that you grew up in Washington.

"First of all, I come from an international background. My mother is from the West Indies. My father is black, from here. We lived on army posts that were predominantly white. Also, my father was an officer, and there were very few black officers, you see, so that separated us from black people. I went to predominantly Catholic schools, all white. I really didn't get exposed to black people until college. I'd not been around black people very much. This is the first time that I've been around so many black people."

How was it to move from a white environment to a mixed environment?

"It's difficult, it still is difficult. Because my mixed background, or the fact that I was raised the way I was, is evident to black people. I'm very aware that I don't quite fit in among black people here collectively. I think one of the reasons is because of my mother's influence. A lot of the attitudes that I have are from her, which is not the American experience. So when I think a certain way about a certain thing, it's strange to black people here, and I think it's because of my mother being raised in a different place. I'm in situations where I'm not accepted by

blacks, because I don't fit into the mold. I don't have a black
dialect supposedly, whatever that is. I've been told on the phone,
'You don't sound black.' Which was really ignorant. It's as ignorant as saying you don't sound white. You know, I've been told,
'We thought you were white.'

   "I think the way I relate to men as a black woman is really
different than most black women. That's where I find most of my
problems."

   Can you tell me about it?

   "This is my bias, okay, but most black American women—I
say black American because I'm not sure it is the same for black
women in other countries—I find that they're very passive with
black men. I find them very subordinate. I think the roles that
they play in the family tend to be more subordinate than I was
brought up with. And I've been told by many black men that I'm
too aggressive. If anything, I am, compared to most black women.
I remember weird things. For instance, when you're with a mixed
group, male and female, and they're talking about intellectual
issues, it seems like most black women are very quiet and won't
participate. They let the men do the talking. But not me. I'll be
engaged in arguing . . . . When I was working on certain commit-
tees, I noticed that most of the black women would sit and let the
men make all the decisions. I never would; I would be right in
there making decisions.

   "But I think most of my problems are as a black female with
black men, because I find black men very difficult sometimes.
And they find me difficult sometimes. I don't play the role that I
think they want a black woman to play. I think black women play
a lot of games. Again, this is my stereotype. I'm talking very
frankly with you. But they play a lot of feminine games, which I
just don't like to play. Like going along with certain things that
protect a man's male ego, which I would never do. Say, a simple
matter where you would disagree, a topic. I would let my mate
know very strongly that I disagree, very directly. Whereas I think
some black women would feel, I really don't agree with him, but
it's not that important, so I'll just let him go ahead and think that
I agree.

   "Or, this is a big one I think, sometimes black women hold
themselves back intellectually and professionally because they're
afraid of losing a man. It's very difficult for a black female
professional to meet someone her equal. A professional black

woman is very frightening to many men. So you have a lot of women who will downplay their intellect, who will subdue their abilities in order to appease their man, which I will never do. Maybe that's why I'm still single."

Have you ever had a white boyfriend?

"No. I've dated whites, though. But I won't anymore."

Why not?

"I want to be with a black man, someone who understands what it is like to be black in this country. You know, there are white people who understand more than most. Or they have a tremendous sensitivity, in spite of the fact that they aren't black. It's just that sensitivity doesn't make up for a black man [who] knows what it's like. Who knows what you're going through, as opposed to somebody who can sympathize. I'm not against interracial marriages at all, but I think it takes two very strong individuals. And I just don't meet people that strong everyday.

"And also, it is too painful for me. There is always that issue of taking you home to mama, and the racism there. I don't think there are too many strong white men, who would value my ethnicity and bring up my children, say, to value what they're worth. So I have made a rule not to become involved with white men. Because I want somebody who understands my experience from my point of view."

Do you think white men find you or other black women attractive?

"Oh yes. Especially if you're working in a professional situation, I think there will be a lot of white men who will be attracted to an attractive, intelligent, professional black woman. They ask you out, they want to take you to dinner, they want to get involved with you. It's obvious. I haven't had to deal with that too much in the past couple of years because I don't know too many white men around here that I associate with as friends. I'm not uncomfortable in social situations with whites. I'm very clear that I'm not one of them, but I'm not uncomfortable.

Did you like college?

"Yes. I felt very secure academically and also in other spheres, because I was raised among whites, and so I know them. There is nothing that they do that shocks me. Academically I was very well prepared, better than some, because I had a very good education. And so I was competing at their level. I think they didn't expect that. I definitely am intelligent, I don't need to put myself down, but I wasn't really different or smarter than them. I just really believe that they weren't used to having a black person who was on their level academically, who could handle things. I was always very verbal in class, and that seemed to impress them. They don't expect a black person to have ideas that you articulate. And so in that sense, I think they were sort of in awe of me.

"I didn't associate with too many people, black or white. I kept a distance. I just think it's funny that I felt so comfortable. I guess I got a laugh out of watching them be surprised at me. There were very few people at college that I felt knew me very well. I would get a laugh out of seeing them wonder what grades I got, seeing me get an A or something. I kind of laughed to myself.

"I felt really good that most people were very curious about me and did not know too much about me. And I kind of liked it that way. I'm so used to not belonging, you see. I'm so used to not belonging in situations that I was real clear that the reason I went to college was not for social reasons, not to interact with whites. It was to get an education. See, having been raised among whites in terms of going to school in predominantly all-white situations, the difference between us economically, socially, and racially was real clear, and my parents helped me to stay clear. That's the only reason I was in this situation with all whites, to get a good education. And I was not one of them."

*It may be a silly question, but do you often **think** about being black?*

"I don't think that's a silly question, I think it's really interesting. I don't think I do. I think I *remember* it; when I'm with black people I'm *conscious* of it. But I don't wear my race on my sleeve. I don't go through the day thinking, I'm black. I'd be interested to see how other people answered that question, because I don't think that way about being a woman either. I'm conscious of it when discrimination happens, conscious of it when I'm in a social situation. But I don't go around real conscious of it in my mind. I'm sure that there are a lot of black people who do, though."

Do you also have white friends?

"Yes, I do. One of my best friends is white."

Do you talk about racism with her?

"No, I never have with this person. She's my best friend and I've never talked about it. I don't talk race with whites, very few.

Because it just gets me in a situation where they can't handle the things I say. I will never expect a white man or woman to be able to understand the black experience. And that's what I mean you have to always remember. My parents told me that. You have to know the white mentality in this country."

What did they teach you about the white mentality?

"One, that they will never expect you to be anything or have anything. They will never expect you to be clean. They will never expect you to be intelligent or articulate. They will never expect you to have high standards or high morals. That's the first thing that I think I remember. They will expect you to be dirty, they'll expect you to be dishonest, they'll expect you to be stupid.

"My parents taught me that white people will never want a black person above them. Again, I'm talking collectively here, I'm not talking about individuals—I'm talking about the mentality. The one thing a white person cannot stand is taking orders from a black person. They will never let you get above them. And that's the truth, I really believe that about the white mentality. I know that if I'm ever in a position where I have to dictate to people, that's not something they will like. Because white people will never like it when black people have any kind of power, especially over them. That's what I was made to remember—they can't stand taking orders from you or being in a subordinate position.

"If you told them, look, when you see me up here in a position of authority, something inside of you may go sick, it would appear they're not even aware of that. I think it's unconscious or subconscious. But that's the truth, they hate that."

I cannot help but compare Pamela's clarity about this issue to *Olga's* situation. After years of harassment as a student nurse, Olga moved into a supervisory position and found herself abused by the students under her. She knew the situation was difficult and unfair, but could not frame it in any way that helped her to cope with it.

"What else? The white mentality is not up front. You know what I mean? They'll never say what's really on their minds. That's something that black people say about whites, and it's true. They can smile in your face and pat you on the back, but you can never be fooled by that. You know it doesn't mean that they consider you an equal. That's how I see it; that's what I was taught. I'm going to teach my children the same things.

"I consider myself a very ambitious woman and I think a lot of times, in school situations, especially, it is held against me. I think the reason it is held against me is because white people expect blacks to just survive. I call it the ghetto mentality. Some black people would really object to me using this term. You know what I call a ghetto mentality? It's somebody who is only content to survive, who only looks at the present. They never think of tomorrow. Well, too many white people *want* blacks to be that way. So when you have a black person who is aggressive and ambitious, that's really held against them. They're called egocentric, they're called all these negative things, because they strive for the best, which to white people is not good. They want a black person who is content.

"I always get such a laugh out of this. Because I feel like I'm a foreigner in a country with foreigners, but I know those foreigners better than they know themselves. I know exactly how they think, because I lived with them. So I feel very secure. It's a funny thing, because I think black people understand white mentality more than white mentality understands itself."

Similarities in the Experiences of Surinamese and African-American Women

In a structural sense, there are important differences in the position of black women in the U.S. and the Netherlands. Slavery of blacks existed within the U.S., and in 1964 segregation was still legal. Consequently, African-American people have a long tradition of liberation struggle, and African-American women appear to be more aware than Surinamese women of the meanings and implications of being a member of an oppressed racial group. This awareness starts at home. African-American mothers or other significant persons at home *prepare* their children to be aware of the "white mentality." Children are told that they are going to be discriminated against and that they will have to deal with that. Sexual violence against black women is a more prominent issue in the U.S. than it is in the Netherlands. This is not surprising, because it is based on a model of oppression taken from slavery. Knowing black mothers warn their daughters against these dangers.

Despite these differences, the two groups of women share many similar experiences on the level of day-to-day interactions.

Racism is expressed in many covert ways in the U.S. as well as in the Netherlands, and the African-American women's descriptions of subtle racism have striking similarities to those of the Surinamese women. Even when whites "don't want to admit it—" says one Surinamese woman, "—we know that it does exist" concludes her African-American sister.

Both groups of women find covert and subtle racism difficult to describe. "They just treat you differently," says Shirley. "But how exactly, I couldn't say." Both groups concur that everyday racism often involves small, apparently minor offenses that are difficult to deal with because one can be accused of oversensitivity. Carla objects to the Dutch argument: "You Negroes always feel discriminated against." Women in the U.S. suffer the same criticism from the dominant group. Pamela: "That is what white people always say about these things, that you are too sensitive."

African-American women point out that one can learn to recognize covert racism. As Audrey said, "It took me a while to really catch on." Bernice adds: "With whites being subtle, you become much more sensitive to and aware of the kinds of things they do." Only a few of the Surinamese women make systematic observations of Dutch behavior. Quite a few say they never pay any attention to discrimination.

In employment and in education, the U.S. has policies of affirmative action. This is not the case in the Netherlands. On the other hand, Dutch society is a social welfare state and the U.S. is not. Despite these and other larger differences, there are many similarities on the level of everyday life at work, in school, and in public situations. This is not surprising, because both countries share Euro-American cultural patterns. I have compared below a range of situations in which the experiences of Surinamese and African-American women are exactly the same.

Housing

African-American women had little to say about racism in the neighborhood, probably because they live in primarily black areas. Both groups of women experience discrimination from housing and rental agencies or owners. There is an interesting connection between the story of Bernice from the U.S. and Mavis from the Netherlands. African-Americans have a longer history of experience with housing discrimination. Covert strategies are exposed when the word spreads among blacks about these forms of discrimination. An obviously racist strategy in the U.S., which Bernice pointed out, is charging prices that are "totally outrageous ... just to discourage [me] from coming to look at all." This would have passed unnoticed in the Netherlands, because this type of discrimination is not commonly known among blacks there. Mavis, in fact, said that she would *rather* have had the housing agency exaggerate about the prices, instead of pretending they hadn't spoken with her over the phone. "Then I could have at least said no." She prefers *not to know* about the discrimination. Of course, it is short-sighted to think that discrimination has less negative impact when you do not know that it is happening. As we shall see from the two interviews with African-American women that follow, a knowledge of racism is a necessary precondition for effectively dealing with and combating the problem.

Work

In their daily experiences with white colleagues, supervisors, clients, and other personnel, both Surinamese and African-American women are confronted with the following forms of racism:

1. Black women are not accepted in leadership positions
2. Supervisors tend to be very watchful about whether black employees get to work on time
3. Black women are belittled (they have to endure humiliation; they are frequently "put into their place; and their objections are not taken seriously.")
4. Black women are treated as servants
5. Black women are asked to do practical, service-type tasks rather than intellectually or socially stimulating ones
6. There is intolerance against women of color speaking their own language (sometimes called "black English" in the U.S.).

Education

Both groups of women face the following impediments to success in school:

1. Black women are more often discouraged from pursuing higher education, while being advised to train for practical work

2. Those who excel are accused of cheating, or face the disbelief of teachers and the jealousy and hatred of white students
3. Contributions by white students are taken more seriously than those of black students
4. Black women are not included by their peers in group assignments
5. Low expectations systematically undermine the women's goals
6. Assertive and radical black students risk being punished with unfairly low grades
7. Supervisors neglect black trainees
8. White students do not know how to communicate with black students.

Public situations

In shops, women in both countries are regarded with suspicion and face accusations of theft. Interestingly, some reactions in the U.S. and the Netherlands to this form of incrimination are similar. "I find that I go into stores with my hands always visible," said Eleanor, an African-American woman. Olga, a Surinamese woman, made it a point to shop with a transparent shopping bag. White shoppers in the U.S. and the Netherlands often respond in a similarly rude fashion to women of color.

Conclusion

The accounts of the African-American women are not only significant because the similarities help to clarify the Dutch situation. Their experiences are also helpful in explaining forms of subtle racism which the Surinamese women are not aware of. I recall, for instance, that Ilse did not understand the racist implications of comments from her colleagues who wondered how she managed to dress well when she earned so little. Pamela from the U.S. knew immediately in the same situation that whites "don't expect a black woman to have these things."

In concluding, it is relevant to mention that, apart from cross-cultural transmission, strategies for recognizing and combating racism are also passed on from generation to generation. Many African-American women emphasized the role of their mothers in teaching them how to resist oppressive circumstances

and behavior. This important factor—the transmission of knowledge about racism and the use of this knowledge in dealing
effectively with racist situations—is addressed in more detail in
the next section.

Back in the U.S.A.: The Script Is Constant

"We have a saying here that goes: The script is constant . . . things really haven't changed. Now, that is a
generalization, because certainly the fact that we're
sitting here comfortably and talking about our university degrees and all of those things [is evidence that]
there have been changes. But still, yes, the awareness
that the script is constant, that's about the systematic
exclusion of black people from participation in the
economy . . . and from the wonderful things that are
[part of] a right to life. I have that awareness. It just
becomes second nature. It is an inner language that I
have that arms me in order to be able to cope."[129]

In 1985 I returned to California. For a study on a larger scale,
I wanted to further round out the information on racism that I
had received from the nine women interviewed in 1981. It would
be a comparative study of everyday racism in the experiences of
women with a higher education in the United States and in the
Netherlands. In this context, I interviewed 55 black Dutch and
American women. My findings about the U.S. can be summarized
in a few words: "The script is constant. The agenda is the same."
The tendency to cover up and deny racism, which Gloria, Eleanor,
Pamela, and others had warned us of in 1981, has become still
more pronounced and now appears to be taking its toll on the
younger generation of blacks. Several women express their concern about this new generation of middle-class youth, considering
them insufficiently aware of the subtler forms of racism and of
the historical foundations of the struggle against racism.[130] At the
same time, the income gap between middle-class and lower-class
blacks is devastating, and a considerable portion of the black
population is permanently unemployed and socially marginalized.

An increasing reluctance to become more involved in, let
alone responsible for, combating racism is itself a new ideological

form of racism.[131] Arguments based on this ideology state that the black population was wrongly and overly privileged by affirmative action, that blacks didn't know how to take advantage of their opportunities, and that they should therefore just stop talking about racism.[132] It is generally assumed that affirmative action programs have mostly benefited and contributed to the development of the black middle class.

In the context of affirmative action programs, black women received access to predominantly white institutions. In the 1985 study, I spoke with black women about some of the side effects of the integration of blacks into white institutions. The central point was the demand for quality in social contact with colleagues, managers, clients, and other personnel. Many women share the opinion that after an institution has met the quota, little is done about the racist social undertones in the institution. Once inside, the women have to struggle against harassment, against being saddled with heavier duties, and against disrespectful or patronizing feedback from colleagues. They find that information relevant to their job is withheld, and encounter other barriers to promotion within the institution.[133] Yet the myth prevails that the black woman's "double disadvantage," a disadvantage based on both race and gender, has been banished from the labor market by virtue of the "double advantage" of affirmative action programs.[134]

As various women commented, "Racism is still rearing its ugly head." Paule P., 39, and Grace E., 22, discuss this. Both are involved in university life. Paule is a professor of history. When I met her, she was about to leave for a year in the Caribbean as coordinator of an international project. Grace is a student of computer science. I have chosen these two women from the interviews I made during 1985–1986 because they specifically discuss racism within the higher education system and the difficulty they have maintaining themselves in an intellectual stronghold that presents itself as liberal, while racism and sexism are the harsh reality.

Paule and Grace delve at length into the problem of "elite racism"—the racism of the more highly educated members of the dominant group. Moreover, they reveal some shortcomings in affirmative action policy. They do not criticize the concept of affirmative action itself, but they do point out its limitations. They show that an excessive attention to numbers has left the quality of social contact between black and white colleagues within the workplace unchanged.

Paule P.

Her office is very small and extremely full. The shelves are lined with rows of books interspersed with African art. On the wall hangs an antique map of a Caribbean island. I am offered the only easy chair. It is late in the afternoon on a Friday, the end of a workweek. The sun is low in the sky, and it shines in streaks through the slits in the window blinds. Right into my eyes. I see only the contours of Paule's face, but I also want to read the language of her eyes. Stepping carefully between piles of papers, we are able to get to the cord of the blinds. It snags, gets caught in a slant, and jams. Just like a comic strip. We finally decide just to turn my chair around. In any case, the incident has certainly broken the ice.

This turns out to be a brief but intense interview. Paule has a very busy schedule and at 5:30 P.M. must chair a discussion on the image of the black woman in American historiography. When we leave her office at a quarter past, the beauty of the almost deserted campus has a chilling effect on me. It is the biting racism beneath the liberal surface.

Could you talk about how it was for you as a black woman in graduate school? In what ways did you have to work harder in order to succeed, for example?

"I don't think that anybody who was in a predominantly white graduate program at that time was in a typical situation, because blacks had simply never been in graduate school. I felt very isolated. Extremely isolated. I had little or nothing to say to my peers or fellow students in the history department. We were not interested in the same kinds of things.

"I took courses in history. All of the people I know from that period in my life are black. For a while, I think I was the only black woman in graduate school there; most of the other blacks were men. And many of them were married to or going out with white women. This created a kind of awkwardness in any kind of friendship. At one point there were a couple of fellows that I liked to be with, to talk to about Afro-American experience and Afro-American history. When I was with them, it was fine as long as it was just me, but when other fellows started coming over, I would be relegated to the kitchen with the women. These were not women who were also in graduate school. The men would go off and talk their masculine talk, and, well, I had nothing in common with their wives. Not only because of race, but also because of the level of education, as I said. I wasn't even sure they had graduated from college. The level of our conversation was severely limited. You know, I couldn't trade recipes with them because I didn't cook! We didn't wear the same style of clothing, so they couldn't even tell me where to shop. I had a son, so unless we talked specifically about the children, there was really nothing to say. Well, my side of that conversation was exhausted quite rapidly. There's only so much you can say about a 2-year-old, you know."

Did you experience discrimination when you were in college?

"I can't really say I did. I think part of that has to do with the time I came along. In the 1960s, certain kinds of white people were becoming very conscious of their actions and were bending over backward not to be racist anymore. And not to be ignorant —I think that's even more to the point, *not to be ignorant*. They were kind of 'on good behavior,' watching themselves.

"It hadn't gotten to the point yet—as it did I think in the later 1960s—where white people were saying, 'Well, fuck this.' I guess you'll clean that one up! [She laughs.]

"You know, they hadn't gotten to the point where they were tired of 'Negroes.' Later they were, and that same old racism started to come out again."

Do you think the expression of racism has become more subtle?

"I think so. Let me just give you an example. A couple of years ago, there was a particular black graduate student in the department of political science. He'd been there for quite some time. It happened that the department was being reviewed; the program was being evaluated. When they do that, they bring in four or five really top-notch people in the field who are also academics, and they say, 'Take a look at this program. What do you think of it?' One of these people happened to be a hotshot journalist. All the graduate students really wanted to meet him. So this black graduate student volunteered his time to be a kind of 'gofer,' to help out at the house with the reception—those kinds of things—under the full expectation that he would be introduced to the hotshot journalist. Well, he was not. He was not introduced despite all he did. He was there all the time, kind of standing around, and people were being introduced right and left, and nobody said, 'So-and-so, this is . . . . '

"Of course, it was a *white* big shot. The person who had given the reception was a friend of mine, and somebody who I felt could only have done this as a real oversight. I thought, he must be under pressure, having people here and so on. Once this is pointed out to him, he'll be sincerely sorry and want to make amends somehow. So I said, 'You know, So-and-so's very hurt because he wasn't introduced, and there's kind of a little racist thing going on here.' He said, 'Well, I'll think about it.' When he came back a couple of days later, he said, 'You know, I thought about this, and there's no racism on my part, none at all.' I said, 'But you didn't introduce him!' 'Oh, well, you know, a lot of people didn't get introduced.' 'Yes, but you know this student has been doing all these things, and . . . . ' 'Oh, no, no, no—no racism on my part,' he said.

"What I'm saying is that it's gotten to the point where people will not admit it. You can point out to them that this is in fact what their actions are saying to you, and they will look you dead in the face and say, no, that's not what it means at all; you cannot read my actions."

I would like to go a little further with this particular example. It illustrates an important problem: **You** *know what is happening, but it's obvious that the person can always deny it by saying, well, don't try to tell me what my own actions mean. I'm wondering whether there are* **other** *cues that told you this was racism.*

"Well, here are some other things that happened. One of the secretaries on support staff was also helping, a black woman. She and the black graduate student were both told specifically which bathroom in the house to use. And of course the bathroom that they were to use happened to have been [attached to] what used to be the maid's room. There are three bathrooms in the house: one off what had been the maid's quarters, one in the bedroom, and another in a more public area. But, 'You use this bathroom.' That's one thing.

"It was taken for granted that they would do these things. Their having taken their time and paid for the gas to go back and forth and to run these errands was not worthy of a thank you. And then to ignore Basil—I mean, he's a really big, tall man, over six feet tall; you *can't* ignore him and you can't be unaware of his presence. To have him there, hovering, just kind of waiting on people, being in the way so he can be introduced to this big shot . . . and then his name is never mentioned.

"These things were serious enough to me that I felt I really had to speak to this person about it. I could not believe that he would not be concerned about them if I called them to his attention, because this was a person who had been very nice to me. One thing especially convinced me of his racism. When I said, 'Oh, you can't be serious; maybe you're not interpreting this correctly,' he would not even talk with me or consider the possibility that this was how his actions were coming over. There was no discussion, just, 'No, this is not what I am, and that's that.' And this proved to me, yes, obviously you did it, otherwise you would be willing to discuss it and, if not defend yourself, at least explain what those actions meant in reality.

"I could tell you many more things. I was chair of this department, so I might as well. It became very clear to me then, as it is clear to me now, that whereas white people on this faculty can do certain things, if I do them, it's cause for immediate cen-sure —precisely because I am black. Now, I don't know whether it's partly because I'm a black *woman*. I guess maybe the generation I'm part of, and where I grew up, and so on . . . . I feel that I have been discriminated against far more on the basis of my blackness than I have on the basis of my sex."

Does it make you nervous to talk about it?

"Oh, it doesn't make me nervous; I'm afraid it's going to make me very angry and that it'll bring up a lot of the pain. I felt like I came into my intellectual own here. A lot of people here were very important to me, and this whole situation was very important. I felt that I had been given something that I needed to give back, something very positive and very good, and I wanted to kind of 'contribute.' When these things began to happen, it was very painful.

What happened exactly with the faculty?

"Well, as I said, I was chair of this department. I had just been promoted to associate professor, and I'd just gotten tenure, so I was really very young and very new. All these things were against me. Have you read Richard Wright's *American Hunger*,[135] where he talks about joining the John Reed Club? The writers in the club try to use him against the painters in the club to take the club over. They know that if they nominate and elect him as executive secretary then nobody will be able to speak against him because that will label them a racist. Of course, they're dedicated to equality for Negroes and all that. Well, I was elected chairman of this department in pretty much the same way. I realized this at the time, but as I say, I really like this place and I really like these people and if I could do something for them, even just a fraction of what they've done for me, then, hey, that's all right. So, I become the chair. And the honeymoon is rapidly over. I inherited a department that was in really, really bad shape. I mean, it was over budget, and there was dissension, and just a host of things.

"They have to do something here called academic files: They review the faculty's performance in terms of their scholarship, teaching, and other professional activities and decide whether or not to award them a salary increase. So they told me, 'Your files are in terrible shape.' I said, 'What do you mean? I'm following the guidelines of my predecessors and putting in those files what the faculty members have done. I've never heard any of them complain about their files.' They said, 'Well, your predecessors did a terrible job of it, too.'

"I had to do 100% better than what these people had been doing in the past. I could not have any typos in any of the correspondence that I sent out, for example; if there were any, this was taken as a sign of my ignorance and incompetence. My unfitness for teaching. They would send things back to me with the typos circled, which I considered extremely insulting. It was as though I were a student who had to be corrected. And I internalized a great deal of this. I mean, I said to myself, obviously it 's you, you're stupid, you're ignorant, you shouldn't be in this job, and on and on.

"When I came into the department, I reorganized the staff duties, and nobody in this department remembers that I did this. You ask anybody who did it, and they will say either that it's always been this way or that George S., the previous chair, did it, or that somebody else did it.

"On this campus, at that time, it was totally unprecedented for an associate professor to become head of a department, particularly a major department like this one. Now, it was obvious that I was, like, this whiz kid. But had I been a *white* whiz kid, I would have been promoted to professor. This did not happen to me. They told me, you can't be promoted on the basis of administrative work. I thought, I can understand that; I'll be promoted on the basis of my publications. Little did I realize what kind of time and energy this job was going to take. That first year, when I was told that I couldn't be promoted on the basis of my position as chair, they didn't even want to give me a salary increase. I couldn't draw on the good job that I was doing as chair as a means of advancing up the ranks.

"The following year when, as I said, the honeymoon was over, the fact that I was doing a "bad job" as chair became the reason that I did not get a salary increase. This despite the fact that during that year I out-published every fucking person in this department, *including* every senior professor. But I didn't get a thing. Even after I got out of the chair, they still did not want to promote me. They said, 'Well, tell me, what have you done as chair?' And I said, 'Just a minute. If you look at the way this department is organized, you'll see what I've done.' 'Oh, did you do that?' Yeah, motherfucker, you were right there when I did it. Over your objections. And now you're taking advantage of it, and getting all the credit and benefits from it.

"There have been other things like that. I was offered a job at a big private university. I ended up not taking it because of family considerations—I couldn't move my family out of state again; it was just really out of the question at that point. But the tradition is that when you are offered a job, you go to your own department chair and say, I have been offered this other job. If they want you to stay, they try to match the salary with an offer of their own, or they try to come up with a close amount. In my case, I was told point blank that there was no way in the world I was going to get this much money. Now, keep in mind that we were only talking about a $5,000 salary increase. And $5,000 is not a great deal of money, not much for a salary increase.

"But I was told point blank that I could not get this. I mean, I was told this by literally everybody, almost from the chancellor on down. Another person, a white man in this department, was given something like a $10–15,000 salary increase when they matched his salary. He has one book. I have four.

Do you get any support in such situations?

"Just me, myself, and I. That's really the truth. [She laughs.] Me, myself, and I. There are a few people in this department whom I care for. A. is one. There are a couple of other people whom I like and admire and respect, but there are not many. I have friends in the community where I live. I also have friends among black scholars and teachers elsewhere."

Do you get support from your black students? Support that makes you feel stronger and happier about the courses you're giving?

"I would prefer having more black students. I have found —especially over the last three or fours years this feeling has intensified—that I've never really wanted to teach African-American history to predominantly white students. I wanted to be on campuses where there was a significant number of black students. These were the people I wanted in the majority of my classes. There was a time, which I hope is coming to an end, when there were more white than black students in the classes. Since by and large the white students tended to be far more self-confident than the black students—just in terms of speaking out in class, of using their whole vocabulary—black students would not say anything. They would not participate in the discussion. Very often, since they would come into the course motivated by experience as opposed to some kind of theory, you know, they just felt that they could not stand up there. So it became very painful for me to teach."

Do you feel like a role model for your black students?

"I haven't felt that way for quite some time. But that may be changing again. I'm not really sure."

Can you elaborate?

"Well, I haven't felt that black students looking at me and my life have felt that this was something they would like to have for themselves. Yes, that's precisely what I mean. At one point there were very few black undergraduate history majors. There was one person, a young woman who was really very, very sharp. I just got the feeling that she looked at my life and saw what was happening and thought, I really don't want this to happen to me. I mean, this is truly the way I felt about it. The pain of that period was such that, as I said, I don't think anybody wanted to make this a model for their life. Looking at it, they could not see how they could do these things and avoid the pain, avoid all that had come in its train. So, no, I haven't felt like a role model. I think now I may be more in control of myself and of my life and of what I want to do, so that I present a more positive image. Somebody looking at me now might think, yeah, I would like to be a college teacher."

✳

The story of Paule P. illustrates how racism operates on a day-to-day basis in the workplace. Discrimination on racial grounds runs through so many relationships and situations: among colleagues, between teachers and students, between professors and staff. Paule is confronted with stereotypical racism in a professor who reserves the maids' bathroom for black visitors. In other situations, racism strikes quite unexpectedly. A colleague who is otherwise friendly turns out to have a racist attitude after all. It is important to see that, contrary to what many white people believe, blacks are *not* oversensitive about racist situations. At first, Paule does not even want to consider the idea that her colleague is behaving in a racist manner. My further questioning, however, elicits other arguments which indicate that racism was indeed involved. In fact, it is the colleague who overreacts because he *lacks knowledge* about racism: He believes that whatever his behavior, it could not have been racist.

Paule's judgment about racial situations is based on a grounded knowledge and understanding of racism. This has developed over the years through many personal experiences as well as through what she witnesses and reads about the African-American experience. She uses this knowledge routinely in interpreting her own day-to-day interactions. A good example of this is her reference to Richard Wright's novel, in which she recognizes her own situation.

The story of Paule P. confirms the point I made earlier that racial problems cannot be solved by affirmative action alone. She was hired as a department chair, but soon found she was on her own amidst racial attitudes that had not kept pace with the progressive racial policies of the 1970s. As a result, dominant group members, from colleagues to the chancellor, systematically undermined her work so as to prove their prejudice that a black was incapable of functioning at that level. Let me recall some examples. When Paule became chair, whites had *exaggerated expectations* about her. She had to perform 100% better than her predecessors, a demand made doubly unrealistic because the same whites were undermining her efforts to do a good job. This is evident from their *unfair evaluations* of her work. She gets no credit for positive achievements such as the reorganization of the administration. It is taken for granted that some other chair must have been responsible for that. Conversely, when she makes even the smallest mistakes, such as a typo in a letter, it is blown out of proportion and used to put her down and to justify the prejudice that blacks are not competent.

One should not need too much imagination to understand, that in a racist context, blacks, even when they excel, are *not meant to move from the margin to the center* of an organization. Even when Paule P. out-published her colleagues, and received another job offer, the university refused to reward the achievements of this black scholar. Faced with these and many other manifestations of racism, it takes an extraordinary ability and tenacity to persevere.

Grace E., the last woman to speak out, looks at similar problems, seen from a student's position. An interesting aspect of her story is that she followed in the footsteps of her mother, who taught her to challenge and resist racial oppression politically.

Grace E.

Grace has sharp eyes and a knowing smile. She talks very quickly, laughing now and then, and has a surprisingly political mind in comparison with other students her age. I learn that she received extensive information from her mother about the history of black Americans and the struggle for civil rights. She learned from her mother to take a clear position against racism. This kept her one step ahead of her classmates. In high school, she was active in organizing political meetings for black students. Now that she is at college, she plays an important role in promoting the interests of black students.

Do you have memories of the period of the civil rights movement in the 1960s?

"Not really; I wasn't born until 1964. I remember the time following the civil rights movement, though. My mother told me what happened. Martin Luther King, Jr. and Malcolm X were most popular when I was very young. I grew up in Washington in the 1970s. My mother got a divorce and started to go back to college. Here she was, a divorced black woman with five kids, going back to school. And she made it through. At that time, especially at college campuses, black students were still very active. Most black students were still in touch with our African traditions—they wore dashikis and they wore their hair in afros and naturals. I remember growing up on the campus. They had apartments for married students or students with children, and near the apartments there was an elementary school. Some cousins and I were practically the only black students there. My mother was constantly telling us we should be proud to be black:

'We are women of color.' I think that's why I'm really happy I grew up there. Otherwise I would never have learned half of it. Most black students who lived in black neighborhoods didn't really see the civil rights action or anything that happened afterwards. But during that time, black students were still united; it was good. And they used to have these rap sessions over at our house, talking about socialism and capitalism and many other things."

You were 6 at the time?

"Around 6, 7 years old, but I do remember it."

When did you really begin to understand what was going on?

"Even back then, even though I was experiencing racism, I really didn't understand it. I don't think I fully understood what was going on until I was in high school in Los Angeles. Apart from that, I was always taught certain things to say, and what to do if somebody used certain words—like nigger. 'Don't let anybody call you that and don't even use it with other blacks.' But I really didn't know what it was all about or why these things happened."

What were your experiences in high school? Did you go to a black high school?

"No, I went to an integrated high school. My high school was strange. It was literally half and half: 50% blacks and 50% whites. But the black students who got bused to the school all came from wealthy neighborhoods in Los Angeles. So the income levels were different, you know—most of the black students there had more money than the white students. But still there was a lot of racism. For instance, one month was declared Black History Month. I remember no one even took the initiative to organize an event or anything. So I was among some students who got together to organize an event, and we arranged for a speaker to come. He was really good. He showed a film on a country in Africa and talked about the traditions there and the similarities to our present culture. He was also talking about different governments, and how people call Africa a jungle, you know, when really this culture in the United States is an even bigger jungle, considering the crime and so on. A lot of the white history teachers were getting all upset. It was wild! They resented me for having gotten that speaker. They started calling me a radical, which I learned to take as a compliment. The speaker had shown pictures of these little girls in Africa with cornrows in their hair.

It was during the time that this white actress, Bo Derek, started wearing cornrows. They tried to make us believe it was a new style from England. And he said, no, cornrows started in Africa."
Were any of your friends white?
"When I first got there, I had a couple of white friends. But it seems like they took my friendship as a token, as if to say, 'No, I'm not prejudiced. See: *she's* my friend and she's black!' Then there were other things they'd say. Once, two people got As on a test, and it was the two of us black students, the only black students in the class. The response from others was something like, 'Gee, you guys really do well.' As if we're not supposed to. Or they would say, 'Why do blacks dance all the time?' 'Well, why don't you have rhythm?' you know? It's just a different tradition.

"I started getting involved in various organizations. The first one was called The Black and Jewish Experience. The idea was to find out what blacks and Jews have against each other. I made some very important friends there. I was really happy to have met those students. Mainly we talked about the different stereotypes of blacks and of Jews, identifying them and discussing which of those stereotypes were positive and which negative."
Can you recall some of the stereotypes?
"I remember the ones mentioned for blacks: We can't speak English well," she laughs. "We dance all the time; we eat watermelon and fried chicken; black people have big butts. And about the Jewish students: You can't trust a Jew because he'll take your money. We just discussed how the stereotypes arise, and that if we keep on believing in those stereotypes, they may actually materialize.

"Before the Bill Cosby show, in the majority of black shows the black woman was always fat, the blacks always lived in the ghetto. They were always happy, and they were always stupid, or they acted stupid. We talked about the fact that little black kids watched these shows and identified with the stereotypes."
What do you like about the Bill Cosby show?
"Well, he offers a more positive image. He shows another side. Here he is, a doctor, his wife is a lawyer, and they're family-oriented. And it's funny. It attracts all age groups and all races. I like that. It's a good show."
You work at the affirmative action office?
"Yes, I'm an intern there. It's a paid position. We're a kind of umbrella organization for all the other affirmative action or-

ganizations, so we can also provide them with funds for certain events. I've had many jobs here as part of my financial aid. I get work study, so I have to work, but this is the job I like the most. It's working at something that I would want to work with anyway. I always worked with the Black Student Organization, or the Third World student alliance, or similar organizations. Now I have an opportunity to work and research certain areas and get paid for it, too."

Did you experience any racism in those jobs?

"I sure did. Last year I worked in the student employment office. I started working before this white girl came to work there. Then it seemed that they had suddenly cut my hours down and increased hers, for some reason. We were doing the same job, except she was assigned the easy, pleasant work, and I had to do the hard, boring work like filing papers. She did work that was more fun, like greeting people at the door, signing people in, you know? So I quit. I got tired of it. I noticed what they would ask each of us to do. The work that I did was more tedious. She was up front and I was always in the back. I think it was racism because she had started the job after I did, and I felt that since I had more experience, I should have been in the position she was in. Those were the clues."

Could you tell me more about your life on campus?

"When I first came here, I think I was more militant than I am now. Most of the friends I made were black, and I didn't feel that comfortable about making friends with whites. But the longer I was here, the more white friends I met. Now I have all kinds of friends. At this campus you sometimes see certain groups of black students always hanging around each other, but, I don't know, maybe I'm more well-rounded. Last year, I had all types of friends. This year, I still have those friends, but mostly I hang out with my roommates, because I'm trying to slow down socially and study more. Most of my friends are black."

Do you think black students are welcome on this campus?

"No, they're not. I'm sure that if they were welcome, there would be more events that would fulfill some of the black students' needs. Every other Saturday we have SWL—Saturday Wild Life—and all the bands they have ever had at the concerts on Saturdays are white bands. Once—oh, this is ridiculous—when they finally got a black band, they got this group called the Bounties. So ignorant. I would not want these people to represent me. They have a song out called "Rednecks," and in the song they always use the word "nigger, nigger, nigger." The white students just love it.

"I don't know, it's ridiculous how racist this school is. You picked the right school to come to. It is very racist. The black students aren't welcome here at all. That's part of my internship, in fact, to try to get resident deans to put on some events at the beginning of the year for black or Latino students and even get some black bands up there, because we pay our fees too, after all. A lot of black and minority organizations ask for funds for an event and they're told that their idea doesn't represent the majority of the school. So it's like, since the whites are the majority, it's not a good event. It's ridiculous. Whites should come to our events, too. They're just on one track, one-sided a lot of the time, some of them. I think that's what makes it doubly hard for us—to deal with the system here and to do well in school. It's hard."

How does that affect your personal life?

"I think we have to do so many extra things.... It's like an outside pressure—we *have* to do well because they don't think we *can* do well, so it's a must. And it's a must to make sure *other* black students are doing well at school, offering help or directing them to the tutorial services. And it's like, I have to be on this committee or organization, because the decisions they make might not take black students into consideration. I better be there to make sure some conservative side doesn't come out on top, because all they talk about is making another slave race. You have to spread yourself around more. So I think that creates added pressure. Even for social activities, for instance, we have to constantly arrange our own.

"That reminds me: Now they have this big issue here on the alcohol policy. Students who are not yet 21 are drinking at parties. They're trying to cut down on the amount of liquor on campus. They have a committee monitoring different parties. One time they came to a black party. Well, when we have dances, we never have liquor. I mean, as long as the music is there, we have fun. At white parties, as long as the *liquor* is there, they have fun. When the beer is gone, the party is over. So they said, 'Wow, your dances are so nice. I never saw anybody with one cigarette or drink.' We don't need alcohol; all we need is music and we have fun. Right?

"The resident dean was so surprised. She said, 'That's the kind of parties I like to see. Students having fun, without all the other unhealthy stuff.' You know, when parties go on with all the beer, a fight always breaks out or some students get sick because they've drunk too much. It's wild here on weekends, it really is. Living on campus with those parties and all those white people getting drunk, you get kind of nervous. You know, how are they going to act when they get drunk? Are they all going to start chasing me or something? So, I get worried.

"I think it's very dangerous. I know it. Me and my friends used to get together and ask each other, 'So whose house you want to spend the night at this weekend? Let's go over to your dorm room, bring your books,' or whatever. It was almost like we were locking ourselves in. Which is really bad, kind of scary."

Did anything actually happen?

"Well, before it even got that far I was afraid of it. I lived in a suite with suitemates; we had two dorm rooms and we shared a bathroom. Some white girls lived in the other dorm rooms, and we'd had a conflict because one of them used to blast her music too loud, and once she claimed I'd slammed my door, and she said when I slammed my door it scratched her album. So she came over and made a big fuss. I said, 'Wait a minute. First of all, I didn't slam my door, and second of all, why don't you move the stereo? You blast your music too loud anyway.' So once they were having a party in her room and her friends were spending the night. One girl went to use the bathroom, and she shut the door and locked it. I guess that scratched the record. So she came over and banged on my door. 'I am sick of you stupid niggers; you look like apes anyway,' she said. After all that happened, when she was sober, her excuse was, "I was drunk; I really didn't know what I was saying." But you know, if she was drunk and she was driving and she hit somebody, she would go to jail anyway. You are still accountable for it.

"My friends and I went to get the resident advisor (RA). We got the black resident advisor. The RA that lives on my floor is white; we didn't feel comfortable about getting her."

So you didn't want to go to the white resident advisor, you wanted to go to the black? Why?

"I felt more comfortable with a black RA, because I felt she'd be more sensitive to what happened, more sensitive to the issue. I really didn't know how the white RA was. She might have thought there was nothing wrong about it at all. She might have thought the main problem was that the girl was banging on my door, and that she called me names, without really thinking about *what* she called me. That's why I went to the black RA. Then, after it happened, this white RA tried to make it clear to me that I could come to her for anything, so I guess she got offended by it. Still, I didn't like her; it seems like even when she was my RA, she was more concerned with the white students and wasn't really concerned with how I was getting along living with all white students. They weren't really trying to understand. You're trying to look after students' needs, but I think the needs are different for a student of color. A black advisor would automatically know that."

How does it feel being in a white environment?

"It feels like I am trying to hold on to my culture as tight as I can and trying not to lose it. I notice some other black students assimilate more into the white culture. They go more into the mainstream; they change their tone of voice: 'I better talk like this and use this slang word and say, wow, groovy,' or whatever, instead of using the slang they were accustomed to from their black neighborhoods. Some black students assimilate and forget about their home environment and their black friends. I thought I would hold on to it as much as I can, because I don't think there is anything wrong with it. And if I want to say this word or do this or do that, that's *me*. And if I want to dance around the room and play rhythm and blues and jazz and soul, that's *me*, you know. There is nothing wrong with it. That's how it is.

"The way I see it, it's almost like you're given two choices. You can either assimilate, become a part of the white majority of students, or you can keep your own culture and hold on to what you've got. And you may be called an oddball, or radical, or something like that, so it's harder.

"White students call me odd, because what I've got is not like what they've got, and to them it's strange, so they automatically call it odd. And to me what they do is strange, but it's not like I would tell them, 'You're odd.' I guess that's what makes it harder. I don't know whether I'm supposed to change my lifestyle. What about this thing I'm doing—is it wrong, is it right, you know? Do I have to start going to these rock and roll parties? Do I have to start drinking beer, or can I listen to my soul or whatever? That's what makes it harder.

"I know a lot of black students who come from families that go to church a lot. But once they come to college they stop going to church. Their [black] church may not be represented in this community, it might be farther away, which makes it harder. So they're not as religious as they used to be. I've never really been that religious anyway, so that never affected me."

It sounds like it's important for your cultural identity that you remain in contact with the black community.

"Yes, that's another thing you have to deal with, trying to keep up with what's going on in the world, or what's going on in your community, because we're so isolated. It's almost like they're trying to reprogram you or something, so you have to really read the papers and try to find out what's going on."

Do you get the support you need here on campus?

"Not the support I would have liked to have when I was a freshman. As far as tutorial services, there are enough TAs [teaching assistants] here, but not enough TAs of color. So when you go to them, it feels like, 'Oh, here I go to this white student who knows everything.' And he kind of makes you feel, 'Here I am, always asking for help.' But if you see another black TA, it gives you motivation.

"There is this real good black professor named Dr. F. He works in Sociology. He gave a speech on how we should go and talk to the professors and make better use of the school. So I went to talk to my math professor, because I had some questions and he was the best person to ask.

"I walked in there, and there's a room full of white males. They looked at me like I came to take out the trash or something. Like I wasn't a student. I mean, everything got quiet, and they looked at me like, 'What do *you* want? Oh, the trash is right there, and can you dump this out, too?' That's the feeling I got even though they didn't say it. So I sat down, took out my notebook, and started asking some questions. But the first two minutes, wow, it was crazy."

And after two minutes, they were just normal?

"Not really. If I asked something, at first they would pay attention, really pay attention to what I was saying, you know, and then after I asked enough questions, it was like, 'Oh, I guess she's one of the special ones; this is not normal for a black student.'"

How would you know that was what they were thinking?

"I wouldn't really know, but that's the feeling I got. I know when I first walked in, everyone stopped what they were doing and suddenly everything was silent. So I know the feeling was there—what do *you* want? And after that, a white student walked in and everybody didn't look and stop, as they had for me. And then another thing: When I asked him a question, it seemed as if everybody was staring down my throat. Most black students don't go and talk to their professors; if they did, those students would not have stared at me so strangely."

Do you have to make more of an effort to get their assistance than white students, or is it just that the tutors and professors are annoyed at having to assist anybody?

"The last thing they want to see is more black doctors. They want us to stay on welfare. So their assistance is virtually nonexistent. It's like a weeding-out process, and we are the first people to be weeded out. That's how the whole country is. They don't want any black professionals here because we'll get too smart, might get to changing things. So when you first come in, there are a thousand students who want to go to med school. By the time you become a junior or senior, there are five hundred, and out of that five hundred, not everybody is going to go to med school. So the first people they are going to eliminate are the students of color."

How can they eliminate them?

"They can't really, but they can do little things. Like you can go see them, and they may help you out, but they never give you a welcome feeling. You get a cold feeling. You may not want to go back to that TA. You want to say, 'Oh, yes, I understand it, I understand it,' when you really don't. So you may not feel as welcome as a white student. To a white student, it's, 'If you don't understand, make sure you come back!' With us, it's, 'This is how you do that, okay? See you later.' You know, *get out of here*. I can't say that about all TAs, but some TAs. But I really never had one that actually would say, 'Come back.'"

Which black woman do you admire?

"I admire almost all black women that have been in this country. We've gone through so much. As far as famous black women, I really admire a lot of black women writers, like Nikki Giovanni, Maya Angelou, Angela Davis, Toni Morrison, and Alice Walker. I admire my mother. I admire other black women.

"I admire their strength; I find black women to be strong. I am not being prejudiced against men, but here in the United

States, a lot of marriages end up in divorce and it's the black women, the majority of the time, who are the ones who take in the children and have to go to work. Even while they *are* married, black women have always had to work *and* take care of the family. One time this white woman, who was into the women's movement, was asking me why so few black women come to the meetings. Women are the same, but still there is a difference. The black woman has to support her race and other black women. It's a different struggle. Now white women are working women, and suddenly having day-care at jobs is a big issue; but before, when black women *always* had to work—my grandmothers always had to work—nothing was even talked about. So I really admire their strength. Even for black families in which the parents stay together, it seems like the person who always manages the money is the woman. She's almost like the head of the family. So I admire them.

"When times get rough, I tell myself: I am a woman of color. I'm tough, I'm strong! I guess at hard times something like that is reinforcement: You can do it. You are a woman of color. Look what everybody else has been through. You know you can do it!"

✳

Like Paule, Grace is sensitive, but not oversensitive, to racist elements in everyday situations. Her judgments are the result of careful reasoning, based on systematic comparisons between her experience and those of white students. A good example is the way she carefully compares her task assignments at the student employment office with those of a white co-worker of the same age and qualifications. While Grace does the tedious work in the back, the white student is asked to do the pleasant and personable work, such as greeting people at the front door. Similarly, she compares the reactions of white TAs to black students and white students: It is "Can I help you?" to the white students and "What do you want?" to the blacks. She compares white students' reactions to *her* joining a question session with the math professor to their reaction when a *white* student enters the room. Because she is black, she not only stands out, she also has to deal with her fellow students' biases. Their expectations about black students are low and they are almost eager to see their views confirmed. Even when Grace asks normal, intelligent questions of the professor, the students can maintain their anti-black prejudices: She must be a non-typical black student! This illustrates the point I made in Chapter I, namely that prejudices are quite resistant to counter-information.

These examples must not be seen in isolation. They are part of the prevalence of Euro-American centrism at U.S. universities. Blacks are tolerated, but not accepted. Grace characterizes the situation very well when she says that if blacks *were* welcome there would be more events that would fulfill some of the black student's needs. As a consequence of this cultural bias, black students have to organize alternative ways to maintain their culture, whereas white (middle class) students automatically get cultural stimuli that are tuned to their needs.

Another problem we have already seen in the story of Paule is that whites usually lack knowledge about racism. They are often *more concerned about maintaining a positive or non-racist self-image than about the injustice of racism itself.* As a result, they either deny or mitigate racism, which makes it more difficult to keep the issue of racism on the social agenda.

In conclusion, black students face a triple burden: like white students, they have to study hard to get through school. Unlike white students, however, they have to do extra work. They must develop coping strategies so that they can survive in a climate of everyday hostility, which also offers them almost no role models. Further, they have to be self-assured, and show great stamina in order to guard against the damaging effect of low expectations. Finally, they must find alternative ways to keep connected to black culture and experience, the source which gives them the strength they need to persevere and to succeed, despite everyday racism.

CONCLUSION

———————— ✳ ————————

Everyday Racism—
A Global Challenge

Though the black woman's situation is far too complex to be explained only by the factor of racism, everyday processes that are experienced as racism form a central part of her life situation. I have tried to focus attention on the *experienced reality*, dwelling on the question of what everyday racism *is* without yet entering into a discussion of the implications of this approach for *combating* racism. That is a study in itself. Its most important premise would be that a problem that is fully integrated into everyday processes —both in interaction within institutional contexts and within informal community situations, in addition to being spread and confirmed by policy makers, the media, school textbooks, and literature—requires a simultaneous attack at all levels of the social system. In other words, the fight against racism must be fully integrated into the same processes by which racism is perpetuated from generation to generation.

Everyday racism includes the situations, attitudes, and customs that produce racial inequality in daily life. The concept of everyday racism therefore includes practices at both the institutional level and the individual level.

The experience of everyday racism is a cumulative process. New situations are explained from the perspective of previous personal experiences with racism, knowledge of others' experiences of racism, and general or abstract knowledge about the problem of racism.

Racism is present everywhere in society. It is experienced in ordinary contact with white people: colleagues, classmates, teachers, neighbors, store personnel, clients, and so on. The patterns recur over and over again, as whites brand people of color inferior, try to avoid certain kinds of social contact with them, and make them into the targets of hostility, hatred, and aggression.

Racism is often expressed verbally. It is apparent in conversations and remarks made about or aimed directly at ethnic groups. Surinamese women are confronted regularly with racist abuse, like remarks that they should go back to their own country, and blacks everywhere hear verbalized prejudices concerning their basic "character." Whites often exchange racist comments and opinions unabashedly in the presence of a black person.

As a byproduct of extensive anti-discrimination legislation in the U.S., racism there has become increasingly subtle since the 1960s. In the Netherlands, subtle racism has begun to take on violent and overt shape. There is still hardly a glimmer of an active policy for legislative action on discrimination. Despite unemployment levels of 40–60% among blacks, the Dutch government refuses to endorse affirmative action policies. A specific "Law for Equal Treatment" will only be finalized in 1994.

Racism in the United States and in the Netherlands is based on the same ideology of white superiority. The opinion heard so often, that racism occurs especially among whites of lower classes, is unfounded. From the experiences of better educated Surinamese and African-American women, it is evident that racism occurs in rich communities and that teachers and professors also express racism, in their own ways. Some women even believe that they experience racism *especially* from rich people or the well educated.

Everyday racism is a coherent complex of various kinds of discrimination and prejudice that are experienced in diverse situations. On the basis of these women's experiences, the characteristics of everyday racism and its effects have become clear:

Everyday racism is defined by the way in which people of color experience living in the same society with whites.

Everyday racism is experienced in a racist environment. That is, it is expressed in a range of events, many of which may appear to be "trivial" or even "normal."

Everyday racism implies that people of color can, potentially, experience racism every day. As a result, people of color learn to systematically observe the behavior of whites. They develop expertise in judging how whites behave toward them. They also gain insight into the white delusion of superiority and the ideology defining people of color as inferior. They have daily opportunities to test new insights, because they have contact with all sorts of whites every day.

Everyday racism can be a source of constant tension. It means being ever-alert to exactly what is going on during one's contact with whites.

Everyday racism means not being able to take for granted that whites will respect you, treat you with courtesy, judge you fairly, or take you seriously. Certain rights, respect, and recognition, which whites take for granted in their own lives, are denied to people of color.

Everyday racism consists of continually recurring patterns of discrimination and prejudice. Racial/ethnic discrimination occurs in school, at the bakery, at work, or in the housing market. This also highlights the ideological basis of racism and the fact that it is not an individual but a group phenomenon.

Everyday racism is often covert, subtle, and seemingly intangible. It often seems to be a matter of incidental and trivial unfairness. And "petty" racism may occur so frequently that people begin to suppress their awareness of the incidents. Consequently, when blacks discuss racism, a typical response is, "That happened to me, too, actually. It happened slightly differently, but it's basically the same thing, now that you mention it."Yet this covert racism can have serious consequences. It can mean being forced to resign from one's job or having to leave school before completing one's education.

Everyday racism in many situations means that whites automatically favor whites, discriminating to their own advantage. History and reality—the judgment of whether something is good, bad, or even just significant—are defined from a white perspective. This is especially obvious in education and the media.

Everyday racism causes people of color to anticipate racism in their contact with whites, regardless of whether they are actually discriminated against in each instance.

Experiencing *everyday racism* means meticulously checking out and considering again and again whether prejudice and discrimination is present in a given situation. In other words, the black person thinks about an incident carefully before labeling it racism. It is not in blacks' interest to see "more" racism than is actually there. A corresponding part of *everyday racism* is the fact that there are whites who do not accept blacks' view of racism. The black's view of racism, coming from experiences that are verified again and again, is often written off as "subjective" and hence unreliable. What is really going on here is that the black's view of the situation is not being taken seriously. Also, if a white person points out existing racism to his or her own people, their anger and aggression toward that person can be very great. One who shows solidarity with blacks may be seen as a traitor.

Experiencing *everyday racism* may come down to "taking" or "putting up with" incidents without protest. When faced with the argument that they are "hypersensitive," blacks often feel that there is nothing they can say. Furthermore, whites often do not recognize their own racism, or simply deny it outright. As a result, blacks who broach the subject of covert racism may feel they are treading on thin ice.

To live with the threat of racism means planning, almost every day of one's life, how to avoid or defend oneself against discrimination. Accordingly, asserting oneself is often condemned as "aggressive" or "hostile," when one is, in fact, refusing to accept racism.

Everyday racism is not limited to strictly personal experiences. People of color feel affected by the racism that is directed against others, as well. When someone uses the defense, "I didn't mean *you*," they emphasize the *essence* of racism, rather than excusing themselves from it. For racism is never directed against blacks as individuals—blacks as people—but against blacks as the "other."

FOOTNOTES

———————— ✳ ————————

For errata, changes, and late additions to the Foototes, please see page 288.

1. The research was carried out from 1981 through 1983, toward completion of my studies in cultural anthropology at the University of Amsterdam. See P. Essed, 1983a.

2. Selltiz, Wrightman, and Cook 1976:321.

3. The Surinamese population includes various ethnic groups: Hindustani, Afro-Surinamese (also referred to as "Creoles"), Javanese, Chinese, Indians, Marrons (traditionally called "bush Creoles"), Lebanese, and Europeans.

4. Tajfel 1981.

5. Simpson and Yinger 1972:106, Farley 1982.

6. Lenders and van de Rhoer 1983:58.

7. Pettigrew 1973:270. See also Pettigrew 1981.

8. See, for example, Montagu 1964, Banton 1967, Jordan 1968, Miles 1982, Kuper 1975. For a discussion of various theoretical approaches to "race relations," see Cox 1948, Van den Berghe 1967, Barrera 1979, Banton 1983.

9. Montagu 1972, Chapter I; Memmi 1983:17.

10. Husband 1982:18.

11. Miles 1982:44.

12. Several scholars prefer to associate ethnic characteristics strictly with sociocultural characteristics. See Farley 1982, Blalock 1982, Rose 1964.

13. See also Allport 1954, Chapter I; Katz 1976, Chapters II and III.

14. See Pettigrew 1982, Van Dijk 1984, Anne Frank Stichting and Dubbelman 1984, Barker 1982, Lawrence 1982a, Miles and Phizacklea 1979, Sivanandan 1982.

15. Jones 1972, Wilson 1973, Hodge et al. 1975, Jones and Kimberley 1982, Blalock 1982, Manning and Ohri 1982, Gundra 1982.

16. Barker 1981.

17. Van den Berg and Reinsch, *Racisme in schoolboeken* [racism in textbooks], 1983. The concepts of cultural and ideological racism are often confused with each other. It would be leading us too far afield to go into the debate over the relationship between culture and ideology. The research on racism generally distinguishes between racism as an ideology (Wellman 1977, Miles 1982) and the different dimensions in which it manifests itself in practice: cultural (Jones 1972, Terry 1975), institutional, and individual (Carmichael and Hamilton 1967, Knowles and Prewitt 1969, Pettigrew 1971, Levin and Levin 1982, Reenen and Pope 1982).

18. See also Jones 1972:148.

19. Jordan 1968. See also Fryer 1984, Chapter 7.

20. Jordan 1968:27.

21. In order of mention, the quotes are excerpted from: *De aarde en haar volken* 1880-1:175; 1880-6:203; 1880-6:208; 1881-6:203; 1882-2:23; 1881-8:250; 1883-9:276. Uitgeverij H.D. Tjeenk Willink, Haarlem.

22. Raymond Corbey, *Wildheid en beschaving* [primitive and civilized culture], 1989.

23. J. Nederveen Pieterse, *Wit over Zwart* 1990 [*Black over White*, U.S. edition forthcoming].

24. Roline Redmond, *Zwarte mensen in kinderboeken* [blacks in children's books], 1980. Similar research has been done in relation to American, British, German, and other Western children's books. See, for example, Stinton 1979, Preiswerk 1980.

25. Redmond 1980:32/33.

26. Redmond 1980:34.

27. Redmond 1980:43.

28. Redmond 1980:41/42.

29. Fox 1975.

30. B. Tate and J. Stinton 1979.

31. Van den Berg and Reinsch 1983.

32. Van den Berg and Reinsch 1983:43/44.

33. Gillian Klein, *Reading into Racism*, 1985.

34. Teun A. van Dijk, *Schoolvoorbeelden van racisme* [school examples of racism], 1987.

35. See Van Dijk and Spaninks 1981.

36. For American and British critical studies on the image of blacks in the media, see Husband 1975, Joseph and Lewis 1981: Chapter V, Schary 1969.

37. Teun A. van Dijk, *Racism and the Press*, 1991.

38. Teun A. van Dijk, *Minderheden in de media* [minorities in the media], 1983.

39. The concept of "institutional racism" was introduced by Carmichael and Hamilton (1967). The concept of "white racism" is used in connection with this, to indicate that racism is firmly anchored in societal structures and determines how the society functions. See Bromley and Longino 1972, *Report of the National Advisory Commission on Civil Disorders* (better known as the Kerner Report) 1968.

40. There have been a few Dutch and many non-Dutch studies carried out on the subject of institutional racism. For a general idea of institutional racism and the specific forms it takes, I recommend reading American and British information on this topic, which is relevant to the Dutch situation as well. Below is a brief bibliography, with annotations indicating the social context in which the institutional racism was studied. Publications accompanied by an asterisk pertain to the Dutch situation.

The housing and labor markets: Daniel 1968, D. Smith 1977, Bovenkerk 1978*, Ratcliffe 1981. The job market and unions: Braham *et al.* 1981. Business: Pico 1974, Fernandez 1981. Science: Ladner 1973, UNESCO 1983, Lawrence 1982b, Mullard 1973, Chapter 6. Education: Piliawsky 1982. Housing, employment, health care, education, the court system, and other areas: Bromley and Longino 1972. Legislation, government policy, law enforcement and the police, education: Glazer and Young 1983. Law enforcement and police: Gordon 1983. Laws, legal status, and government policy: Lester and Bindman 1972, Moore 1975, Ausems-Habes 1983*, *Ars Aequi* 1981-10*, Ali and Hoens 1983*, Werkgroep Knelpunten in het Nederlands Recht voor Etnische minderheden 1983*. Policy on aliens: Moore and Wallace 1975, Ali 1981*. Health care: Willie *et al.* 1973.

41. See also Malone 1980, 1983, Rendel and Bindman 1975:4, Commission for Racial Equality 1980.

42. See also Groenendijk 1980.

43. Portegijs 1983:68.

44. See also Bovenkerk and Breuning-van Leeuwen 1978, Schumacher 1980:120.

45. See also Sint and Nijzink 1980: "Onderaan de Arbeidsmarkt" [At the bottom of the list in the job market] pp. 12–29, Boerma 1981:35.

46. Gewestelijk Arbeidsbureau Utrecht [Utrecht area employment office], August 1981. *Beleidsadvies inzake buitenlandse vrouwen* [policy recommendations concerning foreign women], E.M.M. Wegdam.

47. Bovenkerk 1978:17.

48. Ghazi 1982, Nijzink 1980.

49. The housing project is called Gliphoeve. See Schumacher 1980:84/85.

50. This is apparent from Dutch discussions on ethnic "minorities" in the Netherlands. See also Van Dijk 1984.

51. See Marlene de Vries 1981, Van den Berg-Eldering *et al.* 1980, Appel *et al.* 1980, Groen and Peperstraten 1981, Eijsenring and Bochove 1979, Dors 1984.

52. See, for example, Varina Tjon-Ten 1983.

53. Dors 1982:68, Martens-Elling and Janssen 1979.

54. For example, Marlene de Vries 1981, Raad voor het Jeugdbeleid [Council on youth policy] 1983.

55. Aalberts and Kamminga 1983:63/64. See also Bovenkerk and Luning 1979.

56. Cashmore and Troyna 1982, Joshua and Wallace 1983.

57. Levin and Levin 1982:85.

58. Jones 1972:118ff.

59. See also Essed 1983a.

60. See also Dennis Brooks 1981 and other articles, and Braham, Rhodes, and Pearn 1981.

61. See also Van Duijne-Strobosch 1983:4.

62. See also Essed 1982.

63. Thus in the Netherlands more attention is given to extreme racism than to other forms of racist expression. See, for example, Bouw *et al.* 1981, Van Donselaar and Van Praag 1983, Hagendoorn and Janssen 1983.

64. See also Carmichael and Hamilton 1967 on this point.

65. Van Praag 1983:63.

66. Statistics: Sociaal en Cultureel Rapport 1982:250.

67. Lagendijk in van Praag 1983:63.

68. Crosby, *et al.* 1980.

69. Weitz 1972.

70. This view was at the root of the earliest psychological studies on prejudice, such as those of F. Allport 1920, Bogardus 1925, Katz and Braly

1933. LaPiere (1934) negated this argument, although his experiment, too, can be criticized for carelessness. The essence of his experiment was that certain American restaurant owners did admit customers of color, when it came to the crunch, yet when asked about their attitude, they indicated *not* admitting any customers of color. The customers of color in these experiments were always in the company of whites. The question remains whether they would have been admitted into the restaurants if they had come alone. This criticism, however, does not alter the fact that LaPiere's conclusion—that there is not necessarily a consistent relationship between attitudes and behavior—is true. See also Raab and Lipset 1962:37.

71. See also Richmond 1973, Simpson and Yinger 1972:29, Hendriks 1981:65-67.

72. Lagendijk 1980:2. I.

73. The U.S. Department of Commerce Reports census data of 1988 indicate the following breakup for the total U.S. population: 84.3% white, 12.3% black, and 3.4% other races. The distribution of blacks in the fifty largest metropolitan areas ranges from a high of 41.7% in Memphis, TN to a low of .9% in Salt Lake City. The other six highest urban concentrations are: New Orleans (33.5%); Richmond, VA (29.2%); Birmingham, AL (28.7%); Norfolk/Virginia Beach, VA (28.6%); Washington, DC (26.7%); Baltimore, MD (25.6%).

74. Dummett 1973, Dworkin and Dworkin 1976, Levin and Levin 1982, Littlewood and Lipsedge 1982, Manning and Ohri 1982, Miles and Phizacklea 1979, Phizacklea and Miles 1980: Chapter 7, Satow 1982.

75. See, for example, the terminology in Baker 1970, Aptheker 1982, Hull, Scott, and Smith 1982. Also, the description "Third World person" has often been used in this connection (see, for example, Joseph and Lewis 1981), after the analogy of Carmichael and Hamilton's idea of the (black) colony within the United States (1967).

76. See Lie and Schouten 1983.

77. In Ali and Hoens 1983:38-43.

78. Djadoenath *et al.* 1981. See also Djadoenath 1983, Serkei 1983.

79. Essed 1981, 1982.

80. Examples include Van den Berg-Eldering 1979, Theunis 1979, Benson 1981, Khan 1979, Lenders and Van de Rhoer 1983.

81. See Williams in Phillips 1971:30, Tixier y Vigil and Elsasser 1978, Schuman and Hatchett 1974:119, Watson 1973, Gwaltney 1980, Kochman 1981.

82. An overview of related studies would lead us too far afield at this point, so I will name only a few examples. *The United States:* Parsons and

Clark 1965, Hannerz 1969, McCord *et al.* 1969. *Britain:* Benson 1981, Khan 1979, Watson 1977, Pryce 1979, Wallman 1979. *The Netherlands:* Van den Berg-Eldering 1979, Lenders and Van de Rhoer 1983, Buiks 1983, Biervliet 1978.

83. Ryan 1976. See also Wilhelm 1970, Jackson 1973, Tierney 1982, Muraskin 1975.

84. See Daniel 1968, Weitz 1972, Kramer 1973, Dutton *et al.* 1973, 1974, Wellman 1977, Poskocil 1977, Malone 1980, Milner 1981, Rose 1981, Dummett and Dummett 1982, Van Dijk 1984.

85. See Rowe 1977, Hall 1982.

86. For example, see Smith 1977. See also in Bovenkerk 1978.

87. Daniel 1968:46.

88. McConahay 1983.

89. See Van Dijk 1984. This study of discussions among Dutch people on ethnic groups in the society also reveals the strategies the Dutch use to conceal prejudices or to avoid making prejudiced statements.

90. Smith 1977:138.

91. See Tierney 1982:29.

92. Pettigrew 1971, Cicourel 1978.

93. See, for example, Dummett 1973, Rowe 1977, Wellman 1977, Hall 1982, Van Dijk 1984.

94. See Weitz 1972, Posckocil 1977, Fernandez 1981.

95. J. Katz 1978.

96. Rendel and Bindman 1975, Reubsaet *et al.* 1982:259-262.

97. Black women's studies (or, more generally, women-of-color studies) is an academic area as yet little developed in the Netherlands. Black feminism in the Netherlands is closely tied to its sister movements in the United States and Britain. Publications about and (with a few exceptions) by women of color in the United States, Britain, and the Netherlands include the following. I will limit myself here to work that deals with women of color as belonging to an oppressed "minority group" in a western society.

The United States: Beal 1970, Longaeux y Vasquez 1970, Norton 1970, Weathers 1970, Weisstein 1970, Ladner 1972, Lerner 1972, Reid 1972, Epstein 1973, Jackson 1973, Staples 1973, Murray 1975, Myers 1975, B. Smith 1977, Hamburger and Fowler-Gallagher 1978, Noble 1978, M. Wallace 1978, Bell *et al.* 1979, The Combahee River Collective 1979, *Heresies* 1979, Mirandé and Enriquez 1979, Sterling 1979, Christian 1980, Frontiers 1980, Myers 1980, Rodgers-Rose 1980, P. Wallace 1980, Davis 1981, Hooks

1981, Joseph 1981, Joseph and Lewis 1981, Moraga and Anzaldua 1981, Vitale 1981, Aptheker 1982, *Heresies* 1982, Hull, Scott, and Smith 1982, Baraka and Baraka 1983, B. Smith 1983. (For an extensive bibliography of writings on African-American women, see Sims 1980.)

Britain: Black Women's Action Committee 1972, Harris 1972, James 1975, Sharpe 1976 (Chapter VIII: Black Girls in Britain), Wilson 1978, Kalra 1980, Prescod-Roberts and Steele 1980, Amos and Parmar 1981, Carby 1982, Fuller 1982, Parmar 1982, Bourne 1983, Phizacklea 1983.

The Netherlands: Gaikhorts *et al.* 1979, Axwijk 1980, Nalbantoğlu 1981, Schmitz 1981, Voorbereidingsgroep congres Buitenlandse Vrouwen 1982, Essed 1982, Da Lima 1983, Lenders and Van de Rhoer 1983, Loewenthal 1984.

98. Hagendoorn and Janssen 1983.

99. See also Macciocchi 1977, Kinloch 1979:52/53, Gronings Comité tegen fascisme en racisme 1983.

100. Evans 1979.

101. See also Allen 1974, Davis 1981.

102. Veenman and Jansma 1981:3.

103. Anne Frank Stichting and Dubbelman 1984:8.

104. Simonse 1982:85/86; Portegijs *et al.* 1983:13; Anne Frank Stichting and Dubbelman 1988.

105. This percentage includes the approximately 160,000 Americans, Canadians, Belgians, West Germans, British, and other EEC inhabitants. Entzinger 1982:24, Anne Frank Stichting and Dubbelman 1984:11.

106. Mullard 1982:121.

107. See, for example, Bovenkerk 1978: Chapter 1.

108. Van Praag 1983:24.

109. Bloem 1983.

110. See Milner 1981, Lagendijk 1980:24.

111. *Minderhedennota* 1980:69 [the minorities amendment].

112. In connection with this, Van Duijne Strobosch carried out a critical investigation of the anti-discrimination policies and the role of anti-discrimination institutes in the United States and in various West European countries. Van Duijne Strobosch 1983.

113. See, for example, in the "Summary of the Policy Document on Minorities," Ministry of Home Affairs, 1983.

114. We find the same view reflected in government reports such as that by Penninx (1983) and the study by Entzinger (1984) on the government

policies in various West European countries. In addition to the study by Entzinger, I recommend *Here for Good* by Castles (1984). This study offers a Marxist analysis of government policy and labor positions of ethnic groups in various West European countries.

115. See also Braam 1973:110.

116. Besides the few Dutch publications on discrimination, prejudice, and racism, such as those of De Bruijn 1972, Michon 1973, and Bovenkerk 1978, it is only since the 1980s that we see attention turning to the problem of racism in the Netherlands. This is apparent from the increasing number of studies, congresses, discussion forums, and the like. See, for example: With 1981 (racial preference in choice of partner), *Ars Aequi* 1981 (racism and legal status), Van Dijk 1983 (racism in the daily press), Van den Berg and Reinsch 1983 (racism in school books), *Komma* 1982 (racism and anti-Semitism), Lie and Schouten 1983 (women and racism), Anne Frank Stichting and Dubbelman 1984 (facts and arguments to negate prejudices). It is noteworthy that an inordinately large number of publications are devoted to the right-wing extremist position (e.g., Bouw *et al.* 1981, Donselaar 1983, Hagendoorn and Janssen 1983, van Vliet 1983). This is related to the one-sided association of racism with extremism and fascism.

117. See also Little 1978:62. In Britain as well, the word "racism" has long been suppressed. See Reenen and Pope 1982:14. The same is true of the United States. See Pettigrew 1980: Introduction.

118. Blumer 1958, Thomas and Comer 1973, Ryan 1981:155.

119. Jenkins *et al.* 1979, Katz 1978, Kramer 1973, Manning and Ohri 1982, Satow 1982, Terry 1975, Cottle 1978.

120. See Adorno's (now outdated) theory (Bloom 1971:65ff. and Milner 1983:29ff.) on the authoritarian personality (1950). See Wellman 1977 and Ryan 1981:58, 222 (note 16) on racial/ethnic prejudice and class origin.

121. Carla's statement may be understood in light of the Dutch educational system, which also applies in Surinam. After the child completes elementary school, her teacher decides which of three possible forms of secondary school the child will attend. "Ulo" and "Mulo" are abbreviated names for the two-year and four-year secondary school programs, neither of which are preparatory to university study. "Ulo" and "Mulo" are Surinamese school tracks that are more or less equivalent to the Dutch LBO and MAVO, respectively. (The Dutch tracks are discussed in more detail under "Education" in Chapter II.)

122. See Van Dijk 1983.

123. Daeter 1982.

124. A complete analysis and the construction based on the three main forms of racism may be found in Essed 1983b: Chapter II, pp. 144–163.

125. Budike 1982: Chapters IV, V.

126. Van Praag 1983:59, 63.

127. In 1988, a Southern California hospital directed Filipina nurses not to use Tagalog, a native language, when at work: not during breaks, not in the cafeteria, not even when phoning home. A Filipina assistant headnurse who spoke out against the directive was demoted to emergency room nurse. The hospital denied that the demotion was linked to her objections, and later reversed their language policy. The nurse meanwhile filed suit in U.S. federal and state courts.

   This story and other cases of language discrimination in the workplace were reported by Sarah Henry in a *Los Angeles Times* Magazine article of June 10, 1990: "Fighting Words."

128. Brent 1973.

129. This quote is from an African-American woman who took part in the follow-up study during 1985–86. The information from this research has been incorporated into my book, *Inzicht in alledaags racisme* (Essed 1990).

130. During the course of this study, a fascinating article by Thomas Morgan appeared in *The New York Times* Magazine of October 27, 1985: "A New World Ahead: Black parents prepare their children for pride and prejudice."

131. I discuss this problem more extensively in Essed (1986, 1987, 1988).

132. McConahay 1986, Pettigrew 1985.

133. See Fernandez 1981, Fullbright 1986.

134. See Fullbright 1986.

135. Wright 1977.

BIBLIOGRAPHY

Entries in Dutch are marked with asterisks. For errata, changes, and late additions to the Bibliography, please see page 288.

*Aalberts, Monique M.J. en Evelien M. Kamminga, *Politie en allochtonen*, Staatsuitgeverij, 's Gravenhage, 1983

Adorno, T.W., E. Frenkel-Brunswik, D.J. Levinson, and R.N. Sanford, *The Authoritarian Personality*, Harper, New York, 1950

*Ali, H.A. Ahmad, *Vreemdelingen beleid Surinamers*, Stichting Landelijke Federatie van Welzijnsstichtingen voor Surinamers, Utrecht, 1981

*Ali, Hamied Ahmad en Jan Hoens (red), *Congresbundel: "Congres recht en raciale verhoudingen* (Amsterdam, 21 januari 1983), Willem Pompe Instituut voor strafrechtswetenschappen, Rijksuniversiteit, Utrecht, 1983

Allen, Robert, *Reluctant Reformers*, Howard University Press, Washington, DC, 1974

Allport, F.H., The Influence of the Group upon Association and Thought, in: *Journal of Experimental Psychology 2*, 159–182, 1920

Allport, Gordon W., *The Nature of Prejudice*, Anchor, New York, 1954

Amos, Valerie and Pratibha Parmar, Resistances and Responses: The Experiences of Black Girls in Britain, in: Angela McRobbie and Trishna McCabe (Eds.), *Feminism for Girls*, Routledge & Kegan Paul, London, 1981, pp. 129–148

*Anne Frank Stichting en Jan Eric Dubbelman, *Vooroordelen veroordeeld* Anne Frank Stichting, Amsterdam, 1984 (sixth revised edition, 1988)

*Appel, René, Cees Cruson, Pieter Muysken, en J.W. de Vries (red), *Taalproblemen van buitenlandse arbeiders en hun kinderen* Coutinho, Muiderberg, 1980

Aptheker, Bettina, *Woman's Legacy: Essays on Race, Sex, and Class in American History*, University of Massachusetts, Amherst, 1982

*Ars Aequi, 't is een vreemdeling zeker, 1981–10

*Ausems-Habes, Hansje, *Congres recht en raciale verhoudingen. Verslag van een op 21 januari 1983 gehouden congres*, Gouda-Quint, Arnhem, 1983

*Axwijk, Hilly, *De Surinaamse vrouwen en haar "onvolledig gezin" in Nederland* (Scriptie Hogere beroepsopleiding, maatschappelijk werk), Werkgroep voor het Surinaamse boek, Haarlem, 1980

Baker, Ross K. (Ed.), *The Afro-American*, Van Nostrand Reinhold, New York, 1970

Banton, Michael, *Race Relations*, Tavistock, London, 1967

Banton, Michael, *Racial and Ethnic Competition*, Cambridge University Press, Cambridge, 1983

Baraka, Amiri and Amina Baraka, *Confirmation: An Anthology of African American Women*, Quill, New York, 1983

Barker, Martin, *The New Racism*, Junction, London, 1981 (1982)

Barrera, Mario, *Race and Class in the Southwest*, University of Notre Dame Press, Notre Dame, IN, 1979

Beal, Frances M., Double Jeopardy: To Be Black and Female, in: Robin Morgan (Ed.), *Sisterhood Is Powerful*, Vintage, New York, 1970, pp. 382–396

Bell, Roseann P., Bettye J. Parker, and Beverly Guy-Sheftall (Eds.), *Sturdy Black Bridges: Visions of Black Women in Literature*, Anchor, New York, 1979

Benson, Susan, *Ambiguous Ethnicity: Interracial Families in London*, Cambridge University Press, Cambridge, 1981

*Berg, Harry van den en Peter Reinsch, *Racisme in schoolboeken*, SUA, Amsterdam, 1983

*Berg-Eldering, Lotty van den, *Marokkaanse gezinnen in Nederland*, Samson, Alphen aan den Rijn, 1979

*Berg-Eldering, Lotty van den, Anneke C. Adriaansen en Harmen Grebel, Van kansloos naar kansarm: buitenlandse kinderen in het Nederlands onderwijs, in: M. Sint en T. Nijzink (red), *Tussen wal en schip*, Intermediair, Amsterdam, 1980, 71–82

Berghe, Pierre L. van den, *Race and Racism: A Comparative Perspective*, Wiley and Sons, New York, 1967

Biervliet, W.E., The Hustler Culture of Young Unemployed Surinamers, in: H. Lamur & J. Speckmann (Eds.), *Adaptations of Migrants from the Caribbean in the European and American Metropolis*, ASC, University of Amsterdam, Amsterdam, 1978

Black Women's Action Committee, The Black Women, in: Michelene Wandor, *The Body Politic*, Stage 1, London, 1972, pp. 84–89.

Blalock, Hubert M., Jr., *Race and Ethnic Relations*, Prentice-Hall, Englewood Cliffs, NJ, 1982

*Bloem, Marion, *Geen gewoon Indisch meisje*, In de knipscheer, Haarlem, 1983

Bloom, Leonard, *The Social Psychology of Race Relations*, Allen & Unwin, London, 1971

Blumer, H., Race Prejudice as a Sense of Group Position, in: *Pacific Sociological Review 1*, 3–7, 1958

*Boerma, Nanko, *Migrantenjeugd in Nederland*, VU, Amsterdam, 1981

Bogardus, E.S., Measuring Social Distances, in: *Journal of Applied Sociology 9*, 299–308, 1925

Bourne, Jenny, Towards an Anti-Racist Feminism, in: *Race and Class 25* (1), 1–22, 1983

*Bouw, Carolien, Jaap van Donselaar, Carien Nelissen, *De Nederlandse Volks-Unie: portret van een racistische splinterpartij*, Het wereldvenster, Bussum, 1981

*Bovenkerk, Frank (red), *Omdat zij anders zijn. Patronen van rasdiscriminatie in Nederland*, Boom, Meppel, 1978

*Bovenkerk, Frank en Elsbeth Breuning-van Leeuwen, Rasdiscriminatie en rasvooroordeel op de Amsterdamse arbeidsmarkt, in: F. Bovenkerk (red), *Omdat zij anders zijn*, Boom, Meppel, 1978

*Bovenkerk, F. en M. Luning, Surinamers en grote autos: een "levensecht experiment" om rassendiscriminatie op te sporen, in: *Intermediair 15*, 21 (mei), 59–63, 1979

*Braam, S., *Suriname en de Surinamers*, Kruseman, Den Haag, 1973

Braham, Peter, Ed Rhodes, and Michael Pearn (Eds.), *Discrimination and Disadvantage in Employment: The Experience of Black Workers*, Harper & Row, London, 1981

Brent, Linda [pseudonym], *Incidents in the Life of a Slave Girl*, Harcourt Brace Jovanovich, New York, 1973

Bromly, David G. and Charles F. Longino (Eds.), *White Racism and Black Americans*, Schenkman, Cambridge, MA, 1972

Brooks, Dennis, Race and Labour in London Transport: Some Conclusions, in: Peter Braham *et al.* (Eds.), *Discrimination and Disadvantage in Employment*, Harper & Row, London, 1981, pp. 126–137

*Bruijn, Gerard de (red), *Racisme in Nederland*, NVSH, 's Gravenhage, 1972

*Budike, Fred, *Surinamers naar Nederland. De migratie van 1687 tot 1982*, IVABO, Amsterdam, 1982

*Buiks, P.E.J., *Surinaamse jongeren op de Kruiskade*, Van Loghum Slaterus, Deventer, 1983

Cade, Toni (Ed.), *The Black Woman: An Anthology*, New American Library, New York, 1970

Carby, Hazel V., White Woman Listen! Black Feminism and the Boundaries of Sisterhood, in: Centre for Contemporary Cultural Studies, *The Empire Strikes Back*, Hutchinson, London, 1982, pp. 212–235

Carmichael, Stokely and Charles Hamilton, *Black Power*, Vintage, New York, 1967

Cashmore, Ernest and Barry Troyna (Eds.), *Black Youth in Crisis*, Allen & Unwin, London, 1982

Castles, Stephen, *Here for Good*, Pluto, London 1984

Centre for Contemporary Cultural Studies, *The Empire Strikes Back: Race and Racism in 70s Britain*, Hutchinson, London, 1982

Christian, Barbara T., *Teaching Guide to Accompany "Black Foremothers: Three Lives" by Dorothy Sterling*, The Feminist Press, New York, 1980

Cicourel, Aaron V., Living in Two Cultures: The Everyday of Migrant Workers, in: *Living in Two Cultures*, UNESCO, Paris, 1978, pp. 17–65

The Combahee River Collective, A Black Feminist Statement, in: Zillah Eisenstein (Ed.), *Capitalist Patriarchy and the Case for Socialist Feminism*, Monthly Review, New York, 1979, 362–372

Commission for Racial Equality, *Report of Two Formal Investigations (Broomfield and London Drivers Supplied Services)*, CRE, London, 1980

*Corbey, Raymond, *Wildheid en beschaving*, Ambo, Baarn, 1989

Cottle, Thomas, *Black Testimony: The Voices of Britain's West Indians*, Temple University Press, Philadelphia, 1978 (1980)

Cox, Oliver C., *Caste, Class, and Race*, Modern Reader Paperbacks, New York, 1948 (1970)

Crosby, F., S. Bromley, and L. Saxe, Recent Unobtrusive Studies of Black and White Discrimination and Prejudice: A Literature Review, in: *Psychological Bulletin 87* (3), 546–563, 1980

*Daeter, Caroline (red), *Criminaliteit onder buitenlanders* (literatuurrapport), Regionaal Centrum Buitenlanders, Den Haag, 1982

Daniel, W.W., *Racial Discrimination in England*, Penguin, Harmondsworth, 1968 (1971)

Davis, Angela, *With My Mind on Freedom: An Autobiography*, Bantam, New York, 1974

Davis, Angela, *Women, Race and Class*, The Women's Press, London, 1981 (1982)

*Dijk, Teun A. van, *Minderheden in de media*, SUA, Amsterdam, 1983

Dijk, Teun A. van, *Prejudice in Discourse. An Analysis of Ethnic Prejudice in Cognition and Conversation*, Benjamins, Amsterdam, 1984

*Dijk, Teun A. van, *Schoolvoorbeelden van racisme*, SUA, Amsterdam, 1987

Dijk, Teun A. van, *Racism and the Press*, Routledge, London, 1991

*Dijk, Teun A. van en Pierre Spaninks, Ethnische minderheden in Schoolboeken, in: *Sociale Vorming 10*, 149–154, 1981

*Djadoenath, Lya *et al.* (red), *Zwarte mensen in Londen. Verslag van een oriëntatie-reis*, Werkgroep Zwarte Publikaties, Utrecht, 1981

*Djadoenath, Lya, Zwarte mensen in Nederland (1), in: J. B. Weenink (red), *De Vreemdeling in onze samenleving*, VU, Amsterdam, 1983, pp. 95–98

*Donselaar, Jaap van en Carlo van Praag, *Stemmen op de Centrumpartij*, Centrum voor Onderzoek naar Maatschappelijke Tegenstellingen, Leiden, 1983

*Dors, Henry G., *En daarom zijn ze hier* (doctoraalskriptie), Universiteit van Amsterdam, Subfakulteit opvoedkunde, Amsterdam, 1982

*Dors, Henry G., *Rond de conceptualisering van intercultureel onderwijs*, Amsterdam, 1984

*Duijne Strobosch, A. J. van, *Bestrijding van discriminatie naar ras. Enkele ervaringen met de bestrijding van raciale discriminatie in andere landen*, Staatsuitgeverij, 's Gravenhage, 1983.

Dummett, Ann, *A Portrait of English Racism*, Penguin, Harmondsworth, 1973

Dummett, Michael and Ann Dummett, The Role of The Government in Britain's Racial Crisis, in: Charles Husband (Ed.), *"Race" in Britain*, Hutchinson, London, 1982, 97–127

Dutton, D.G. and R.A. Lake, Threat of Own Prejudice and Reverse Discrimination in Interracial Situations, in: *Journal of Personality and Social Psychology 28*, 94–100, 1973

Dutton, D.G. and V.L. Lennox, Effect of Prior "Token" Compliance on Subsequent Interracial Behavior, in: *Journal of Personality and Social Psychology 29*, 65–71, 1974

Dworkin, Anthony Gary and Rosalind J. Dworkin, *The Minority Report*, Holt, Rinehart & Winston, New York, 1976 (1982)

*Eijsenring, A.I. en N.E. Bochove, *Taal- en communicatieproblemen bij allochtone jongeren in Nederland*, Staatsuitgeverij, 's Gravenhage, 1979

Eijsenstein, Zillah R. (Ed.), Capitalist Patriarchy and the Case for Socialist Feminism, *Monthly Review*, New York, 1979

*Entzinger, H.B., Migratie- en miderhedenbeleid in Europees perspectief, in: J.M.M. Van Amersfoort en H.B. Entzinger (red), *Immigrant en Samenleving*, Van Loghum Slaterus, Deventer, 1982, 20–39

*Entzinger, H.B., *Het minderhedenbeleid*, Boom, Meppel, 1984

Epstein, Cynthia Fuchs, Positive Effects of the Multiple Negative: Explaining the Success of Black Professional Women, in: Joan Huber (Ed.), *Changing Women in a Changing Society*, University of Chicago Press, Chicago, 1973, pp. 150–173

*Essed, Philomena, Feminisme en racisme, in: M. Beelaerts, S. Grotenhuis, M. Grunell (red), *congresbundel Zomeruniversiteit Vrouwenstudies*, Zomeruniversiteit Vrouwenstudies, Amsterdam, 1981, pp. 16–17

*Essed, Philomena, Racisme en feminisme, in: *Socialisties Feministiese Teksten 7*, 9–40, 1982

*Essed, Philomena, Hoe racisme eruit ziet (lezing, congres tegen Racisme, 12–13 nov. 1983), in: Kitty Lie en Marja Schouten, *Antiracisme: Een andere richting*, Stichting Ombudsvrouw, Amsterdam, 1983a, pp. 56–67

*Essed, Philomena, *Alledaags racisme* (doctoraalscripte), Univeriteit van Amsterdam, ASC, Amsterdam, 1983b

Essed, Philomena, *The Dutch as an Everyday Problem: Some Notes on the Nature of White Racism*, Working paper 3, Centre for Race and Ethnic Studies, Amsterdam, 1986

Essed, Philomena, *Academic Racism: Common Sense in the Social Sciences*, Working paper 5, Centre for Race and Ethnic Studies, Amsterdam, 1987

Essed, Philomena, "Understanding Verbal Accounts of Racism," *Text 8* (1), 5–40, 1988

*Essed, Philomena, *Inzicht in alledaags racisme*, Het Spectrum, Utrecht, 1990

Evans, Sara, *Personal Politics: The Roots of Women's Liberation in the Civil Rights Movement and the New Left*, Vintage, New York, 1979 (1980)

Farley, John E., *Majority-Minority Relations*, Prentice-Hall, Englewood Cliffs, NJ, 1982

Fernandez, John P., *Racism and Sexism in Corporate Life*, Lexington Books, Lexington, MA, 1981

Fox, Paula, *The Slave Dancer*, Dell, New York, 1975

Frontiers, Chicanas in the National Landscape, special issue, vol. 5, no. 2, 1980

Frye, Marilyn, On Being White: Thinking Toward a Feminist Understanding of Race and Race Supremacy, in: Marilyn Frye, *The Politics of Reality: Essays in Feminist Theory,* Crossing Press, New York, 1983, pp. 110–127

Fryer, Peter, *Staying Power: The History of Black People in Britain,* Pluto, London, 1984

Fullbright, K. The Myth of Double-Advantage: Black Female Managers. in: M. C. Simms and J. Malveaux (Eds.), *Slipping Through the Cracks: The Status of Black Women,* Transaction Books, New Brunswick, NJ, 1986 pp. 33–45

Fuller, Mary, Young, Female, and Black, in: E. Cashmore and B. Troyna (Eds.), *Black Youth in Crisis,* Allen & Unwin, London, 1982, pp. 87–99

*Gaikhorts, Laetitia *et al.* (red), *Buitenlandse Vrouwen in Nederland (DIC map 73),* de Horstink, Amersfoort, 1979

*Gewestelijk Arbeidsbureau Utrecht, *Beleidsadvies inzake buitenlandse vrouwen* (E.M.M. Wegdam), 1981

*Ghazi, Hassan Bel, *Over twee culturen, uitbuiting en opportunisme,* Futile, Rotterdam, 1982

Glazer, Nathan and Ken Young (Eds.), *Ethnic Pluralism and Public Policy,* Heinemann Educational, London, 1983

Gordon, Paul, *White Law: Racism in the Police, Courts and Prisons,* Pluto, London, 1983

Green, Phillip, *The Pursuit of Inequality,* Pantheon, New York, 1981

*Groen, M.A. en I. van Peperstraten (red), *No wegi pikin na ai (Weeg geen kinderen door te schatten, vind eerst uit wat zij bevatten),* Stichting Landelijke Federatie van Welzijnsstichtingen voor Surinamers, Utrecht, 1981

*Groenendijk, C.A. van, Van gastarbeider tot medeburger, in: M. Sint en T. Nijzink (red), *Tussen wal en schip,* Intermediair, Amsterdam, 1980, pp. 30–40

*Gronings Comité tegen Facisme en Racisme, *Het vrouwbeeld bij extreemrechts in Nederland,* Konstapel, Groningen, 1983

Gundra, J., Approaches to Multicultural Education, in: John Tierney (Ed.), *Race, Migration and Schooling,* Holt, Rinehart & Winston, London, 1982, pp. 108–119

Gwaltney, John Langstone, *Drylongso: A Self Portrait of Black America,* Vintage, New York, 1980 (1981)

*Hagendoorn, Louk en Jacques Janssen, *Rechts-omkeer,* Ambo, Baarn, 1983

Hall, Roberta M., *The Classroom Climate: A Chilly One for Women?* Project on the Status and Education of Women, Association of American Colleges, Washington, DC, 1982

Hamburger, Robert and Susan Fowler-Gallagher, *A Stranger in the House,* Macmillan, New York, 1978

Hannerz, Ulf, *Soulside: Inquiries into Ghetto Culture and Community,* Columbia University Press, New York, 1969

Harris, Hermione, Black Women and Work, in: Michelene Wandor (Ed.), *The Body Politic,* Stage 1, London, 1972, pp. 166–174

*Hendriks, J., *Emancipatie. Relaties tussen minoriteit en dominant,* Samson, Alphen aan den Rijn, 1981

Henry, Sarah, Fighting Words, *Los Angeles Times Magazine,* June 10, 1990

Heresies, Third World Women. The Politics of Being Other, special issue, vol. 2, no. 4, iss. 8, 1979

Heresies, Racism is the Issue, special issue, vol. 3, no. 4, iss. 12, 1982

Hodge, John L., D. Struckman, and L. Dorland Trost, *Cultural Bases of Racism and Group Oppression,* Two Riders, Berkeley, 1975

Hooks, Bell, *Ain't I a Woman? Black Women and Feminism,* South End, Boston, 1981

Hull, Gloria T., Patricia Bell Scott, and Barbara Smith (Eds.), *But Some of Us Are Brave. Black Women's Studies,* The Feminist Press, Old Westbury, NY, 1982

Husband, Charles (Ed.), *White Media and Black Britain,* Arrow, London, 1975

Husband, Charles (Ed.), *"Race" in Britain. Continuity and Change,* Hutchinson, London, 1982a

Husband, Charles, Introduction: "Race," The Continuity of a Concept, in: Charles Husband (Ed.), *"Race" in Britain,* Hutchinson, 11–23, London, 1982b

Jackson, Jacquelyne Johnson, Black Women in a Racist Society, in: C. Willie, B. Kramer, and B. Brown (Eds.), *Racism and Mental Health,* University of Pittsburgh Press, Pittsburgh, 1973 (1977), pp. 185–268

James, Selma, *Sex, Race and Class,* Falling Wall Press, Bristol, 1975

Jayawardena, Kumari, *Feminism and Nationalism in the Third World,* ISS, Den Haag, 1982

Jenkins, D., S. Kemmis, B. MacDonald, and G. Verma, Racism and Educational Evolution, in: G. Verma and C. Bagley (Eds.), *Race, Education, and Identity,* Macmillan, London, 1979

Jones, C. and K. Kimberly, Educational Responses to Racism, in: John Tierney (Ed.), *Race, Migration and Schooling*, Holt, Rinehart & Winston, London, 1982, pp. 134–160

Jones, James M., *Prejudice and Racism*, Addison-Wesley, Reading, MA, 1972

Jordan, W.D., *White over Black: American Attitudes toward the Negro 1550–1812*, Norton, New York, 1968 (1977)

Joseph, Gloria, The Incompatible Menage à Trois: Marxism, Feminism, and Racism, in: Lydia Sargent (Ed.), *Women and Revolution*, Pluto, London, 1981, pp. 91–107

Joseph, Gloria and Jill Lewis, *Common Differences: Conflicts in Black and White Feminist Perspectives*, Anchor, New York, 1981

Joshua, Harris and Tina Wallace, *To Ride the Storm: The 1980 Bristol "Riot" and the State*, Heinemann, London, 1983

Kalra, S.S., *Daughters of Tradition. Adolescent Sikh Girls and Their Accommodation to Life in British Society*, Diana Balbier, Birmingham, 1980

Katz, D. and K. Braly, Racial Stereotypes of 100 College Students, in: *Journal of Abnormal and Social Psychology* 28, 280–289, 1933

Katz, Judy, *White Awareness: Handbook for Anti-Racist Training*, University of Oklahoma Press, Norman, 1978

Katz, Phyllis A. (Ed.), *Towards the Elimination of Racism*, Pergamon, New York, 1976

Khan, Verity Saifullah (Ed.), *Minority Families in Britain*, Macmillan, London, 1979

Kinloch, Graham C., *The Sociology of Minority Group Relations*, Prentice-Hall, Englewood Cliffs, NJ, 1979

Klein, Gillian, *Reading into Racism*, Routledge and Kegan Paul, London, 1985

Knowles, Louis L. and Kenneth Prewitt, *Institutional Racism in America*, Prentice-Hall, Englewood Cliffs, NJ, 1969

Kochman, Thomas, *Black and White Styles in Conflict*, University of Chicago Press, Chicago, 1981

Komma, Racisme/Anti-Semitisme, special issue, vol. 3, no. 2, 1982

Kramer, Bernard M., Racism and Mental Health as a Field of Thought and Actions, in: C. Willie, B. Kramer, and B. Brown (Eds.), *Racism and Mental Health*, University of Pittsburgh Press, Pittsburgh, 1973 (1977), pp. 3–23

Kuper, Leo (Ed.), *Race, Science and Society*, Allen & Unwin, London, 1975

Ladner, Joyce, *Tomorrow's Tomorrow: The Black Woman*, Anchor, New York, 1972

Ladner, Joyce (Ed.), *The Death of White Sociology*, Vintage, New York, 1973

*Lagendijk, *Publieksmeningen over nieuwe landgenoten*, Lagendijk Opinie-onderzoek, Apeldoorn, 1980

LaPiere, R.T., Attitudes versus Actions, in: *Social Forces 13*, 230–237, 1934

Lawrence, Errol, Just Plain Common Sense: The "Roots" of Racism, in: Centre for Contemporary Cultural Studies, *The Empire Strikes Back*, Hutchinson, London, 1982a, 47–94

Lawrence, Errol, In the Abundance of Water the Fool Is Thirsty: Sociology and Black "Pathology," in: Centre for Contemporary Cultural Studies, *The Empire Strikes Back*, Hutchinson, London, 1982b, pp. 95–142

*Lenders, Maria en Marjolein van de Rhoer, *Mijn God, hoe ga ik doen?* SUA, Amsterdam, 1983

Lerner, Gerda, *Black Women in White America: A Documentary History*, Vintage, New York, 1972 (1973)

Lester, Anthony and Geoffrey Bindman, *Race and Law in Great Britain*, Harvard University Press, Cambridge, MA, 1972

Levin, Jack and William Levin, *The Functions of Discrimination and Prejudice* (second edition), Harper & Row, New York, 1982

*Lie, Kitty en Maria Schouten (red), *Anti-racisme. Een andere richting*, congresverslag 12–13 nov. 1982, Stichting Ombudsvrouw, Amsterdam, 1983

*Lima, Julia da, "Voor racisten ben je niet wit en daarom niet goed", in: Hamied Ahmad Ali and Jan Hoens (red), *Congresbundel: "Congres recht en raciale verhoudingen,"* Rijksuniversiteit, Utrecht, 1983, pp. 38–43

Lindsay, Beverly (Ed.), *Comparative Perspectives of Third World Women, The Impact of Race, Sex, and Class*, Praeger, New York, 1980

Little, Alan, Schools and Race, in: Commission for Racial Equality, *Five Views of Multi-Racial Britain*, London, 1978, pp. 56–65

Littlewood, Roland and Maurice Lipsedge, *Aliens and Alienists*, Penguin, Harmondsworth, 1982

*Loewenthal, Troetje, De witte toren van vrouwenstudies, in: *Tijdschrift voor Vrouwenstudies 17*, jrg. 5, no. 1, 5–17, 1984

Longauex y Vasquez, Enriqueta, The Mexican-American Woman, in: Robin Morgan (Ed.), *Sisterhood Is Powerful*, Vintage, New York, 1970, pp. 426–432

*Luning, Margreet, *Politie en Surinamers*, ASC, Universiteit van Amsterdam, Amsterdam, 1976

*Macciocchi, Maria A., *Vrouwen en facisme*, Sara, Amsterdam, 1977

Malone, Michael, *A Practical Guide to Discrimination Law*, Grant McIntyre, London, 1980

Malone, Michael, *Racial Discrimination: Your Right to Equal Opportunity*, Ross Anderson, Boston, 1983

Manning, Basil and Ohri, Ashok, Racism—The Response of Community Work, in: A. Ohri, B. Manning and P. Curno (Eds.), *Community Work and Racism*, Routledge & Kegan Paul, London, 1982, pp. 3–13

Marable, M. *Race, Reform and Rebellion*, Macmillan, London, 1984

*Martens-Elling, Agnes en Raf Janssen, *Jongeren die tot hun recht willen komen*, Commissie Orienteringsdagen, Utrecht, 1979

McConahay, John B., Modern Racism, Ambivalence, and the Modern Racism Scale, in: J.F. Dovidio and S.L. Gaertner (Eds.), *Prejudice, Discrimination and Racism*. Academic Press, Orlando, FL, 1986, 91–125

McConahay, John B., *Modern Racism and Modern Discrimination. The Effects of Race, Racial Attitudes and Context upon Stimulated Hiring Decisions*. Paper delivered at the sixth annual scientific meeting of the International Society for Political Psychology, St. Catherine's College, Oxford University, July 1983

McCord, William, John Howard, Bernard Friedberg, and Edwin Harwood, *Lifestyles in the Black Ghetto*, Norton, New York, 1969

*Memmi, Albert, *Racisme hoezo?* Masusa, Nijmegen, 1983

*Michon, Mary, *Oordeel, vooroordeel, veroordelen*. Anthos, Baarn, 1973

Mies, Maria and Rhoda Reddock (Eds.), *National Liberation and Women's Liberation*, ISS, The Hague, 1982

Miles, Robert, *Racism and Migrant Labor*, Routledge & Kegan Paul, London, 1982

Miles, Robert and Annie Phizacklea (Eds.), *Racism and Political Action in Britain*, Routledge & Kegan Paul, London, 1979

Milner, David, *Children and Race: Ten Years On*, Ward Lock Educational, London, 1983

Milner, David, Racial Prejudice, in: J. Turner and H. Giles (Eds.), *Intergroup Behaviour*, Blackwell, Oxford, 1981, pp. 102–143

*Minderhedennota, *Staatsuitgeverij*, 's Gravenhage, 1983

Mirandé, Alfredo and Evangelina Enriquez, *La Chicana: The American-Mexican Woman*, University of Chicago Press, Chicago, 1979, pp. 150–173

Montagu, Ashley, *Man's Most Dangerous Myth, the Fallacy of Race*, Oxford University Press, London, 1964 (1974)

Montagu, Ashley, *Statement on Race* (third edition), Oxford University Press, London, 1972

Moody, Ann, *Coming of Age in Mississippi*, Dell, New York, 1968

Moore, Robert, *Racism and Black Resistance in Britain*, Pluto, London, 1975

Moore, Robert and Tina Wallace, *Slamming the Door*, Martin Robertson, London, 1975

Moraga, Cherrie and Gloria Anzaldúa (Eds.), *This Bridge Called My Back: Writings by Radical Women of Color*, Persephone, Wattertown, MA, 1981

Morgan, Thomas, A New World Ahead: Black parents prepare their children from pride and prejudice, *New York Times Magazine*, October 27, 1985

Morgan, Robin (Ed.), *Sisterhood Is Powerful*, Vintage, New York, 1970

Moynihan, Daniel P., *The Negro Family: A Case for National Action*, Government Printing Office, Washington, DC, 1965

Mullard, Chris, *Black Britain*, Allen & Unwin, London, 1973

Mullard, Chris, Multiracial Education in Britain, from Assimilation to Cultural Pluralism, in: John Tierney (Ed.), *Race, Migration and Schooling*, Holt, Rinehart & Winston, London, 1982, pp. 120–133

Muraskin, William Allen, *Middle-Class Blacks in a White Society*, University of California Press, Berkeley, 1975

Murray, Pauli, The Liberation of Black Women, in: Jo Freeman (Ed.), *Women: A Feminist Perspective*, Mayfield, Palo Alto, CA, 1975, pp. 351–363

Myers, Lena Wright, *Black Women: Do They Cope Better?* Prentice-Hall, Englewood Cliffs, NJ, 1980

Myers, Lena Wright, Black Women and Self Esteem, in: M. Millman and R. Moss Kanter (Eds.), *Another Voice*, Anchor, New York, 1975, pp. 240–250

*Nalbantoğlu, Papatya, *Aysel en anderen, Turkse vrouwen in Nederland*, Sara, Amsterdam, 1981

*Nederveen Pieterse, J., *Wit over Zwart*, KIT, Amsterdam, 1990. (English translation: *Black over White*, Yale University Press, New Haven, CT, 1991)

*Nijzink, Ton, De woningnood treft buitenlanders dubbel, in: M. Sint en T. Nijzink (red), *Tussen wal en schip*, Intermediair, Amsterdam, 1980, pp. 71–82

Noble, Jeanne, *Beautiful, Also, Are the Souls of My Black Sisters: A History of Black Women in America*, Prentice-Hall, Englewood Cliffs, NJ, 1978

Norton, Eleanor Holmes, For Sadie and Maude, in: Robin Morgan (Ed.), *Sisterhood Is Powerful*, Vintage, New York, 1970, pp. 397–404

Ohri, Ashok, Basil Manning and Paul Curno (Eds.), *Community Work and Racism*, Routledge & Kegan Paul, London, 1982

Parmar, Pratibha, Gender, Race, and Class, Asian Women in Resistance, in: Centre for Contemporary Cultural Studies, *The Empire Strikes Back*, Hutchinson, London, 1982, pp. 236–275

Parsons, Talcott and Kenneth B. Clark (Eds.), *The Negro American*, Beacon, Boston, 1965 (1967)

Penninx, Rinus, *Migration, Minorities and Policy in the Netherlands*, WVC, Rijswijk, 1983

Pettigrew, Thomas F., *Racially Separate or Together?* McGraw-Hill, New York, 1971

Pettigrew, Thomas F., Racism and the Mental Health of White Americans: A Social Psychological View, in: C. Willie, B. Kramer, and B. Brown (Eds.), *Racism and Mental Health*, University of Pittsburgh Press, Pittsburgh, 1973 (1977), pp. 269–298

Pettigrew, Thomas F. (Ed.), *The Sociology of Race Relations*, Free Press, New York, 1980

Pettigrew, Thomas F., The Ultimate Attribution Error: Extending Allport's Cognitive Analysis of Prejudice, in: Elliot Aronson (Ed.), *Readings about the Social Animal* (third edition), Free Press, San Francisco, 1981

Pettigrew, Thomas F., Prejudice, in: T. Pettigrew, G. Frederickson, N. Glazer, and R. Ueda, *Prejudice: Dimensions of Ethnicity*, Belknap, Harvard University Press, Cambridge, MA, 1982, pp. 1–29

Pettigrew, Thomas F., New Black-White Patterns: How Best to Conceptualize Them? in: *Annual Review of Sociology 11*, 329–346, 1985

*Phillips, Derek L., De rectificatie van onrechtvaardigheid, Het geval van Surinamers en Antillianen in Nederland, in: *Beleid en Maatschappij 9* (5), 129–137, 1982

Phillips, Derek L., *Knowledge from What? Theories and Methods in Social Research*, Rand McNally, Chicago, 1971

Phizacklea, Annie (Ed.), *One Way Ticket, Migration and Female Labour*, Routledge & Kegan Paul, London, 1983

Phizacklea, Annie and Robert Miles, *Labour and Racism*, Routledge & Kegan Paul, London, 1980

Picó de Hernandez, Isabel *et al.*, Study to Determine the Extent and Ramification of Color, Sex and National Origin Discrimination, in: *Private Employment in Puerto Rico*, Center for Environmental and Consumer Justice, Puerto Rico, 1974

Piliawski, Monte, *Exit 13, Oppression and Racism in Academia*, South End, Boston, 1982

*Portegijs, Nico (samenst.), *De nieuwe Amsterdammers*, Amsterdams Centrum Buitenlanders, Amsterdam, 1983

Posckocil, A., Encounters Between Black and White Liberals: The Collision of Stereotypes, in: *Social Forces 55*, 715–727, 1977

*Praag, Carlo S. van, *Vooroordeel tegenover etnische minderheden*, Sociaal Cultureel Planbureau, Rijswijk, 1983

Preiswerk, Roy (Ed.), *The Slant of the Pen: Racism in Children's Books*, World Council of Churches, Geneva, 1980

Prescord-Roberts, Margaret and Norma Steele, *Black Women: Bringing It All Back Home*, Falling Wall, Bristol, 1980

Pryce, Ken, *Endless Pressure: A Study of West Indian Life Styles*, Penguin, Harmondsworth, 1979

Raab, Earl and Seymour Lipset, *The Prejudiced Society*, in: Earl Raab (Ed.), *American Relations Today*, Anchor, New York, 1962, pp. 29–55

*Raad voor het jeugdbeleid, *Aarden in Nederland, een beleidsadvies over jongeren uit etnische groeperingen*, WVC, Staatsuitgeverij, 's Gravenhage, 1983

Ratcliffe, Peter, *Racism and Reaction: A Profile of Handsworth*, Routledge & Kegan Paul, London, 1981

*Redmond, Roline, *Zwarte mensen in kinderboeken*, Nederlands Bibliotheek en Lektuur Centrum, Den Haag, 1980

Reenen, Lionel and Maggie Pope, Racism and AWC's Development, in: A. Ohri, B. Manning, and P. Curno (Eds.), *Community Work and Racism*, Routledge & Kegan Paul, London, 1982, pp. 14–26

Reid, Inez Smith, *Together Black Women*, Third Press, New York, 1972 (1975)

Rendel, Margherita and Geoffrey Bindman, *The Sex Discrimination Bill: Race and the Law*, Runnymede Truse, London, 1975

Report of the National Advisory Commission on Civil Disorders, Dutton, New York, 1968

*Reubsaet, T.J.M., J.A. Kropman, en L.M. van Mulier, *Surinaamse migranten in Nederland, deel 2. De positie van Surinamers in de Nederlandse samenleving*, Instituut voor toegepaste sociologie, Nijmegen, 1982

Rich, Adrienne, Disloyal to Civilization: Feminism, Racism, and Gynephobia, in: *Chrysalis 7*, 9–27, 1979

Richmond, Anthony H., Race Relations and Behaviour in Reality, in: Peter Watson (Ed.), *Psychology and Race*, Aldine, Chicago, 1973 (1974), pp. 287–308

Rodgers-Rose, La Frances (Ed.), *The Black Woman*, Sage, Beverly Hills, 1980

Rose, Peter, *They and We: Racial and Ethnic Relations in the United States*, Random House, New York, 1964

Rose, Terrence L., Cognitive and Dyadic Processes in Intergroup Conflict, in: David L. Hamilton (Ed.), *Cognitive Processes in Stereotyping and Intergroup Behaviour*, Erlbaum, Hillsdale, NJ, 1981, pp. 259–302

284   E V E R Y D A Y   R A C I S M

Rowe, Mary P., The Saturn Rings Phenomenon: Micro-Inequities and Unequal Opportunity in the American Economy (MIT Preprint), in: P. Bourne and V. Partners (Eds.), *Proceedings*, University of California, Santa Cruz, 1977

Rubin, Lillian B., *Busing and Backlash, White Against White in an Urban School District*, University of California Press, Berkeley, 1972a

Rubin, Lillian B., Maximum Feasible Participation: The Origins, Implications and Present Status, in: Arnold Rose and Caroline Rose (Eds.), *Minority Problems* (second edition), Harper & Row, New York, 1972b, pp. 169–182

Ryan, William, *Blaming the Victim* (revised), Random House, New York, 1976

Ryan, William, *Equality*, Pantheon, New York, 1981

Satow, Antoinette, Racism Awareness: Training to Make a Difference, in: A. Ohri, B. Manning, and P. Curno (Eds.), *Community Work and Racism*, London, Routledge & Kegan Paul, 1982, pp. 34–42

Schary, Dore, The Mass Media and Prejudice, in: Charles Glock and Ellen Siegelmann (Eds.), *Prejudice U.S.A.*, Praeger, New York, 1969, pp. 96–111

*Schmitz, Lucy (red), *Geboortenregeling en Turkse, Marokkaanse en Surinaamse vrouwen in Nederland*, Stimezo, Den Haag, 1981

*Schumacher, Peter, *De minderheden*, Van Gennep, Amsterdam, 1980

Schuman, Howard and Shirley Hatchett, *Black Racial Attitudes, Trends and Complexities*, University of Michigan, Ann Arbor, 1974

Seale, Bobby, *Seize the Time: The Story of the Black Panther Party*, Arrow, London, 1968 (1970)

Selltiz, Claire, Lawrence S. Wrightsman, and Stuart W. Cook, *Research Methods in Social Relations*, Holt, Rinehart & Winston, New York, 1976.

*Serkei, C., Zwarte mensen in Nederland (2), in: J.B. Weenink (red), *De vreemdeling in onze samenleving*, VU, Amsterdam, 1983, pp. 99–103

Sharpe, Sue, *Just Like a Girl*, Penguin, Harmondsworth, 1976 (1981)

*Simonse, Joop, *De tafelrand blijft*, Samson, Alphen aan de Rijn, 1982

Simpson, George E. and J. Milton Yinger, *Racial and Cultural Minorities: An Analysis of Prejudice and Discrimination* (fourth edition), Harper & Row, New York, 1972

Sims, Janet L., *The Progress of Afro-American Women*, Greenwood, Westport, CT, 1980

*Sint, Marjanne en Ton Nijzink (red), *Tussen wal en schip*, Intermediair, Amsterdam, 1980

Sivanandan, A., *A Different Hunger: Writings on the Black Resistance*, Pluto, London, 1982

*Sloot, Ben, Legitimatie van positieve discriminatie, Twee redeneerpatronen, in: *Ars Aequi 10*, 655–663, 1981

*Sloot, B.P., Wat verstaat men onder positieve discriminatie? in: H. Ausems-Habes (red), *Congres recht en raciale verhoudingen*, Gouda-Quint, Arnhem, 1983, pp. 185–186

Smith, Barbara, *Toward a Black Feminist Criticism*, Out & Out Books, New York, 1977 (1980)

Smith, Barbara, *Home Girls: A Black Feminist Anthology*, Kitchen Table/Women of Color Press, New York, 1983

Smith, David J., *Racial Disadvantage in Britain*, Penguin, Harmondsworth, 1977

Sociaal en Cultureel Rapport, Staatsuitgeverij, 's Gravenhage, 1982

Staples, Robert, *The Black Woman in America*, Nelson-Hall, Chicago, 1973 (1976)

Sterling, Dorothy, *Black Foremothers: Three Lives*, The Feminist Press, New York, 1979

Stinton, Judith (Ed.), *Racism and Sexism in Children's Books*, Writers and Readers, London, 1979

Summary of the Policy Document on Minorities, Staatsuitgeverij, 's Gravenhage, 1983

Tajfel, H., *Human Groups and Social Categories*, Cambridge University Press, Cambridge, 1981

Tanner, Leslie B. (Ed.), *Voices from Women's Liberation*, Mentor, New York, 1971

Tate, B. and J. Stinton, Racism and Distortions Pervade "The Slave Dancer," in: Judith Stinton (Ed.), *Racism and Sexism in Children's Books*, Writers and Readers, London, 1979, pp. 54–59

Terry, Robert W., *For Whites Only* (revised), Eerdmans, Grand Rapids, MI, 1975

*Theunis, Sjef, *Ze zien liever mijn gezicht dan mijn handen*, Het Wereldvenster, Baarn, 1979

Thomas, Claudewell S. and James P. Comer, Racism and Mental Health Services, in: C. Willie, B. Kramer, and B. Brown (Eds.), *Racism and Mental Health*, University of Pittsburgh Press, Pittsburgh, 1973 (1977), pp. 165–181

Tierney, John (Ed.), *Race, Migration and Schooling*, Holt, Rinehart & Winston, London, 1982a

Tierney, John, Race, Colonialism and Schooling, in: John Tierney, John (Eds.), *Race, Migration and Schooling*, Holt, Rinehart & Winston, London, 1982b, pp. 1–43

Tixier y Vigil, Yvonne, and Nan Elsasser, The Effects of the Ethnicity of the Interviewer on Conversation, a Study of Chicana Women, in: special issue, American Minority Women in Sociolinguistic Perspective, *International Journal of Sociology and Language 17*, 91–102, 1978

*Tjon-A-Ten, Varina, *Als ze maar geen dag tegen me zeggen, ik ben niet hun collega*. Paper gepresenteerd op de Studiedag Caribische Minderheden in Nederland, ASC, Universiteit van Amsterdam, Amsterdam, 7 okt. 1983

Turkse Vrouwenkrant 5 (15) 1983

UNESCO, *Living in Two Cultures: The Socio-Cultural Situation of Migrant Workers and Their Families*, UNESCO, Paris, 1982

UNESCO, *Racism, Science and Pseudo-Science*, UNESCO, Paris, 1982

U.S. Department of Congress, Bureau of the Census, *Statistical Abstract of the United States 1990*, Government Printing Office, Washington, DC, 1990

*Veenman, J. en L.G. Jansma, *Molukkers in Nederland*, Van Loghum Slaterus, Deventer, 1981

Verma, Gajendra K. and Christopher Bagley (Eds.), *Race, Education, and Identity*, Macmillan, London, 1979

Vitale, Sylvia Witts, A Herstorical Look at Some Aspects of Black Sexuality, in: *Heresies 3* (4), iss. 12, 63–65, 1981

*Vliet, Nico van, *Minderheid of Medelander, Immigratie, discriminatie en racisme*, Donker, Rotterdam, 1983

*Voorbereidingsgroep Congres Buitenlandse Vrouwen, *Verschillende vrouwen uit verschillende landen*, Verslag Congres Buitenlandse Vrouwen, Nederlands Centrum Buitenlanders, Utrecht, 1982

*Vries, Marlene de, *Waar komen zij terecht? De positie van jeugdige allochtonen in het onderwijs en op de arbeidsmarkt*, Staatsuitgeverij, 's Gravenhage, 1981

Wallace, Michele, *Black Macho and the Myth of the Superwoman*, Calder, London, 1978 (1979)

Wallace, Phyllis A., *Black Women in the Labor Force*, MIT Press, Cambridge, MA, 1980 (1982)

Wallman, Sandra (Ed.), *Ethnicity at Work*, Macmillan, London, 1979

Wandor, Michelene (Comp.), *The Body Politic: Writings from the Women's Liberation Movement in Britain 1969–1972*, Stage 1, London, 1972

Watson, James L. (Ed.), *Between Two Cultures: Migrants and Minorities in Britain*, Blackwell, Oxford, 1977

Watson, Peter (Ed.), *Psychology and Race*, Aldine, Chicago, 1973, (1974)

Watson, Peter (Ed.), Some Mechanics of Racial Etiquette, in: Peter Watson, *Psychology and Race*, Aldine, Chicago, 1973, (1974), pp. 267–285

Weathers, Mary Ann, An Argument for Black Women's Liberation as a Revolutionary Force, in: Leslie Tanner (Ed.), *Voices from Women's Liberation*, Mentor, New York, 1970, pp. 303–307

*Weenink, J.B. (red), *De Vreemdeling in onze samenleving*, VU, Amsterdam, 1983

Weisstein, Naomi, Women as Nigger, in: Leslie Tanner (Ed.), *Voices from Women's Liberation*, Mentor, New York, 1970, pp. 296–303

Weitz, S., Attitude, Voice and Behaviors: A Repressed Affect Model of Interaction, in: *Journal of Personality and Social Psychology* 24, 14–21, 1972

Wellman, David T., *Portraits of White Racism*, Cambridge University Press, Cambridge, 1977

*Werkgroep Knelpunten in het Nederlands Recht voor Etnische Minderheden, *Rechtsmiddelen tegen rassendiscriminatie*, Nederlands Centrum Buitenlanders, Utrecht, 1983

Wilhelm, Sidney, *Who Needs the Negro?* Anchor, New York, 1970 (1971)

Willie, Charles, Bernard Kramer, and Bertram Brown (Eds.), *Racism and Mental Health*, University of Pittsburgh Press, Pittsburgh, 1973 (1977)

Wilson, Amrit, *Finding a Voice: Asian Women in Britain*, Virago, London, 1978

Wilson, William J., *Power, Racism and Privilege*, Free Press, New York, 1973 (1976)

Winston, Henry, *Class, Race, and Black Liberation*, International Publishers, New York, 1977

*With, Julian S., *Rassenvoorkeur bij partnerkeuze*, Utrecht, 1981

Wright, Richard, *American Hunger*, Harper & Row, New York, 1944 (1977)

To order please see last page

ORDER FORM

10% DISCOUNT on orders of $20 or more —
20% DISCOUNT on orders of $50 or more —
30% DISCOUNT on orders of $250 or more —
On cost of books for fully prepaid orders

NAME

ADDRESS

CITY   STATE   ZIP

COUNTRY (outside USA)   POSTAL CODE

TITLE	QTY	PRICE	TOTAL
The Amnesty International Handbook	@	$14.95	
The Amnesty International Report (hard)	@	$25.00	
The Amnesty International Report (soft)	@	$15.00	
Bitter Fruit (soft cover)	@	$12.95	
Bitter Fruit (hard cover)	@	$21.95	
Everyday Racism (soft cover)	@	$12.95	
Everyday Racism (hard cover)	@	$19.95	
Helping Teens Stop Violence (soft cover)	@	$11.95	
Helping Teens Stop Violence (spiral)	@	$14.95	
Human Rights for Children (soft cover)	@	$10.95	
Human Rights for Children (spiral bound)	@	$12.95	
Spirit of Change	@	$ 9.95	

Shipping costs:
*First book: $2.00
($3.00 for Canada)
Each additional book:
$.50 ($1.00 for Canada)
For UPS rates and
bulk orders call us
at (510) 865-5282*

TOTAL
Less discount @_____%
TOTAL COST OF BOOKS
Calif. residents add sales tax
Shipping & handling
TOTAL ENCLOSED
Please pay in U.S. funds only

(   )

❏ Check   ❏ Money Order   ❏ Visa   ❏ M/C

Card # _____ Exp date _____

Signature _____

Complete and mail to:
Hunter House Inc., Publishers
PO Box 2914, Alameda CA 94501-2914
Phone (510) 865-5282 Fax (510) 865-4295

❏ Check here to receive our book catalog